The Ultimate Guide to

Natural Health

Quick Reference

Acknowledgments
The authors wish to thank the following people for sharing their inspiration, wisdom, insight, and support in making this book possible:

Bruce Ditchfield
Alfred J. Ferro
Bill Gladstone
Amy Trejo
Gary Spivey
Arthur Rollé
Lynn M. Rollé
Robert R. Rollé
Dolores J. Veith
Lisa Marie Wark
Steven J. Wark
Christopher Van Buren

The Ultimate Guide to Natural Health

Quick Reference

By Reno R. Rollé
Dr. James William Forsythe M.D., H. M. D.

This book is a product of:
Boku International
374 Poli Street, Suite 206
Ventura, CA 93001

www.bokusuperfood.com

Cover design by Brent Nimms
Internal Design & Formatting by: Christopher Van Buren
Managing Editor: Christopher Van Buren
Copy Editor: Debi Schepers

Additional technical editing by Scott Olson, ND

ISBN: 978-1-933754-28-4

10 9 8 7 6 5 4 3 2

How to Use This Book

Welcome to ***The Ultimate Guide to Natural Health, Quick Reference.*** We hope you will find this an essential addition to your health and wellness library and an indispensable resource for information on common ailments and the natural ways to cure them. Naturally, we could not include every possible ailment in this volume, nor could we include every possible cure or natural remedy associated with a problem. Instead, we have tried to include the best and most important information on each entry, including the causes and essential elements involved in its treatment.

Treatments may combine a variety of approaches, from food and diet to homeopathic remedies and alternative therapies. You should not use the information in this book as a replacement for sound medical advice from your doctor. Instead, the information provided is intended as opinion.

Besides the main information in each entry, we have added special elements, like sidebars and humorous quotations. Finally, don't forget that our complete volume, ***The Ultimate Guide to Natural Health Deluxe Edition*** contains additional entries and more information in each entry, including healthy recipes, special added sidebars, and tips. It contains over 650 pages of information on natural health in a hardbound, reference edition. It's the perfect book to keep in your library for years to come. For more information visit the publisher's site at www.ultimatenaturalhealth.com.

Contents

Preface

By Reno R. Rollé

> **"You could have been a doctor, you could have been a teacher."**
> Lucky Dube, international recording artist

I'll never forget the impact of first hearing Lucky sing these words. The idea that teachers and doctors, in certain parts of the world, might be considered equal and held in the same esteem resonated with me and still does to this day. Here in the United States, we're probably more apt to group doctors with lawyers. These are both, after all, highly regarded professions with great earning potential. Teachers, on the other hand, though providing one of society's most critical services, earn very modest salaries. In fact, I believe they're probably the most underpaid professionals in America. Lucky didn't sing, "You could have been a doctor, you could have been a lawyer." Instead, the song pairs doctors with teachers and considers them equal. Not for the amount of money they earn but for their powerful ability to help people and positively impact lives.

Although people tend to think of doctors as scholars or those trained in the healing arts and licensed to practice medicine, perhaps surprisingly, the Latin root of the word doctor actually means "teacher." As is probably the case with most of you reading this book, I am neither trained in nor licensed to practice medicine. But as a business executive, marketing consultant, and parent, I also teach, which really, is just a form of sharing. I believe that knowledge and wisdom are amongst the most powerful things a person can possess, but even more powerful than possessing great knowledge and wisdom is the act of sharing it, which is my primary goal in creating this book.

My sincere hope is that the information contained in this book will help bring all of us a bit closer to nature, revealing a path to healthier and happier lives. It's here, close to nature, where so many answers to the questions and problems we face can be found. Often hidden in plain sight! When I was growing up, I despised artificial sweeteners. I had no idea why. I wasn't armed with the information to understand that they were harmful, even poisonous.

According to advertisements I saw and read, if I used artificial sweeteners, I'd never get fat or have cavities. Dentists even recommended them! I hated them and couldn't get them past the tip of my tongue. Though I wasn't consciously aware that these ingredients were poisonous, my subconscious was keenly aware and in control of my decisions. This is the universal language of nature. It's one we all know and understand; we have only to open our minds and listen.

The one thing I absolutely do not want to do with The Ultimate Guide to Natural Health is mislead a single person. If you are sick or have been diagnosed with a disease, you should see a licensed health care practitioner at once. Please do not interpret this book as a replacement for professional medical care.

The idea of a natural "cure" is very enticing. When considered in relation to a disease or ailment, a cure might be thought of as a very quick, simple, and, ideally, permanent solution. Like a shot of anti-venom for a deadly snakebite. Sickness however, doesn't usually occur as suddenly as a snakebite, but often evolves in a more gradual process resulting from a cycle of negative events—stress, poor diet, lack of exercise, bad habits, and so forth. It's often years of abuse that leads to a toxic body and sickness. Though the human body has an amazing capacity to heal, it is only reasonable to expect that resolving or curing these disorders will take some time as well.

For this reason, the act of curing should also be considered in the context of a process. Instead of a pattern of negative habits and behavior leading to sickness, a similar pattern of repeated positive habits and behavior can lead directly to wellness. This is where the connection between cure and prevention becomes obvious. A healthy lifestyle with a commitment to repeated positive habits and behavior will provide the very foundation for prevention. An ounce of which, we all know, is priceless! I strongly recommend keeping this book close by with the hope that you will be encouraged to open your mind and experience a world of natural possibilities and positive change.

My grandfather had a favorite saying: "Every day, every day, every day!" This was his mantra for the virtues of consistency. It's true that lasting solutions do come from a commitment to doing what is right and what is good—consistently. I think it's also important, though, to remember that no one is perfect and yet we're all amazing! Some people are blessed with lightning-fast metabolisms and seemingly bulletproof immune systems. It appears they can eat or drink anything and never exercise—without ever gaining weight or getting sick. Though most of us have to work much harder to stay healthy, we are indubitably blessed in other ways. In a perfect world, we would all eat only organic foods. We would have no stress, drink pure water, and exercise every day. No one would smoke, be overweight, or ever get sick. The world is, however, clearly not perfect, and yet it too, is amazing and beautiful! Life is a perpetual act of balance. It is in our best interests to embrace a similar commitment to balance and moderation, while enjoying all the wonderful things life has to offer.

The medical model in the United States has many of us conditioned to "follow doctor's orders" at all times, unconditionally. I respect medical doctors a great deal. I believe they mean well, provide invaluable service, and truly do want to help people. That said, I am a realist and know that as in every profession, some doctors are better than others. I also understand that no one person knows everything and that change is constant.

I remember my first visit to a chiropractor in 1979. I slipped and hurt my back terribly while loading a truck. The pain was severe and I did the only thing I knew to do at the time, which was to go see our family doctor. The doctor, of course, prescribed painkillers, which I took quickly in hopes of finding relief. What a fascinating sensation it was as I drifted into a state of numbness and shuffled around the house without a care in the world. With the exception of the fact that I couldn't speak, think, or see straight, everything was wonderful! Until the pills wore off. The pain returned immediately and stayed, until I took more pills. This cycle continued and had me thinking I would never be out of pain or return to normal.

Thankfully, I listened to my body and knew the drugs were not helping me. After a couple weeks of pure misery, my older brother recommended that I see his friend Doctor Mark, the chiropractor. He assured me that his friend would fix my back. Contrary to the advice of our family doctor, who insisted that chiropractors were quacks and could not be taken seriously, I elected to visit my brother's friend. The result of this, my first chiropractic treatment, was astounding. This man put his hands on me and gently moved my body in ways I had never moved before, causing an immediate transformation from excruciating pain to absolute relief. I had never experienced anything like this. I was ecstatic! The point of this story is that, back in 1979, many medical doctors and the medical community as a whole considered chiropractors to be little more than witch doctors! Even though this medicine has been practiced since the early 1900s, with its roots dating back much further than that, all the medical doctors I spoke with about chiropractors back then rolled their eyes and quickly discredited the practice.

Now things have really changed! There are chiropractors in practically every town in the United States and major insurance companies cover their care. Why do you suppose this is? Because many people just like me have experienced the benefits of this hands-on natural approach to treating the cause of back pain and learned that it works! If I followed my family doctor's advice back then, I might still be taking pain pills . . . or worse! Not because the doctor wanted anything other than what was best for me, but because he simply didn't know any better. He was an MD and had not trained in chiropractic medicine. He didn't know everything! No one knows everything, and change is constant.

I believe that health and wellness are ultimately our personal responsibility and that preventing or curing illness is something we do for ourselves.

Knowledge is power! With it, we can begin to participate more effectively in the critical decisions that concern our well-being.

I often reflect on the announcement we've all heard the flight attendant make just before takeoff: "In the unlikely event of a loss in cabin pressure, an oxygen mask will drop from the ceiling." The flight attendant goes on to explain that adults are to place the mask over their faces first, then help their children. There is an amazing message here that many of us may not immediately grasp. Helping yourself is not selfish. It's vital! We must first love and help ourselves so we are able to love and help others.

As the massive trend back to nature continues, there has never been a better time than now for *The Ultimate Guide to Natural Health.* People from all walks of life are learning to better help themselves and those around them, by empowering the doctor and teacher within all of us.

I have been blessed with the assistance of Dr. James W. Forsythe and my dear friend Bruce Ditchfield. Without their help, creating this book would not have been possible. Together, we have tried to make *The Ultimate Guide to Natural Health* a comprehensive A to Z directory of nature's most powerful natural cures for the most common diseases and ailments. I hope you find the book as helpful as we designed it to be, and I can't tell you what an honor and pleasure it is to share!

By James W. Forsythe, M.D., H.M.D.

> "After years of fighting a debilitating disease through conventional medicine, I finally turned to a direction I should have sought in the very beginning, a natural cure. I now realize, after these painful years, that nature held the key to my recovery."

This quote is from a 62-year-old patient of mine who has diabetes. As a board certified internist, medical oncologist, and homeopathic physician, I have heard these encouraging statements from hundreds of my patients over the past 15 years. Even my advanced cancer patients claim that if it were not for natural alternative remedies, they would have given up and not survived.

Just recently, a patient of mine with stage IV ovarian cancer visited an emergency room in her Northern California community. A young doctor came into the examination room and, without even introducing himself or fully understanding her treatment protocol, said, "You know you're going to die soon. Have you considered hospice care?" Meaning, my patient had six months or less to live. My patient was heartbroken and could not get over his devastating, cold, and rude bedside manner. No, she is not about to give up, and she deserves hope, not pessimism. Today, she is doing well on natural therapies and low-dose chemotherapy and looks forward to living each day.

More cancer patients are experiencing the benefits of natural alternative medicine. Supplementing their conventional cancer therapy with alternative medicines has been beneficial in their cancer treatment. In addition, patients with advanced cancer, who are no longer able to continue with conventional cancer care, that is, chemotherapy, have another option available to them as a last-ditch attempt to fight their cancer.

I always give my cancer patients three options:

1. conventional therapy alone,
2. conventional therapy combined with alternative therapy, or
3. alternative therapy alone. The important message here is to always provide hope.

I have come to see firsthand the benefits of many of the simple and natural remedies cited in this book. As the owner and medical director of the Century Wellness Clinic in Reno, Nevada, I strive to ensure that my medical clinic delivers both hope and healing to those seeking medical care for a variety of degenerative diseases as well as generalized infectious diseases and environmental illnesses. Our alternative therapies are natural and designed to activate the body's immune system so that the body's self-healing ability can be restored.

Our main message in this book is simple and straightforward: Americans need to be more proactive in taking good care of their health. They need to start making the lifestyle choices that enhance their quality of life. The information in this book enables readers to take the first step in healthy living. Good health can be maintained and many disease conditions managed and even alleviated by natural medical remedies. Certainly, if you have a heart attack, stroke, uncontrolled diabetes, or an advancing cancer, conventional medical care should be first and foremost.

Reno Rollé has graciously asked me to participate in this "little bible of natural medical remedies," which, if you had only one book on a deserted island, this would be the one to have. While you may never find yourself on a deserted island, you may find yourself informed and uplifted by the words in these pages.

"Knowledge is of two kinds: we know a subject ourselves, or we know where we can find information upon it."
Samuel Johnson

Introduction

Nutrition: The Ultimate Cure

CAN NUTRITION REALLY BE THE ULTIMATE CURE? Yes, it can. It may sound too simple, but lack of proper nutrition can cause everything from low energy and a weak immune system to virtually every disease known to man! It's no wonder more people are dying now from chronic diseases than ever before in history—no surprise that diabetes and obesity have soared to startling rates. Based on these alarming statistics, some experts are actually predicting for the first time in history, that parents will outlive their children!

According to USA TODAY, one third of children and teens in the United States, about 25 million kids, are either overweight or on the brink of becoming so, the highest number ever recorded! Nutrition provides the foundation for every living cell, every organ and every metabolic chemical in your body. Nutrition defines what you are made of. Abundant nutrition provides the key to enabling good health. It supplies your body with the very fuel for existence. Nutrition provides strength, energy, and vitality while empowering you to fight disease and illness. It's the reason we eat in the first place.

Why We Gain Weight and Get Sick

Hunger is more than just a craving to consume food. Hunger is really your body communicating its desire and basic need for vital nutrition! Taste buds are actually nutrient receptors designed to tell you what foods are nutritious and good for you. We are constantly fooling these receptors with sugar, salt, chemical food additives, and artificial flavorings that make nutrient-depleted foods taste good and appear healthy and nutritious. Your body doesn't want to be fooled—your body craves fuel! When you eat and fill up on nutritionally deficient food, of course you feel full but there's a huge difference between being full and being satisfied. When you eat natural, nutrient-dense foods, you satisfy your body's need for fuel.

> *I attend a health retreat in Calabasas, California, for one week each year. This incredible facility has been described as a yoga, hiking, exercise, and nutrition boot camp. During this one-week stay, we do three hours per day of yoga, hike an average of 12 miles per day in the mountains (mostly straight up hill!), do water exercise classes, dance classes, weight lifting, and more. With the exception of a break for a massage in the afternoon, we basically don't stop moving all day. For the entire week, everyone is restricted to a diet*

> *of only 1200 calories per day of pure, organic vegetarian food and a Super Food elixir, which I'll talk about later. No coffee, no soda, only decaffeinated teas and pure water. Lots of pure water and NO EXCEPTIONS!*
>
> *The most amazing thing about this experience is that while we are working out and performing non-stop, at levels we didn't even know we could achieve, we eat only tiny little plates of food and yet NEVER FEEL HUNGRY. Not only do we not feel hungry, we feel energy like we haven't felt since childhood. We don't feel full (we couldn't because the portions are too small) but once we've eaten, we are completely satisfied and don't feel hungry. There's no desire for snacks, no desire for something sweet or salty. The foods we consume are so nutrient dense and health-creating, so rich with beautiful nutrition that they don't suppress the appetite and hunger—they satisfy it! On this diet of organic, super foods, we are empowered to go further and do more than we ever thought possible. This is an incredible example of how powerful nutrition is. Once you experience this the way I have, you will probably never look at food the same way again!*
> --Reno R. Rolle

Every day we consume processed, garbage food that lacks the vital nutrition our body is screaming for and what happens? We feel full temporarily but we have not satisfied our body's fundamental need for nutrition. As our body struggles to digest what we've eaten, it doesn't find this vital nutrition because IT'S NOT THERE. So we are still hungry. We may be full, but we are not satisfied. We haven't supplied the fuel for our bodies. So the hunger alarm sounds again, we feel hungry and WE EAT AGAIN. By filling ourselves with this processed, nutrient-deficient food, we continue the vicious cycle that has us eating more and more, causing unnecessary weight gain, sickness, and disease.

Try This Simple, Amazing Experiment

The next time you're hungry and ready for a meal, start by eating a few leaves of fresh, organic kale, collard greens, or turnip greens. These are all nutrient-dense foods that will fill your body with nutrition. Within ten or fifteen minutes, you should notice that you have satisfied a great part of your appetite even though you haven't eaten much food. You might notice that you have more energy too. When your body receives high nutrition, it adjusts your appetite accordingly, signaling your stomach that you have received enough fuel.

The next day, try this instead: When you get hungry, have some pasta with crème sauce or tomato sauce from a jar. Or have a sandwich with mayonnaise and lunch meat or a burger at a fast food joint. These are all meals with low nutritive value and you'll notice that even though you eat plenty of food, you'll still want something else after your meal. Maybe something with sugar to increase your low energy. Your body craves more nutrition and you feel this craving.

You will notice that many of the diseases and ailments listed throughout this book recommend a nutrient-dense, health-forming food as a component and often the very foundation of the natural cure. This underscores the significance and vitality of nutrition in general and its direct correlation to health, wellness, and vitality. Where there is mention of nutrient-dense, health-forming foods, you will also notice the **Boku** symbol shown to the right. Boku is an amazing, organic super food. While there is an emerging trend toward super food products, we are absolutely certain that there is no better, more effective, or higher-quality formulation available anywhere on the planet. Boku is a great tasting super green powder that you simply mix with fruit juice or pure water. It contains the most powerful, nutrient-rich foods on earth including:

BōKU

- **Maca root:** An incredible super food from high in the mountains of Peru. Maca has been used for 10,000 years for intensive adrenal, thyroid, and hormonal support. It provides amazing energy from pure nutrition and without the potentially harmful side effects of caffeine.
- **Stinging nettles:** For increased circulation in the respiratory system, causing increased flow of alkalinizing, essential oxygen, stinging nettle is also known to help build the body's resistance to allergens. Nettles are also very high in minerals and vitamin C.
- **Spirulina:** The single most valuable source of B vitamins and most concentrated protein of any food. Spirulina has been discovered to be one of the most nutritious foods on the planet. Grown using water pumped from 2000 feet deep in the ocean, this spirulina is also one of the richest sources of minerals anywhere.
- **Chlorella:** Another blue-green algae, it is also an extremely concentrated source of nutrition and complements Spirulina well. While nutritionists argue over which one is better to use, Spirulina or Chlorella, we put them both in Boku Superfood.

- **Purple dulse seaweed:** Seaweeds are the richest source of assimilable minerals on the planet. They contain all the minerals and trace minerals that are found in the oceans and in the earth's crust.
- **Probiotics:** Health-forming bacteria that are the building blocks of a strong immune system.

And many more!

There are a variety of nutrient-dense, health-forming foods you can try, and you'll see them mentioned throughout this book. But we believe that the special combination in Boku Superfood will give you a powerful and complete set of nutrients that will get you on the road to health and vitality quickly and easily.

The Power of Cleansing

Along with getting good nutrition, there's one other important way to improve your overall health and wellness...something that can help clear away years of bad eating habits and actually help you get more nutrients from the foods you eat. It's no secret. It's simply the addition of a colon and intestinal cleanse. The colon is one of our main detoxification routes and sluggish or unclean bowels breed toxicity that can seriously affect your health.

You'll see colon and intestinal cleansing suggested often throughout this book and that's because a clean and healthy intestinal tract can improve your health in so many ways. Years of sludge and gunk in the colon and intestines can potentially be at the root of numerous ailments, from acne to weight gain.

Look for this **Boku Super Cleanse** symbol throughout this book. It indicates treatments that benefit from colon and intestinal cleansing. Boku Cleanse Steps 1 and 2 work to simultaneously nourish and cleanse the colon and all the body's cells. They are effective and gentle and do not disrupt your normal life activities.

Some of the powerful herbs and healing plants found in Boku Super Cleanse include peppermint leaf, fennel seed, Nopal cactus, and oregano leaf (Step 1), plus slippery elm, marshmallow root, fenugreek seed, activated charcoal, and bentonite clay (Step 2)...plus many other natural ingredients.

For more information on BOKU SUPERFOOD and BOKU SUPER CLEANSE, please visit www.bokusuperfood.com

Natural Health

Acne

Pimples

Though it is often worse in adolescence, and to be somewhat expected due to hormonal changes at that time, acne can happen to anyone at any time, and is a signal the body gives that something is out of balance. Getting embarrassed just adds to stress, which is one of the causes of acne -- so smile anyway!

Causes of Acne

Acne begins in the follicles in the skin. At puberty, testosterone starts to circulate in the oil glands of the face and other parts of the body (but the face is the greatest concern). More oil (sebum) is produced. Everyone's pores react differently to this increase in oil. For some, skin cells proliferate at an increased rate near the opening of the oil ducts. This higher production of cells, mixed with the higher production of oil, clogs the pores of the skin.

Here's a summary of the causes:

- Hormonal cycles of not only adolescence, but also of women's menstrual cycles, can cause acne, as well as stress, poor elimination (constipation), drugs, too much sugar leading to overgrowth of bacteria, and overly acidic blood.
- Blackheads and whiteheads can worsen, not only from the skin not being cleaned often or thoroughly enough, but also because of deficiencies such as magnesium, vitamin A, and B vitamins.
- Poor digestion can cause a buildup of toxins throughout the body, which often comes out through the pores; irritating the skin and leaving it open for acne infection.
- Anything put on the face can clog the pores, especially commercial products that are filled with chemicals that can cause the skin to react.
- Food allergies can manifest as acne.

Treatments for Acne

There are many natural treatments for acne, but not all of them are effective. Here are some of the essentials for clearing up your complexion:

- Cut down on the problem foods: sugar, fried foods, meat, processed food, soft drinks, and dairy products.
- Increase water, raw foods, and eat plenty of watermelon. Add C and B-complex vitamins to your supplement list.
- Reduce stress. (See also Stress.)

Internal Work

Whatever the severity, one aspect of controlling acne is to interfere with the retention of the faster-forming, extra cells clogged with the extra oil in the pore. First, avoid eating foods that add to the problem. This means staying away from foods high in trans-fatty acids and animal fats, as well as refined carbohydrates. Many experts say that acidic blood is a main cause of acne, and this is a product of ingesting too much fried food, meat, sugary foods, white flour products, and soft drinks (big shocker!). Trans-fatty acids, such as margarine and heated oils prevent you from digesting the vitamins and minerals necessary for smooth skin. Avoid eating foods you are allergic to, the most common being wheat and dairy. And reduce stress and slow down when you eat.

Once you stop consuming foods and beverages that add to the problem, the next step is to fix the acne already on your skin. Here are some suggestions:

- It is important to drink eight 12-ounce glasses of pure water per day. This helps your skin flush out oil, cells, and bacteria. Remember, water is the universal solvent.
- Watermelon juice is another skin-healthy beverage.
- Another way to help your body eliminate wastes that help cause acne is by adding a variety of fiber-rich foods to your diet. Lightly cooked or, better yet, raw vegetables are a great source of fiber. They make a healthy contribution to any meal and they also make a satisfying and tasty midday snack to ward off hunger. Complex carbohydrates such as brown rice, whole-grain bread, and legumes are also great sources of fiber. These fiber-rich foods keep your digestive tract moving and clean, leading to acne-free skin and a healthier body overall.

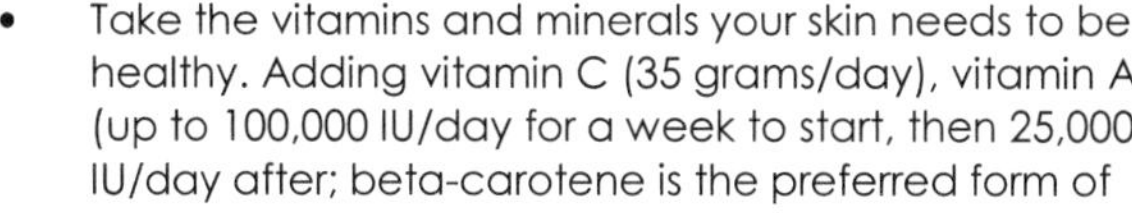

- Take the vitamins and minerals your skin needs to be healthy. Adding vitamin C (35 grams/day), vitamin A (up to 100,000 IU/day for a week to start, then 25,000 IU/day after; beta-carotene is the preferred form of vitamin A) can go a long way toward clearing up your acne. NOTE: Women who are pregnant or may become pregnant should not take more than 8,000 IU/day of vitamin A. Consult your doctor if you fall into this category.

External Cleansing

In order to beat acne, you also need to fight the buildup of excess oils on your skin from the outside. Wash your skin with a mild soap and rinse with hydrogen peroxide, let dry, then wash with clean water again. Finish your washing regimen by spraying your face generously with lignite-activated water (also known as Willard Water). The addition of alpha hydroxy acid (fruit acid) speeds up the removal of dead cells, leaving a smoother complexion. At night, you can cover your face with a bentonite clay mask and let dry, and then wash off -- pulling out impurities.

You're Just Making it Worse

The more you touch your acne, the worse it will get. Oils and bacteria from your fingers can infect acne or, at the least, cause it to spread. Resist the temptation to touch your face. If you must squeeze a pimple, be sure to do so under sterile conditions. Wash your hands with an alcohol-based antibacterial gel and be sure to have witch hazel ready for cleanup. Better yet, have a professional do it for you. That's what they are paid for.

Avoid shaving if you have serious acne on your face. If you must shave, use an electric razor if possible.

ADD / ADHD

Attention Deficit Disorder (ADD) / Attention Deficit Hyperactivity Disorder (ADHD) / Developmental Coordination Disorder (DCD)

All children can be rowdy and hyper-energetic from time to time. And they all have times when it's difficult for them to sit still and concentrate. But if these behaviors reach chronic levels, or measurably interfere with their ability to learn and cope with their lives, then it's possible the child has attention deficit disorder (ADD), most recently referred to as attention deficit hyperactivity disorder (ADHD).

ADHD starts in childhood and affects approximately 12% of children under 16 -- and is on the rise. Around 60% of children with ADHD will still have symptoms by the time they reach adulthood. Many sources go on and on about the types of behaviors that are symptomatic of ADHD, but they mostly boil down to the following:

- Hyperactivity (inability to calm down)
- Impulsive behavior (extremely low impulse control)
- Inattention and lack of ability to concentrate
- Learning disabilities (largely due to the above symptoms)
- Defiant or disruptive behavior, angry outbursts

What Causes ADD/ADHD?

ADHD is considered to be a neurological disorder or, more specifically, a neurodevelopmental disorder, meaning that it is a problem with brain development. However, scientists and healers are divided on the subject and many natural healers believe that ADD and ADHD is just the pharmaceutical industry's label for a range of symptoms that largely come from poor nutrition, specifically from the Standard American Diet (SAD). Other natural health practitioners believe that ADHD is a set of symptoms that come from dysfunctional environments (home, school, church, etc.). Following is a summary of the most accepted theories:

- Genetic predisposition
- Brain injury during pregnancy, at birth, or in early childhood
- Environmental toxins during pregnancy and in early childhood
- Lack of nutrition combined with excess of bad foods
- Dysfunction in a child's key environment
- Mercury toxicity from vaccines

Treatments for ADD/ADHD

Most medical experts say that there is no cure for ADD/ADHD, only treatments that help keep ADD-related behaviors in check and improve cognitive functioning. Whether or not that's true depends on your definition of what, exactly, ADD/ADHD is. There's a good chance that one or more of these natural cures will help or even cure the problem. Therefore, the best therapy involves a combination of cognitive, nutritional, and psychological treatments, including the following:

- Replace sugary, fatty foods like cheese, candy, sodas, and fried foods with nutrient-rich, health-

forming foods like green leafy vegetables, Spirulina, kelp, bee pollen, and maca. Studies prove that children with better diets are able to concentrate and relax more, and have higher achievement levels.
- Increase omega fatty acids in the diet and through supplements.
- Add vitamin C and E supplements and start an antioxidant-rich diet.
- Avoid food additives and foods known to cause allergies, including wheat, dairy products, and processed meats.
- Reduce stress at home and in school and implement relaxation and calming practices.
- Reduce dysfunction at home through emotional support treatments for the entire family.

Other Considerations

The herb skullcap has been shown to help children with ADHD symptoms, and a daily dose of 500 mg of magnesium relieves symptoms by promoting a calm feeling. If you have trouble getting your child off a sugar- and junk-food-dependent diet, try getting away from the source of the temptation. Take a healthy, good-foods vacation for the entire family.

Adrenal Imbalance

Adrenal Depletion / Adrenal Fatigue / Burnout

See also Chronic Fatigue, Diabetes, Energy Enhancement, Stress, Thyroid Imbalance

The most common form of adrenal imbalance is overuse of the adrenal glands, resulting in adrenal exhaustion. This condition is often associated with Chronic Fatigue Syndrome and it is implicated in a number of maladies, including hormone imbalances, poor metabolism and digestion, blood sugar imbalances, and heart disease.

Stress, excess use of stimulants (including caffeine), and viruses (including herpes virus 6 and Epstein-Barr virus) can all cause adrenal exhaustion. When you have to drink more and more caffeine and artificial stimulants to get the same effects, you are on the path toward adrenal exhaustion. At first, you may experience an accelerated energy that is often "speedy" or "wired." This is a sign of excess cortisol and other hormones activated by the adrenal glands pumping adrenaline into your system. You may lose your appetite and have trouble concentrating. Later, when your adrenal glands are exhausted, cortisol is absent and symptoms may include:

- Constant fatigue, no matter how much sleep you get
- Difficulty mustering energy for normal functions
- Tenderness of the lymph nodes
- Depression
- Drowsiness
- Light-headedness
- Mental cloudiness
- Back pain
- Low blood sugar
- Reduced libido

You may also experience disturbed sleep patterns, mood swings, headache, and loss of appetite.

What Causes Adrenal Imbalances?

Adrenal imbalance is, by definition, a hormone imbalance. The adrenal glands produce several hormones essential to our energy levels and our "fight or flight" reactions in case of emergency. The most important of these is cortisol, the hormone that helps us deal with stress and fear. These hormones affect other chemicals in the body, including blood sugar, sodium, potassium, and magnesium, creating a chain reaction within the body. So what causes this imbalance to begin with?

- Chronic stress
- Excess caffeine and other artificial stimulants
- Excess adrenal cortex supplementation
- Digestive problems
- Food allergies, including wheat and gluten sensitivities
- Lack of proper sleep

Treating Adrenal Imbalance

The most important thing you can do for adrenal exhaustion is to change your lifestyle choices that are causing the condition, and create healthier lifestyle habits. Here are the essential treatment choices:

- Reduce the amount of caffeine you consume through coffee, sodas, and artificial stimulants.

- Reduce stress through relaxation of the mind and body and through lifestyle changes, bodywork, and meditation.
- Take pure organic maca root from a super-food supplement. Maca is an incredible super-food from the mountains of Peru, where it's been used for 10,000 years for adrenal, thyroid and hormonal support.
- Add a DHEA supplement (approximately 200 mg daily).
- See the Stress entry later in this book.
- Avoid saturated fats, trans-fats and other food toxins. Reduce sugars and carbohydrates. Increase protein consumption.
- Supplement your body chemistry with magnesium; potassium; vitamins B, C and E; and Pantothenic Acid.

Allergies

See also Adrenal Imbalance, Bee Stings & Insect Bites, Candida, Hives, Immune System Health, Liver & Gallbladder Health

Your immune system is designed to fight off potentially dangerous foreign substances that enter your body. In some people, certain substances called allergens cause the immune system to go overboard trying to fight them off, while in other people, the same allergens cause no reaction at all. Allergens can enter the body from the air (inhalant), from contact (hypersensitivity), or from foods (ingestion). Common allergens include the proteins in pollen, animal dander, dust, mold, synthetic chemicals (including household chemicals and food preservatives), and foods (dairy products, wheat, and nuts). As the immune system attacks the allergens, a series of biochemical processes designed to help in the fight begins: secretion of mucus, blood flows to specific areas of the body, inflammation occurs in certain areas of the body, causing teary eyes, itching, sneezing, coughing, and congestion. Serious allergic reactions can include swelling in the mouth, difficulty breathing, and massive inflammation—and can be life threatening.

What Causes Allergies

Allergies are caused by imbalances or deficiencies in the immune system. These deficiencies can be caused by dietary or nutritional imbalances, or a buildup of toxins in the body.

Treatments

Here are the first steps to controlling allergies:

- Build you immune system with high-potency foods, such as bee pollen, Spirulina, and alfalfa. Drink plenty of water to hydrate your cells.
- Cleanse your colon and liver and use liver-supporting foods and herbs.
- Avoid common food allergens, such as dairy and wheat products.
- Avoid toxic chemicals and get off long-term prescriptions medications, including birth control pills.
- Take Echinacea and goldenseal; vitamins A, C, and E; ginseng; and Astragalus to strengthen your immune system.

For airborne allergies, local, raw bee pollen (which must be kept frozen) has been miraculous for many people. Start with a tablespoon, then increase the dose as it feels right. To avoid making matters worse, you should also refrain from smoking (including being exposed to secondhand smoke) and reduce your exposure to other forms of air pollution where possible.

Adrenal cortex extract (150 mg twice daily with food) with 1 gram of pantothenic acid and 2 grams of vitamin C in the morning and before bed may help rebuild the adrenal glands, which will help to ameliorate allergies. Skullcap herb also can help ease allergies.

Your liver plays a large role in allergies as well. An unhealthy liver means that blood is not being processed and cleaned well, which leads to allergies. Use milk thistle and apple juice to support your liver, and consider a liver cleanse.

Additionally, some health experts believe that an undiagnosed, underlying allergy to dairy products is the root of upper respiratory allergies such as hay fever and asthma. You may want to try eliminating dairy products such as milk and cheese from your diet for a while to see if it helps.

Other Considerations

To relieve allergy symptoms naturally, use the herb marshmallow root to reduce mucus, burdock root (tea or tincture) and pine oil (essential oil) for congestion, stinging nettle for hayfever symptoms, and rosemary essential oil and grape seed extract as anti-inflammatories.

Alzheimer's Disease

Senile Dementia

See also Inflammation

Most people know Alzheimer's disease as the "old age disease" that results in sometimes severe loss of memory. In fact, Alzheimer's is a form of Senile Dementia, a condition often associated with old age. It is a progressive, degenerative disease that affects the brain, causing memory loss, decreased brain function (intellectual and emotional functions), and even physical deterioration of the brain. Although the disease is not exclusively found in older adults, in the United States it affects approximately 10% of adults over the age of 65 and almost 50% of those over the age of 85.

Besides memory loss and forgetfulness, those affected by Alzheimer's disease may experience depression, fatigue, disorientation, and even aggression and paranoia. Following is a summary of characteristic Alzheimer's symptoms:

- Increased memory loss (both short-term and long-term)
- Difficulty in remembering vocabulary
- Very short-term memory loss (repeating questions or comments)
- Difficulty understanding numbers
- Time disorientation
- Difficulty speaking fluently

What Causes Alzheimer's Disease?

The exact cause of Alzheimer's disease is not yet fully understood, but the most probable causes include:

- **Genetic tendencies:** There is some evidence that Alzheimer's has a genetic component.

- **Heavy metal poisoning:** Aluminum is in cookware, baking powder, antiperspirants, drinking water, and household products. Mercury comes from fish, dental fillings, and environmental pollutants.
- **Hormonal imbalances:** High cortisol levels and low melatonin levels have been linked to Alzheimer's disease.
- **Nutritional deficiencies:** Folic acid; niacin (vitamin B3); thiamin (vitamin B1); vitamins B6, B12, C, D, and E; magnesium; selenium; zinc; and tryptophan must be present for proper brain function.
- **pH Balance:** In addition, a proper pH balance must be maintained.

Treatments for Alzheimer's Disease

Although there is currently no cure for Alzheimer's, there are plenty of preventative measures to take now that weren't known ten years ago. If someone in your family had or has Alzheimer's, the chances that you might have it are higher and you would be wise to implement preventive measures.

- Take anti-inflammatory supplements, including vitamins C and E, and spices such as tumeric, cumin, curry, and cayenne.
- Eat a high-protein diet with plenty of amino acids and antioxidants for good brain function. Consider adding an antioxidant juice supplement to your daily regimen.
- Eat plenty of chelating herbs and foods, including garlic, cilantro, Spirulina, alfalfa, and spinach. Consider supplements of lipoic acid and EDTA for their chelating powers.
- Reduce stress, using exercise, yoga, saunas, and other stress-busting techniques.
- Exercise the brain with challenging activities. Studies show that speaking a second language past the age of 60 reduces risk of dementia by 50%.
- Exercise the body to increase healthy blood flow.

Other Considerations

Some experts link the onset of Alzheimer's to the age-related decline of the essential fatty acid phosphatidylserine, which can also be taken as a supplement. Also, consider taking acetylcholine, glutamine powder (which is an acetylcholine precursor), B12 (methylcobalamine B12 is best because it has a higher absorption rate than normal cyanocobalamine B12). Research shows that supplementation with the amino acid acetyl-L-carnitine (ALC) can also do wonders in slowing the progression of Alzheimer's disease.

Another way to improve the symptoms of Alzheimer's and delay its progression is by increasing the brain's energy and maintaining nourishing, oxygen-rich blood. Coenzyme Q10 (Co-Q10) does both. Similarly, a 1995 study showed that herbal extracts from the Chinese Ginkgo biloba tree increased memory and attention span in Alzheimer's patients.

Anxiety

Anxiety Disorder / Panic Attack

See also Stress

Everyone feels anxiety from time to time, sometimes caused by specific environments (like speaking in public) and other times coming upon us seemingly for no reason whatever. For some people, however, anxiety is a frequent visitor and can cause physical symptoms such as heart palpitations (racing heart), excessive sweating, nausea, and dizziness. Other symptoms include nervous shaking, paleness of the skin, and disorientation. A full-blown anxiety attack, or panic attack, can be a major disruption, causing mood, sleep, and nervous system disorders. If anxiety becomes chronic enough that it interferes with normal life functions, then it may be diagnosed as anxiety disorder. This can express itself as an inability to concentrate, inability to sit still, paranoia, depression, and even suicidal tendencies.

What Causes Anxiety?

Although anxiety is always associated with some kind of fear or foreboding, quite often there is no external cause for the fear. Anxiety and panic attacks are almost always motivated internally, by stored emotions. Anxiety can also be triggered by stress, psychological or emotional depletion, or even physical depletion.

Treatments to Reduce or Eliminate Anxiety

The key to treating anxiety is to uncover the underlying emotional patterns causing it. This may be difficult, depending on two major factors: your willingness to delve into emotional issues and the tools you use to do so. Besides treating the causes of the anxiety, you may also require some assistance during an "attack." Here are some helpful keys:

- Avoid caffeine and stress. Implement a regular stress-reduction program.
- Reduce sugar and carbohydrate intake while increasing proteins and amino acids. Add one or more super foods to help maintain good nutrition.
- Use calming herbs and foods, such as passionflower and passion fruit, chamomile, and valerian root.
- Keep calming and grounding essential oils with you to help during attacks: lavender oil, myrrh, cedarwood, and spruce oils are helpful.
- Take regular St. John's wort supplements for their calming and depression-fighting qualities. Pure cocoa is also a great anti-depressant.
- Consider emotional clearing techniques, such as psychotherapy, Neuro-emotional Technique (NET), and Neuro Linguistic Programming (NLP). Many other techniques are also available.
- Alternative therapies like laughter, breath work, meditation, and yoga (for stress reduction) may also help.
- Exercise can help raise serotonin and dopamine (your brain's "feel-good" chemicals), which may help alleviate attacks.
- People who have not had luck with other treatments have gotten results using past life therapy.

Arthritis

Joint Pain

See also Adrenal Imbalance, Bursitis, Hormonal Imbalance, Infection, Inflammation

Arthritis can affect anyone. Almost 20% of Americans have some form of the disease, including many children and young people—and almost twice as many women as men. Symptoms can range from mild pain or aching of the joints to severe and disabling joint pain. If you feel stiffness in the joints when you get up in the morning or experience swelling, discomfort, sensitivity to climate changes (a symptom of arthritis, not a cause), or lack of flexibility in the joints, then you may have a mild form of arthritis. More serious forms can lead to total body weakness, severe joint pain, lack of mobility, fatigue, depression, and even deformed joints.

What Causes Arthritis?

Arthritis has many causes. Here is a quick summary of the current wisdom:

- **Immune system dysfunction:** A weak immune system can lead to arthritis because bacteria are allowed to flourish in the body, including the types of bacteria that cause some forms of arthritis, such as septic, rheumatoid, and psoriatic arthritis.
- **Genetic predisposition:** Degenerative joint disease, known as osteoarthritis, is by far the most common type of arthritis. Studies show that it has some genetic preconditions. This type of arthritis is more common in older people.
- **Overuse and injury:** Although not a common form of arthritis, long-term joint stress can lead to certain forms of joint cartilage degeneration. This can be caused by repetitive motion, overuse, and injury.
- **Hormonal imbalance:** Imbalance of hormones, especially excess cortisol—often caused by stress, excess caffeine, and adrenal imbalance—can lead to some forms of arthritis because of the detrimental effect on the immune system.
- **Inflammation:** Excess inflammation around the joints and tendons is linked to arthritic symptoms.

Treatments for Arthritis

Make sure you're getting good vitamins and minerals from nutritional foods, but be especially sure that you're getting enough of the vitamins B6, C, E, and niacin and the minerals magnesium and zinc. Vitamin E, in particular, helps people with arthritis increase mobility and reduces pain, and research suggests that vitamin C not only reduces inflammation, but also actually helps cartilage grow back. Here are some additional keys:

- Remember that arthritis is an autoimmune disease, so supporting the immune system will help you fight it. Try maca root, olive leaf extract, and Spirulina to help support your immune system.
- Add digestive enzymes in higher than suggested use. If you have ulcers, check with your doctor first.
- Bovine and shark cartilage are rich in glucosamine and chondroitin, which help stimulate the production of cartilage in humans, a feat never before thought possible.

- Take glucosamine sulfate and chondroitin sulfate supplements. Add S-adenosylmethionine (SAMe), which helps the body absorb glucosamine and sustain its effects longer.
- Green-lipped mussels and high-potency fish oils are powerful assistants for arthritic inflammation and help the body grow cartilage.
- Krill supplements can be helpful in regrowing cartilage.
- Drink as much lignite-activated water as you want.
- Methylsulfonylmethane (MSM), a form of dimethyl sulfoxide (DMSO), is used for various forms of arthritis. It is extremely safe and effective in osteo- and rheumatoid forms of arthritis and has minimal side effects.

Other Considerations

The connection between arthritis and stress, including mental/emotional imbalances, is gaining more credibility all the time. Stress-related immune system imbalances can result in the infections that lead to arthritis. This is more evidence to suggest that we implement stress reduction techniques in our lives and limit the use of artificial stimulants.

Many natural health practitioners use oatmeal for fast pain relief. Mix 2 cups of oatmeal and 1 cup of water in a bowl and warm, cool slightly, and apply the mixture to your hands for soothing relief from arthritis pain.

Asthma

Bronchial Spasms

See also Allergies, Bronchitis

More young people under the age of 17 suffer from asthma than from any other medical condition. In adults, asthma is in the top ten leading causes of disease and hospitalization. Each year more than 5,000 Americans die from asthma-related suffocation. Symptoms include difficulty breathing, feelings of suffocation, tightness in the chest, wheezing, and increased mucus in the lungs. Asthma attacks may also cause heart palpitations. Asthma may be either chronic or acute. Acute asthma causes severely restricted breathing and can appear suddenly, with little or no warning. These acute attacks often last only a few hours. Chronic asthma is often less severe than acute asthma, but it has constant symptoms.

What Causes Asthma?

There are two main reasons why the the bronchial passages may spasm and seize up. First, airborne allergens may enter the lungs (generally through the mouth, not the nose), and cause a systematic reaction. In concert with this, a poor immune system or hypersensitivity to certain allergens increases the chances that these allergens will affect the lungs. The specific causes listed below are all variations of these two ideas:

- **Exertion:** Heavy breathing through the mouth due to exertion can trigger the allergic reactions the cause asthma.
- **Poor Nutrition:** Without proper nutrition, the immune system cannot defend the body from allergens and other antigens that enter the body—especially through the mouth.
- **Cold Air:** Especially when breathed through the mouth, cold air can cause constriction of the bronchial passageways.
- **Stress:** Another enemy of immune system, stress causes hormone imbalances that make us more susceptible to allergens and antigens that enter our bodies.
- **Food Allergies:** Specific foods can trigger allergic reactions, especially in the mucus membranes of the body.

Treatments

Asthma treatments take many forms, but they all tend to work in these basic areas:

- **Strengthen the immune system:** Since asthma is a type of allergy, a healthy immune system helps minimize its hold on the body. Try olive leaf extract, Spirulina, Echinacea, and nutrient-rich foods.

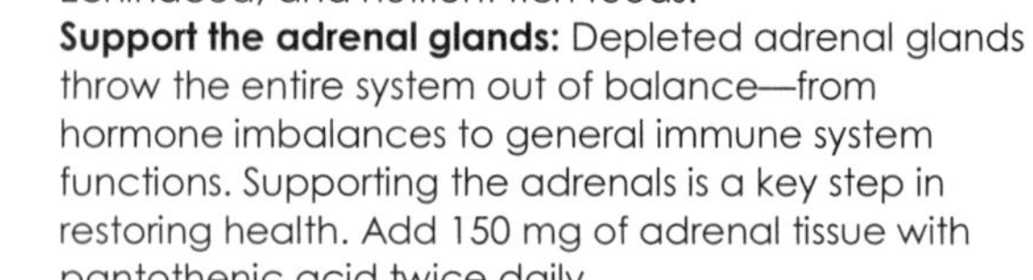

- **Support the adrenal glands:** Depleted adrenal glands throw the entire system out of balance—from hormone imbalances to general immune system functions. Supporting the adrenals is a key step in restoring health. Add 150 mg of adrenal tissue with pantothenic acid twice daily.
- **Take oxygenating supplements:** Herbs and supplements that stimulate the amount of oxygen in

the bloodstream help minimize asthma symptoms. Aloe vera gel (non-rind variety) is a great drink, as it contains more oxygen than any other plant. Add dimethyl-glycine (50 mg 3 times a day). B vitamins, vitamin A, beta-carotene, and Ginkgo biloba all help with circulation and opening tiny blood vessels, allowing oxygen to be carried to all parts of the body. Many have gotten relief by drinking carbon activated water (CAW).

- **Avoid irritating foods:** Dairy and wheat products are two common food groups that exacerbate allergies, including asthma. The long-standing mainstream medical belief is that dairy products such as cow's milk worsen asthma by increasing the body's production of mucus, which then congests the nasal passages.
- **Get relief with natural bronchodilators:** Herbs, essential oils, and other substances can be used to open up the bronchial passageways, providing relief from asthma symptoms. Add a healthy dose of skullcap herb. Herbal teas containing theophylline-like compounds are potent bronchodilators. Other natural bronchodilators include peppermint, spearmint, and pine essential oils. Chamomile essential oil may also help to relax bronchial spasms.

Other Considerations

Many people have gotten positive results from a white powder from Africa called yamoa, which is taken in honey or in capsule form. It takes about ten days of use to take effect and thousands of sufferers have reported remarkable results with improved breathing and diminished symptoms. It is also beneficial for bronchitis and hay fever.

Other remedies can be added to a regimen already set by your doctor. The combination of vitamin C and B15 (pangamic acid) is purported to increase oxygen in the bloodstream. Play with the dosage. When you get relief with the B15, cut back slightly. Work at improving by using less of the supplements so that your body gets stronger on its own.

Many people report that concentrated breathing techniques can help with asthma. These techniques focus on deep, relaxed breaths and an increased awareness of your breathing. In other words, pay attention to your breathing and use the power of the mind to help relax and breathe easier.

Astigmatism

See also Cataracts, Macular Degeneration

Astigmatism is a common condition causing poor vision, and is a distortion of the cornea that leaves the eye oval or football-shaped, rather than round. Round eyes are normal and are important for good eyesight. In cases of astigmatism, the eye focuses on two points instead of one; this happens because rays of light do not form a single point of focus as they enter the eye. The word astigmatism is derived from the Greek alpha, meaning 'without' and stigma meaning 'point.'

The most common symptoms of astigmatism are:

- Blurred vision
- Fatigue
- Headaches
- Eye pain

Straight lines may seem crooked and even distorted. People with astigmatism may complain about blurry or fuzzy lines, and develop severely distorted depth perception over time.

What Causes Astigmatism?

Since astigmatism is a distortion of the cornea, it is difficult to pinpoint its exact cause. Over time, the cornea of the eye can lose its natural roundness. In addition, poor posture, and frequent tilting of the head can lead to astigmatism and problems with perception.

Treatments for Astigmatism

Many treatment options for astigmatism are available, but some have higher risks than others. Surgical procedures developed in recent years include Lasik surgery and photo reactive keratomy (PRK). Both of these are invasive procedures that carry a risk of damage. Side effects may include:

- Feelings of 'halos' around lights
- Tears in the retina, and damage to the optic nerve
- Chronic dry eye, and a diminished capacity to produce tears
- Free radical damage
- Impaired visual acuity

There are natural remedies and cures available as an alternative to surgery. Ayurvedic theory indicates that vision problems are related to digestive imbalances. As a result, some options include regular eye exercises, consumption of Ayurvedic herbs such as amla, triphala, and licorice, and a diet rich in carrots, spinach, and antioxidant vegetables.

Nutritional supplementation can also be helpful; extra supplements high in Vitamin A, Vitamin B complex, Vitamin E, beta-carotene, flavonoids, N-acetyl-cystine (NAC), riboflavin, selenium, taurine, zeaxthanin, and zinc can significantly improve eye health when taken on a regular basis.

The Bates Method involves re-educating the eye to improve healthy eyesight. This works by taking frequent breaks where the mind and body are in a relaxed state. This can involve a peaceful walk or meditation, closing the eyes but improving receptive awareness, and focusing on detailed but pleasant scenery. Over a period of time, this can help train the eyes, mind, and body to work in harmony.

Eating a balanced and healthy diet also can significantly improve eye health. Diets that are good at reducing eye degeneration include food such as:

- Those high in antioxidants, such as Acai berries, Goji berries, red grapes, cherries, mangos, and citrus fruits. Unsweetened cocoa is also an excellent choice that is rich in antioxidants and natural flavonoids.
- Organic egg yolks for the high carotenoid content
- Green leafy vegetables, including leaf lettuce, chard, kale, collard greens, spinach, and parsley
- Those low in unhealthy hydrogenated and partially hydrogenated oils. This includes avoiding processed and fried foods, refined sugars, alcohol, and simple carbohydrates.

Other Considerations

Eye exercises throughout the day can significantly improve your eye health. Resting your eyes for five minutes every 30 minutes can help relax your gaze and improve your overall energy.

Other exercises to try include:

- Blinking your eyes regularly to reduce eyestrain
- Taking regular breathing breaks and meditative rest periods
- Rapidly switching focus from near to far for 20 to 30 minutes
- Rolling eyes up and down in a full circular motion for five minutes, five times a day

Athlete's Foot

See also Infection (Bacteria), Nail Fungus

If you work out, play sports, run, or engage in frequent exercise, you're liable to know what athlete's foot (or foot fungus) is like. It's a common fungal infection that affects millions of people on a frequent basis. It is characterized by fungal growth on the skin of the foot, and sometimes on toenails. Symptoms include itching, burning, stinging, cracking, and scaling of the affected skin. Inflammation of the skin between the toes and soles of the feet are also common.

What Causes Athlete's Foot?

People with athlete's feet may be suffering from candidiasis (systemic yeast overgrowth) in their gastrointestinal tract, which can cause natural imbalances throughout the body that can lead to fungal infections. Sometimes correcting this imbalance is all it takes to relieve long-term athlete's foot. Other causes can be improper foot hygiene, and general skin infections that spread easily in indoor swimming pools and gym locker rooms.

Treatments for Athlete's Foot

Natural essential oils can be applied topically to infected areas. These include tea tree, geranium, and patchouli oils. Flower essences such as Rescue Remedy Cream™ and crab apple can also be helpful. Other herbal extracts and combinations include:

- Tea tree oil diluted with calendula or lavender oil, especially for sensitive skin
- Grapefruit seed extract applied topically, or as a supplement taken orally (it's necessary to dilute this oil)

- Myrrh, garlic, oregano, and pine oils are all antifungal (these should be used topically only)
- A mixture of honey and crushed garlic applied to the area
- Pau D'Arco (a wet tea bag soaked for ten minutes then applied to the area)

Dietary Treatments

Diets rich in raw food, whole grains, and limited dairy products can help reduce the growth of fungus, while yeast-producing foods, such as beer, bread, wine, cheese, and pickled foods can exacerbate the problem. Excess sugar (including honey, fruit, and juice) should be avoided when you are trying to get rid of any fungus.

Add a few important supplements to your dietary routine to help eradicate the fungal infection. Acidophilus; bifidobacteria; vitamins C, E, A, and B complex; and zinc have all proven helpful.

Autoimmune Disorder

See also Immune System Health

Normally, your body's immune system knows to attack foreign agents and leave your own tissues alone. Sometimes, however, a person's immune system can no longer differentiate between foreign cells and the body's own cells; it then and attacks the body it is supposed to protect. This is called autoimmune disorder.

Autoimmune disorders encompass a number of diseases: rheumatoid arthritis, lupus, Sjogrens syndrome, vitiligo, polymyalgia rheumatica, pernicious anemia, Addison's disease, thyroiditis, multiple sclerosis, Lou Gehrig's disease, chronic thyroiditis, Crohn's disease, and sprue. Additionally, some experts suspect that Type 1 diabetes may be an autoimmune disorder. Autoimmune disorder can result in the immune system attacking one of the body's organs, tissues, or cells, such as red blood cells, endocrine glands, thyroid, pancreas, or muscles. The symptoms and outlooks of these conditions vary according to their severity, but they all stem from the same underlying problem: the immune system failing to distinguish between self and non-self.

What Causes Autoimmune Disorders?

Why the immune system attacks healthy body tissues is not completely understood. Scientists expect a genetic predisposition or subtle change to cells within the body tissues such that the immune system no longer recognizes them as "self." This may be caused by toxic build-up or subtle viruses.

Treatments

- Eliminate gluten from your diet by switching from wheat-based cereals to quinoa or rice-based cereals in the morning, use rice bread as your bread of choice for sandwiches and toast, and switch to gluten-free pasta.
- Get more omega-3 fatty acids from chia seeds (from the salvia plant) and cold-water fish such as wild salmon. Other sources include flaxseed oil, walnuts, and tofu.
- Take vitamin B12 and folic acid supplements to help improve vitiligo. Additionally, vitamin D (1,000 IU for chronic disease) helps autoimmune disorders by inhibiting immune system overactivity, and vitamin C may slow the progression of autoimmune disorders. Vitamin E supplements may also help some people.

Back Pain

Backache

See also Arthritis, Liver & Gallbladder Health, Muscle Cramps

The second leading reason for visits to the doctor in the United States is back pain. Almost 80% of the U.S. population will suffer from back pain at some point in their lives. Many of them will end up on dangerous and potentially addictive pain medications and will eventually end up having surgery, steroid injections, and other invasive procedures—often continuing for years.

Research shows that most of the 25,000 back surgeries performed each year may not be necessary, and the condition often reappears in four years or less. Holistic medicine offers alternative options for curing back pain. Instead of just masking symptoms that often leads to failed results, chiropractic adjustments and other measures can be taken for successful treatment. Back pain can worsen over time, and prevention and maintenance of a healthy lifestyle are essential building blocks for aligning the body for optimal performance.

What Causes Back Pain?

The back is a complex mechanism. It has bones, joints, ligaments, muscles, and tendons; these are all held together by connective tissue called fascia. Soft tissue, nerves, skin, and collagen also play their part in the formation of the back. Imbalance or injury to any of these components can result in back pain. Some causes of back pain include:

- Poor posture
- Lack of exercise or physical activity
- Muscular strain from exercise, excessive body weight, or sleep posture
- Lack of movement and exercise
- Liver disease or liver toxicity (including from drinking alcohol)
- Misalignment of the spine, shoulders, and hips that can lead to a chronic condition
- Inflammation of the fascia, joints or tendons from injury, medications, or deterioration of surrounding ligaments
- Scoliosis (curvature of the spine) and other spinal problems

Treatments for Back Pain

Prevention is the best treatment for back pain—and a solid prevention plan includes staying in good physical condition, eating a healthy diet, and stretching frequently. Paying attention to movement and posture is essential. Be sure you have a firm and spacious sleeping arrangement, and that your back is supported in the car (most car seats are not good for the back) and at work. This is especially important if you are overweight. Also, abusing alcohol or prescription medications (including antihistamines) can cause back pain from liver and kidney toxicity.

For easing back pain, you first need to identify the type of pain. Sharp, pointed lower back pain is often a symptom of muscular imbalance. This can easily be cured with long, slow stretching exercises done on the floor. If stretching and movement make your pain more acute afterward, then your back pain may be related to spinal or tissue damage. Use anti-inflammatories as described below.

Dull, aching back pain located in the lower and mid back may be related to the kidneys, and may require a cleanse of the kidneys and liver (see appropriate sections in this book). Powerful herbs that may help include milk thistle (liver tonic and detoxifier), Devil's Claw (back pain relief), boldo, and green tea and extract (diuretic and anti-inflammatory).

Next, focus on inflammation with the best anti-inflammatories available in the natural world: fish oil supplements, garlic, cinnamon, and tumeric supplements. Nutritional supplementation helps prevent back pain and improve overall health. Use calcium and magnesium along with vitamin C, vitamin E, evening primrose oil, coenzyme Q10, and Glucosamine.

Other Considerations

Herbs such as lobelia and cramp bark can be rubbed on the affected area to reduce pain, and other useful herbs include cat's claw, feverfew, rosemary, wild yam, and yucca root. If your back pain is related to kidney toxicity, then massage is not suggested. Instead, use saunas and detoxifying treatments. Other options for treating back pain include:

- Inversion therapy: Now accepted as one of the more successful treatments for certain types of back pain, inversion therapy involves hanging upside-down (at gradually increasing increments of time) on an inversion table. This helps your back muscles to completely relax and allows your spine to naturally correct itself. The extra blood flow to your head is another benefit of this treatment.
- Acupuncture to increase blood flow to stressed muscles
- Bodywork, including massage and deep tissue work, helps create balance and reconnect tissue.
- Feldenkrais Method to correct posture and improve range of motion
- Chiropractic to detect and correct spinal misalignments
- Hydrotherapy that applies water, ice, and steam to restore health
- Other alternative methods including oxygen therapy, Traditional Chinese Medicine, and Ayurveda.

Prolotherapy

Prolotherapy is a semi-natural treatment that stimulates the body's production of collagen and consequently the growth of ligaments and other connective tissues. This has been useful in curing some back problems caused by ligament damage. The therapy involves injecting an irritant solution into the desired area. This causes an intense inflammatory response, which triggers a chain reaction of healing events in the body leading to the rebuilding of connective tissues. Some studies show that the new connective tissues are actually stronger than the original tissues. The treatment is generally repeated several times for full regeneration.

Bad Breath

Halitosis

See also GERD

Bad breath, also known as halitosis or oral malodor, is something of a preoccupation for many people. Almost everyone suffers from occasional "temporary" bad breath in the morning (morning breath) or during the day because of certain foods. Americans spend millions of dollars each year on products designed to "cover up" the bad smell in their mouths, to keep from offending friends and colleges. Breath mints, chewing gum, mouth wash, concentrated drops and strips—most of which have very little effect on the actual causes of bad breath. Their good scents are designed to overpower the bad ones. Without better answers, most people believe they're the best we've got.

What Causes Bad Breath?

Temporary bad breath is generally caused by foods or bacteria in the mouth, and is often nothing more than a reminder that it's time for a little oral hygiene. Brushing and cleansing the mouth generally clears it up. But bad breath can also be caused by stomach acids flaring up from lack of eating, or from lack of normal fluids in the mouth, which allows bacteria to grow and proliferate. Dry mouth can be caused by dehydration or certain prescriptions drugs and poses a threat to your dental health as well as causing bad breath. Chronic bad breath may also be caused by chronic poor oral hygiene.

Breath Treatments

- Drink plenty of pure water to hydrate your body and mouth, eliminating the foul-smelling bacteria that can form on your tongue.
- For temporary bad breath, such as morning breath, try sucking on a whole clove or piece of cinnamon bark. These both have antibacterial properties and pleasant odors, and they are a healthy substitute for sugary, refined, candy breath mints, which can also cause tooth decay.
- Using your toothbrush, brush your tongue with hydrogen peroxide and baking soda—especially way back near the throat where food particles and bacteria sit undisturbed. Floss with dental tape each night.
- For chronic bad breath caused by dry mouth, it's important to stimulate the production of saliva. Start by drinking more pure water, so that saliva can be produced. You can also try saliva-enhancing products (gum, rinses, toothpaste, etc.), such as those produced by Biotene. If this doesn't help, then you may have to stop whatever it is that is causing the dry mouth syndrome (usually drugs).
- For all other types of chronic bad breath, a change in diet, followed by a cleanse, is recommended. Cleanse the colon, intestines, liver, and kidneys—in that order.

Bee Stings & Insect Bites

Bee Sting Hypersensitivity

For most of us, bee stings present only temporary discomfort and a few normal, physical reaction to the sting venom: swelling, redness, and itching around the sting area. Children are often inflicted with bee stings because of their proclivity for playing outdoors and possibly disturbing the bees. Normally, bees and even wasps are not aggressive and you can walk around them without fear of being stung. If they land on you or buzz around you, don't panic! They will usually fly away again once they have determined that you do not have what they want. They are attracted by bright colors. However, bees may also be attracted to certain hairsprays, perfumes, or foods you carry, although they are not likely to sting you just to check out your perfume.

If you do get stung, you can minimize the discomfort through natural means.

Bee Sting Symptoms

Approximately one person in every thousand has a hypersensitivity to bee sting venom and could be at risk of a serious allergic reaction or even death from stings. Normal reactions to bee stings include swelling, burning, or throbbing pain that lasts for a few hours; redness; and itching around the sting area. More serious reactions that warrant medical attention include swelling of the tongue, difficulty breathing, nausea, and impaired vision.

Repeated stinging or multiple stings may cause fever, joint pain, or swelling of the lymph glands in some people. These symptoms generally appear around eight hours after the stinging. If this happens, seek medical attention.

Other insect bites produce symptoms similar to bee stings, unless they are from very venomous insects. Watch for these signs: dizziness, nausea, fainting, sweating or fever, difficulty breathing, swelling around the neck, and diarrhea. Seek medical attention if any of these symptoms appears.

Treatments for Bee Stings and Insect Bites

- DON'T grab the extruding part of the stinger. Instead, quickly take a knife tip or other object with an edge (a credit card, for example) and flick the stinger out.
- Put ice or ammonia on the wound. Ice slows down the spread of poisons and provides cooling relief.
- Next, apply an alkali paste on the sting wound. Toothpaste works well, as does bentonite clay, meat tenderizer, or a paste made of crushed aspirin and a few drops of water.
- For more pain relief, try taking an antihistamine.

Beriberi

Wernicke-Korsakoff Syndrome

Beriberi is a vitamin deficiency condition that can lead to mental, physical, and cardiovascular problems over time. Symptoms can range from mild to severe, and may include:

- Memory loss
- Heart pain
- Poor cold tolerance
- Slow learning and mental confusion
- Vomiting
- Nausea
- Poor digestion
- Tachycardia (rapid heart rate)
- Fatigue and irritability
- Whiteheads on the face and upper torso

Extreme cases can lead to heart attack. Cardiovascular beriberi (Wernicke-Korsakoff syndrome) manifests as a marked reduction of blood flow to the head. At this point, B1 injections up to 100 mg two times daily are necessary.

What Causes Beriberi?

Beriberi is caused by a deficiency in thiamine (vitamin B1), which can be a result of parasites, food allergies, severe stress, or gastrointestinal and liver disease. Primary beriberi can be triggered by inadequate supplies of vitamin B1 in the food you eat. Secondary beriberi is caused by underutilization and loss of B1 in the body. This can be a result of:

- Hyperthyroidism (overactive thyroid)
- Breastfeeding
- Severe fever
- Stress
- Parasites or intestinal damage from toxins, drugs, or alcohol
- Food allergies, including wheat intolerance
- Genetic predisposition

Treatments for Beriberi

Take a good B-complex supplement, preferably a liquid version (vitamins in liquids enter your blood and cells faster than from capsules). Eating a diet rich in B vitamins is helpful, including foods such as brown rice, whole grains, raw fruits, leafy green vegetables, seeds, nuts, and yogurt. Avoiding raw fish is a good idea, and drinking too much water at meals may flush out needed B vitamins and thiamine.

Sulfur can help reduce the symptoms of beriberi, and flower essences such as Rescue Remedy can reduce emotional discomfort and stress.

Taking a thiamine supplement, along with vitamin B complex, vitamin C, or a multivitamin is a natural way to improve symptoms of beriberi.

A good nutrient-dense super food can help with this ailment, such as spirulina, bee pollen, maca, and others.

BōKU

Bird Flu

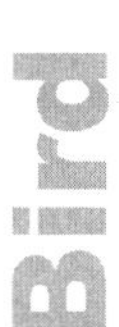

Avian Flu / Avian Influenza

See also Immune System Health, Infection (Viral)

Each year, 36,000 Americans and approximately one million people worldwide die from influenza (flu). These numbers, however, pale in comparison to the influenza pandemic of 1918, which first swept like wildfire through Europe, then claimed an estimated 675,000 Americans and 50 million worldwide.

Many experts agree that the world may be due for another influenza pandemic.

The buzz surrounding the H5N1 strain of avian influenza, a.k.a. bird flu, avian flu, or bird influenza, would have you believe the pandemic is already here and is ready to unleash its deadly talons at any moment. Due to its alleged high mortality rate in humans (50% in adults and a horrifying 89% in children), several global organizations, including the World Health Organization and the U.S. government, are closely monitoring the mutations of this virus. A mutation that allows human-to-human transmission is thought to have the potential to fuel a global epidemic.

In fact, there are many divergent opinions about this illness, and some experts believe that its danger has been completely blown out of proportion. Reports have even been made that the entire thing is a hoax, proliferated by pharmaceutical companies to keep the public buying drugs. Much fear has been generated around this flu because of its alleged mutability, but so far the epidemic has remained a predominately bird-to-bird problem with a relatively small number of documented bird-to-human cases. However, those numbers are supposedly increasing each year.

The truth is, we don't know if there will ever be an epidemic of this flu, or if the reports of human deaths are truly confirmed. Since the cases thus far are almost completely in third-world countries, it's very difficult to get disinterested reports. But because of the elevated concern about this possible epidemic, we felt it was worth offering some information about viral infection and prevention from a natural perspective.

How Does Bird Flu Spread?

Infected birds pass on H5N1 through their saliva, nasal secretions, and feces. Other birds may pick up the virus through direct contact with these excretions or by contact with surfaces contaminated with this material. Because migratory birds are among the carriers of the H5N1 virus, it may spread to all parts of the world. Past outbreaks of avian flu have often originated in crowded conditions in East and Southeast Asia, where humans, pigs, and poultry live in close quarters. In these conditions, a virus is more likely to mutate into a form that more easily infects humans.

Bird flu infections in humans are generally caused by bird-to-human transmission of the virus. A few isolated cases of suspected human-to-human transmission exist, but there is no proof either way in those cases. There is also concern, although no definitive proof, that other animals, particularly cats, may be able to act as a bridge for the virus between birds and humans. So far, several cats have been confirmed to have died from H5N1, and the fact that cats have regular close contact with both birds and humans indicates that monitoring of H5N1 in cats will need to continue.

Preventative Treatments

As with any influenza virus, the key to prevention is loading up on antiviral nutrients and increasing alkaline levels of the blood, thereby creating a hostile environment (healthy blood) for the virus. Here are some nutrients that can help do just that:

- Nutrient-rich, immune-boosting foods, including dark green leafy vegetables and dark red and purple berries
- Olive leaf extract
- Indian Echinacea extract (from the Indian and Asian shrub Andrographis; this herb was the single nutrient credited with reversing the spread of the worldwide influenza pandemic when it hit India in 1919)
- Skullcap herb (interferes with and, in some cases, inhibits the growth and replication of the virus)
- Eleutherococcus senticosus (Siberian ginseng) a natural adaptogen
- Raw garlic or garlic oil (Garlic is a natural germicide, capable of killing nearly any microbe; bacteria, parasites, viruses, and fungi all wilt under its powers. It was even found capable of killing notoriously difficult-to-eradicate skin fungi, such as those that cause athletes foot)
- Picolinated zinc, thymus glandular (zinc and thymus build T cells; when zinc is low, the population of killer T cells necessary to fight infection plummets), N-acetylcysteine (NAC), lysine, colloidal silver, vitamin C (mega doses up to 5 grams daily or until diarrhea results), and Citricidal grapefruit seed extract
- Oregano oil (In a recent study, oregano oil has killed 91% of the Bird Flu virus in a Petri dish within 20 minutes.)

Other Considerations

For better immune system health, don't smoke, drink, take excess caffeine or drugs, or eat dairy products (dairy creates excessive mucus, making your body a Petri dish for breeding more viruses).

Remember, with any virus, washing your hands is critically important in stopping the spread of this flu. Keep in mind that the bird flu is a virus, not a bacterial infection, so antibiotics will not help in preventing this or other forms of the flu.

Blood Pressure (High)

Hypertension

See also Cardiovascular Health, Weight (Over), Cholesterol

Blood pressure is measured by two types of blood activity: the pressure of the pulses of blood in your veins (systolic) and the pressure between pulses (diastolic). Experts now believe that there is not a single normal blood pressure for everyone, but that "normal" may vary depending on the person. The values considered safe and normal for most people, however, ranges from 90/60 to 139/89. If you are on the high side of this range, it's time to take notice and keep an eye on your blood pressure health.

Hypertension generally has few symptoms except a tendency of shortness of breath after mild exertion. The causes of hypertension are much more recognized as signs of health issues: nervous stress, excess weight, and bad eating habits. Hypertension can develop into heart and kidney failure, and even brain damage. And as we all know, high blood pressure puts a person at greater risk for heart attack, stroke, and blindness.

What Causes High Blood Pressure?

High blood pressure is commonly associated with aging because we normally see the arteries begin to stiffen after around age 60. This causes the lower of the two numbers to go up. But not all sexagenarians show these signs.

Other causes of high blood pressure include high stress levels, smoking, and coffee drinking. Smoking and coffee are both stimulants, which raise blood pressure, and stress increases nervous tension, which can cause hypertension. Excess weight can exacerbate the problem by putting more pressure on the heart. A diet of starchy or sugary foods also increases blood pressure, as do saturated and trans fats. All of these causes are related to the same basic factor: putting more pressure on the heart to beat faster and/or harder to get the same amount of oxygen to the blood.

Treatments

You can do many things to lower your blood pressure. Most of them include lifestyle and diet choices. Here are basic changes that can help lower blood pressure:

- Stop smoking.
- Lower stress and eliminate caffeine.
- Lose weight and exercise more (when beginning an exercise program, start slowly and increase gradually).
- Decrease sodium and increase potassium.
- Eat less sugar and fewer starches (you'll get thinner too!).
- Eat foods that help regulate blood pressure, including pure cocoa (or dark, bitter-sweet chocolate), raw garlic, and raw onion. Also eat plenty of potassium-rich foods, like bananas, cantaloupe, peaches, pears, asparagus, and prune juice. Include plenty of sesame oil in your diet, as this oil has been found to dramatically lower hypertension.

Other Considerations

Herbal teas and asparagus supplements are excellent natural diuretics and hypotensives (lower blood pressure). Seaweed and kelp also can help reduce high blood pressure, as can hawthorn berries or hawthorn extract. Too little vitamin C, potassium, magnesium, or calcium in your diet can raise your blood pressure, so be sure to take them in supplement form if your diet tends to lack these important vitamins and minerals.

Hot baths and saunas can help reduce stress and induce sweating that can eliminate toxins from the system. Practices such as meditation and yoga are also excellent for reducing stress and blood pressure.

Blood Pressure (Low)

Hypotension

See also Energy Enhancement, Thyroid Imbalance

Low blood pressure is not as common or as potentially serious as high blood pressure and many consider it a healthy condition. But low blood pressure can be problematic in terms of low energy, sensitivity to cold (and cold extremities), dizziness when suddenly sitting or standing, and circulation disorders, such as baldness and skin problems.

What Causes Low Blood Pressure?

Low blood pressure generally is considered to be hereditary, but other factors may be involved, including diet and breathing habits (chronic low or shallow breath).

Treatments

You have several options that can help raise your blood pressure to normal levels, mostly involving lifestyle and diet choices. Here are some things that can help alleviate low blood pressure:

- Pure cocoa (dark chocolate) helps to regulate blood pressure (both high and low).
- Increase your intake of spices like cumin, curry, tumeric, and cayenne.
- Check for thyroid imbalance and treat with kelp, walnuts, and selenium supplements.
- Get plenty of vigorous exercise.

Body Odor

Bromhidrosis

The antiperspirant industry is worried that people may boycott their products because of the toxic metals they contain, and they should be worried. But how can we continue to smell sweet and fresh unless we use them? Must we cover up our natural odor with highly scented oils or perfumes? Is bad body odor a sign of bad health?

To answer these questions, it's important to realize that body odor is caused almost entirely by the presence of bacteria on the skin and in the body hair. Areas that are moist and kept inside clothing are, therefore, going to be the worst offenders: the armpits, groin area, and feet.

What Causes Body Odor?

Unless a person js very toxic from alcohol, drugs, heavy metals, or other substances, body odor is not caused by sweat, as it generally does not have much odor by itself. However, sweat and other moisture on the body does increase bacteria growth on the skin and, especially, in the hair. The bacteria actually cause the odor. The sweat located in the underarms, groin, breasts, and anal area is different than the sweat on the rest of your body, such as your forehead or palms. The underarm sweat contains more fats and is, therefore, thicker and more "sticky." It also tends to be a yellowish color. This sweat, when left in the hair follicles under the arm, can quickly produce body odor, though the particulars of that odor are influenced by weather, personal biology, and diet. Some people's body odor is not offensive, while others' can be.

What causes a particular body odor to smell bad? Generally diet, use of medications, smoking, and alcohol consumption cause the bad smells. It is said that animals can smell "meat-eating" on other animals and humans. No doubt the consumption of meat and animal fat influences your body odor. Likewise, the excessive consumption of fish, garlic, or other spices can show up in a person's body odor.

If you don't drink enough water, it's possible that your internal organs and skin are not properly "rinsed," and may produce more toxic-smelling odors when you sweat.

Antiperspirant vs. Deodorant

Pretty much all antiperspirants contain deodorizing agents, but deodorants are not the same as antiperspirants. Deodorants simply mask or cover up the odors associated with underarm sweat. Antiperspirants, on the other hand, contain coating agents that reduce the amount of sweat released by the skin in the area where it is applied. The most common coating agent is ACH (aluminum chlorohydrate). Some sticks and gels may use AZAG (aluminum zirconium tetrachlorohydrex GLY).

Sweating is a natural function of the body; it is the body's way of cooling itself off. So even if antiperspirant products weren't loaded with toxic heavy metals, the idea of stopping your body from performing a natural and necessary function is rather misguided. Use natural deodorants and oils to keep yourself smelling fresh, but let your sweat glands do their job by avoiding antiperspirants.

Breast Cancer

See Hormone Imbalance, Weight (Over)

One out of every 8 women in the United States will develop breast cancer. It is the second most prominent cancer in women, next to lung cancer. A serious and almost epidemic problem in the U.S., it makes the top ten list of causes of death for women in this country. Although breast cancer affected less than 1%of the U.S. population in 1960, today it affects almost 12%. Women over the age of 50 are at highest risk, as are those who have close relatives with the disease.

Because of these alarming statistics, we've heard a lot of noise about regular self-examination. And there's a reason for that—breast self-examination is one of the best things you can do to catch this cancer before it catches you. Self examination involves a simple process of pushing on the breast to feel for irregularities: unusual lumps, soft or hard, that were not previously present. Other symptoms to check for include:

- Swelling in the breast or dimply skin around the breast
- Pain in the nipple, changes in the nipple formation, or unusual discharge
- Pain or sensitivity in the lymph node under the arm, or lumps in the armpit

What Causes Breast Cancer?

While there are certain genetic predispositions to getting breast cancer, and some statistical evidence of a family tendency, more than 80% of women with breast cancer have no family member with the disease. Likewise, although more women over 50 develop breast cancer than women under 50, there is no proof that the disease has any connection to hormonal changes at menopause. More likely, factors such as late childbearing, early puberty and obesity contribute to the risk of developing breast cancer. Women who smoke, drink, or take certain long-term medications (such as progesterone and estrogen combinations like Prempro) also have a higher risk of contracting the disease. Poor nutrition may also play a part.

Treatments and Prevention

Many things can be done do to prevent cancer, including breast cancer. Cancer rates have increased in step with the increase of artificial foods and additives in the American diet. Naturally, preventative treatments that focus on removing harmful toxins and adding supportive supplements can be helpful. Here are some of the essentials:

- Stop using chemical antiperspirant products and switch to natural deodorants.
- Stop drinking milk, which is loaded with artificial hormones and pus from factory-farmed cattle.
- Get plenty of vitamins B and E from food and supplements.
- Get extra vitamin D by taking short walks in the sun without sunscreen. In fact, studies show that women who live in sunny climates have a 30% to 40% decreased risk of developing breast cancer.
- Take cayenne pepper in gel caps and eat plenty of chili pepper in your foods.
- Eat plenty of nutrient-rich whole foods for overall immune system health.

Soy products are natural phytoestrogens and are useful in both prevention and an adjuvant therapy in active breast cancer. Also, a number of supplements may help prevent not just breast cancer, but cancer in general. These include antioxidants, selenium, adrenal hormone, the algae Chlorella and Spirulina, and conjugated linoleic acid (CLA) supplements.

Maitake mushroom extract is high in enzymes and beta-glucans, known to fight fungus, virus, and bacteria in the body, as well as cancer. And antioxidants, such as Pycnogenol and green tea helps build the NK and T cells in the immune system that fight cancer.

Other Considerations

If you're worried about breast cancer, you're probably already getting a mammogram done regularly. This is a controversial topic in alternative health circles, as some experts believe that mammograms increase your risk of developing breast cancer. In fact, one Canadian study found that women who receive annual mammograms have a 52% increased risk of ultimately dying from breast cancer. On the flip side, however, the American Cancer Society still loudly advocates regular mammogram screening. The choice is yours, but keep in mind that mammograms do expose your body to radiation, a cause of cancer. An effective alternative is a thermogram, a noninvasive, nonradiation exposure test that relies on detecting the greater infrared radiation from malignant breast lesions.

Bronchitis

See also Asthma, Coughs

That deep, dry or wet cough associated with inflammation of the bronchial airways might be bronchitis. Even minimal symptoms of bronchitis can lead to chronic bronchitis, and if left untreated, could develop into pneumonia. Acute bronchitis usually results from a cold, flu, sinusitis, or viral infection. Chronic bronchitis (long-lasting and severe) can develop after a case of acute bronchitis (severe), and can include wheezing or breathlessness. Other symptoms include chills, fever, and excessive production of mucus and phlegm.

What Causes Bronchitis?

Both acute and chronic bronchitis can develop from bacteria, viral infections, food allergies, and environmental toxins. Smoking and regular exposure to secondhand smoke can also contribute to the development of bronchitis. Short and relatively mild bouts of bronchitis can lead to large-scale infections and pneumonia, if not well treated.

Treatments for Bronchitis

Bronchitis may be prevented with a change in diet, aromatherapy techniques, herbs, improved air quality, and juice therapy. People with recurring bronchitis should be screened for food allergies. Diet improvements and changes before and during a bronchitis episode should include:

- Avoiding sugar, starch, soy, corn, wheat, and soft drinks
- Limiting eggs, dairy, and caffeine
- Eliminating some fruits such as bananas, as they encourage mucus production
- Opening up the air passages with intake of chili peppers, garlic, ginger, and onions; also helpful with the elimination of mucus
- Eating a diet filled with organic, whole foods
- Plenty of pure, fresh water
- Adopting a vegan diet that eliminates meat and dairy completely

Herbs can successfully reduce or treat bronchitis. These are best consumed as a tea or tincture form (tincture works more quickly and with fewer barriers to entering the system):

- Propolis (drop directly into the throat area and breathe in the vapors)
- St. John's wort
- Echinacea tincture
- Grapefruit seed extract (diluted)
- Anise
- Astragalus
- Coltsfoot
- Garlic
- Ginseng
- Goldenseal
- Peppermint

Other Considerations

Nutritional supplementation is recommended for reversing or preventing recurring bronchitis. Recommended nutrients include vitamin A, vitamin C, beta-carotene, zinc, and selenium. Other suggestions include colloidal silver, N-acetylcysteine (NAC), thymus gland extract, and bromelain. Alternative therapies may include detoxification therapy, oxygen therapy, and acupuncture.

Bruising

Contusions / Ecchymoses

Bruising is often associated with physical activity, sports, or youthful activities. But any substantial bump or fall can generate damage to the blood capillaries, causing blood to spread into surrounding tissues. Minor bruises caused by injuries generally go away in three to 10 days, depending on the seriousness of the injury and external factors (diet, for example). Some people are more susceptible to bruising and may benefit from an increase in vitamin C and antioxidants.

Bruising that appears often and without cause should be examined by a health care practitioner. Note that bruising may not reflect an underlying clotting disorder. It is more common in patients on steroids and blood thinners. Also, patients with low blood platelet counts (lack of blood clotting) associated with bone marrow cancers, leukemia and certain chemotherapy protocols frequently experience bruising. Because of thinning skin and more fragile blood vessels, bruising is more common after the age of 60.

Treatments for Bruising

Most treatments for bruising involve some kind of topical substance to help reduce or prevent discoloration and pain.

- Eat foods high in vitamin C and antioxidants, such as fresh fruit, berries, and green leafy vegetables.
- Apply propolis tincture or cream to the surface of the wound. Lavender oil, hyssop, and camphor are also used in the same way; they also can be mixed with the propolis cream.
- Foods rich in bioflavonoids, such as fruit, seabuckhorn (or seaberry), and mango, help repair capillaries.
- You can also try putting white or apple cider vinegar on the bruise.

Other Considerations

Many homeopathic remedies help alleviate bruising. Here are some of the more useful ones:

- Arnica can reduce discoloration and even prevent bruises if applied early. It can also reduce the time a bruise lingers.
- Ledum can be used for dark bruises to help healing and skin discoloration.
- Sulfuric acid homeopathic can be used for dark bruises that are slow to heal.

Homeopathic remedies should be taken every 4 to 6 hours until symptoms recede.

Burns

Blisters

See also Sunburn

The most common form of burn is from simple heat from the sun, fire, or other hot object. The same heat that can cook your food can dry out and burn your skin, causing redness, blistering, tissue damage, and scarring. Burns can also be caused by chemicals, electricity, and radiation.

A first-degree burn damages only the skin tissue. These can usually be treated at home with natural remedies and normally heal in a few days. Second-degree burns damage the nerves and tissues under the skin and often result in blistering. These also usually can be treated at home (sedond-degree burns in children should be treated at a medical facility). Third-degree burns cause serious damage to the skin and can remove large portions of skin from the body. These burns should be treated by health care practitioners at a specialized burn unit. But even with third-degree burns, there are some things you can do to help stop the burning and help the healing process.

Treatments

First-degree or second-degree burns can be treated at home, using one or more natural remedies to ease the pain, reduce blistering and scarring, and clean the burned area. Here are the essentials:

1. Immediately run cold water over the burn or soak the burned area in cold water. Continue for as long as necessary until the pain subsides—the longer the better. The cold water also helps keep blisters from forming. A burned area of skin also is a massively dehydrated area. For the best rehydration of the skin, use Willard Water or other carbon-activated water (CAW).
2. Apply aloe vera pulp or papaya pulp to the wound. Add a few drops of lavender or calendula oil for their extra healing properties.
3. Keep the wound clean using St. John's wort oil (a few drops diluted in a cup of water).

Other Considerations

You can apply plantain pulp or extract or potato pulp to the burned area. The starches in these plants cool and soothe as they help add moisture, thus minimizing scarring and blistering. Plantain also helps clean the area. Replace minerals that escape your body through the burn by taking a mineral supplement, bee pollen, or Spirulina. A few drops of oregano oil can help disinfect broken blisters from the burn (remember, a blister is a burn caused by friction).

Bursitis

See also Arthritis, Inflammation

Bursitis is an inflammation of the cavities around your body's muscles and tendons. These cavities are filled with a lubricating (synovial) fluid, and are the area where friction is most likely to occur, especially over the bony regions of the body. The inflammation can cause severe and long-term pain if in an advanced state. Symptoms include:

- Localized pain and muscle ache
- Swelling and redness
- Low range of motion in shoulders, hips, elbows, and other joints
- Complete loss of range of motion in shoulders, hips, elbows and other joints

What Causes Bursitis?

Misalignment of the joints and areas around specific joints can cause bursitis. Other causes include:

- Trauma or physical injury
- Chronic overuse of joints
- Magnesium and vitamin B12 deficiencies
- Allergies
- Osteoarthritis
- Rheumatoid and inflammatory arthritis
- Calcium deposits in the joints
- Gout
- Infection
- Environmental toxins

Treatments for Bursitis

Bursitis can be treated with topical applications, hydrotherapy, aromatherapy, and diet changes. Changing your eating habits can improve overall health and maintain optimal joint function, and can include:

- Eating foods high in magnesium, such as dark, leafy green, and yellow vegetables
- Drinking filtered water, apple cider vinegar, and honey first thing in the morning or right before bed

- One tablespoon of cod liver oil one to two hours before meals to aid digestion
- Avoiding foods such as tomatoes, potatoes, and eggplant, all vegetables from the nightshade family
- Juice supplements of equal parts carrot, celery, cucumber, and beet juice

Flower essences such as Rescue Remedy cream can be applied to the painful areas a minimum of four times a day. Herbal remedies that are taken as tinctures or as a tea include:

- Meadowsweet
- Horsetail
- Willow bark
- Lobelia and cramp bark rubbed on the affected area
- Aloe vera
- Chamomile tea to relax and soothe the muscles and relieve pain

Homeopathic treatments such as Belladonna, Arnica, Ruta grav., and Silicea also may be helpful

Other Considerations

Vitamin B12 injected intra-muscularly can reduce pain over time. Other healing supplements include vitamin C and bioflavonoids, magnesium, calcium, and proteolytic enzymes taken between meals. Alternative health care therapies such as acupuncture, bodywork, chiropractic therapy, and Traditional Chinese Medicine have been shown to reduce or relieve the symptoms of bursitis.

Butter vs. Margarine

Hydrogenated Vegetable Oil / Trans Fat

The age-old controversy about the use of butter or margarine continues, even though studies are now conclusive about the negative effects of margarine. The price you pay for a few grams' reduction in saturated fats by using margarine could be catastrophic to your health. The following are some sobering facts about butter vs. margarine:

1. Both butter and margarine have the same amount of calories.

2. Butter is slightly higher in fat at 8 grams (saturated fats) per tablespoon compared to 5 grams of fat for margarine (2 grams of saturated fats and 3 grams of trans fat).
3. Eating margarine can increase heart disease in women by 53% over eating the same amount of butter, according to a recent Harvard Medical Study.
4. Eating butter increases the absorption of many other nutrients in other foods.
5. Butter has many nutritional benefits, whereas margarine has a few only because they are mechanically added!
6. Margarine is very high in trans-fatty acids. In the United States alone, about 30,000 people per year die early due to diets high in trans-fatty acids. Trans fats are worse for your heart than saturated fat, tripling the risk of coronary heart disease.
7. Margarine increases total cholesterol and LDL cholesterol (the unhealthy cholesterol).
8. Margarine lowers HDL cholesterol (the healthy cholesterol).
9. Margarine increases the risk of cancers up to fivefold.
10. Margarine lowers the quality of breast milk.
11. Margarine decreases immune response.
12. Margarine decreases insulin response, enhancing the possibility of diabetes.

Here are the most disturbing facts: Margarine is only one molecule away from being plastic. The process of hydrogenating vegetable oil to make margarine is the same process used to turn oil into plastic. Plastic is just slightly more hydrogenated than margarine.

Hydrogenated oils slather the arterial walls of your body with a slick sludge. Constant bombardment with hydrogenated oils helps cause arterial blockage.

The process of adding hydrogen to oil turns the oil black. That's right—margarine is initially black, and then dyed yellow to look like butter. Dyes are toxic and cause an allergic reaction in practically everyone. Many cases of hyperactivity, ADD, and ADHD in children have been directly linked to food coloring and other dyes.

Still not convinced? Try this: Purchase a tub of margarine and leave it open in your garage or a shaded area. Within a couple of days, you will see a couple of things. First, no flies—not even those pesky fruit flies—will go near it. That should tell you something immediately. Second, you'll notice that the margarine does not rot or smell any different. This is because it has no nutritional value. Nothing will grow on it; even those teeny microorganisms will not make their home in margarine because microorganisms cannot grow on something that is nearly plastic.

If you still insist on using margarine, go to a garage sale, buy a boatload of Tupperware, melt it down, and spread some of that on your toast. Sound inviting? Yuk!

Cancer

See also Breast Cancer, Prostate Health

We all have cancer cells. The disease we call cancer means that the immune system has failed to kill these naturally occurring cancer cells before they got out of control and proliferated. Overwhelming evidence suggests that cancer is location-specific. That is, it's associated more with environment (foods and exposure to different substances) than with heredity. Since cancer rates are highest in developed countries, an obvious conclusion is that it stems from artificial substances created to make our lives more convenient, such as cleaning products, food preservatives, and artificial sweeteners, colors, and flavors.

The good news is that most cancers can be treated and even cured.

What Causes Cancer?

We know that cancer is a mutation of DNA that causes cells to mutate and divide rapidly. These damaged cells can invade other tissues in the body and spread, causing systemic disease. What causes these mutations? Studies have shown that artificial influences that come with living in a modern society—radiation, artificial food additives, carcinogenic substances (such as asbestos), and viruses—are major factors. In addition, some cancers are associated with specific substances or conditions:

- Alcohol consumption is associated with oral, esophageal, breast, prostate, bladder and stomach cancers.
- Tobacco use and exposure is associated with lung, oral, esophageal, and other cancers.
- Obesity is associated with prostate, colon, and breast cancers.
- A sedentary lifestyle is associated with prostate, colon, breast, and other cancers.

- Poor nutrition is associated with a weak immune system, and therefore almost any type of cancer, especially breast, prostate, stomach, and colon cancers.
- Immune deficiency diseases (such as HIV) are associated with various types of cancer.
- Hepatitis viruses are associated with liver cancer.
- Certain parasitic infections are associated with bladder and liver cancers.

In addition to these influences, risk of cancer is increased by exposure to carcinogens and infectious or toxic chemicals. This includes anabolic steroids and other hormone treatments, radiation and ultraviolet radiation, and toxic household chemicals.

Treatments

Here's a summary of some of the natural treatments for the prevention and control of cancer:

- Avoid exposure to carcinogens and toxic chemicals, including industrial chemicals, hormone treatments and steroids, food additives, artificial sweeteners, and tobacco smoke.
- Reduce alcohol consumption.
- If you are overweight, increase amino acids, proteins, and enzymes in your diet, and reduce saturated fats, red meat, sugars, starches, and processed foods.
- Eat more quality foods known to fight cancer, including carrots, tomatoes, oranges, broccoli, kale, romaine lettuce, watercress, and spinach, all of which are high in lutein, an antioxidant known to lower the risk of breast and other cancers. Soy and soy products such as tofu are effective against colon cancer, as well as hormone-based cancers such as breast and prostate cancer. Studies suggest that it may even directly block malignant cell growth. Also, garlic, onions, broccoli and Astragalus are rich in methylselenocysteine, a cancer preventative.
- Add a regimen of healing herbs and dietary supplements using the information below as a guide.

Herbs & Supplements

For starters, large amounts of antioxidants from red and purple berries, green tea extract, grape seed extract, vitamins C and E, and beta-carotene are essential for a healthy immune system, and for reducing the effects of toxicity in the body that can lead to cancer. Vitamin E is known to cut the risk of prostate cancer in half. Skullcap herb, olive leaf extract, and mistletoe extract are other great additions.

Several plants and herbal extracts can be used alone or with chemotherapy to improve remission rates. These include: mushroom extracts (maitake, shiitake, reishi), mistletoe extract, cats claw, pau d'arco, paw-paw, Poly-MVA (contains palladium, alpha-lipoic acid, trace minerals, amino acids, and vitamins B1, B2, and B12), Carnivora (an extract from the Venus flytrap plant), Essiac tea, mangosteen, and transfer factor.

The alga Spirulina seems to be an extremely potent cancer fighter. Experts believe that it boosts the immune system's natural killer (NK) cells to help them more efficiently defeat cancer cells that naturally form in everyone's body. The alga Chlorella helps fight cancer by increasing the immune systems effectiveness and increasing blood alkaline levels; but it also packs an extra powerful punch against cancer by increasing levels of the antioxidant albumin in the blood.

Research suggests that supplements of the adrenal hormone dehydroepiandrosterone (DHEA) can help prevent and treat cancer in the colon, breast, and lung, and when applied topically, prevent skin cancer.

Other Considerations

Some experts say that cancer cannot grow in a systemic pH above 7. Here's a jingle: Keep your pH around 7.5 and cancer can't survive. This is only partially true in the case of certain cancers. Blood cancers have a hard time in alkaline blood. If there's one theme everyone should apply to all aspects of life, it is balance. Check your pH. If it's below 7, stop eating the Standard American Diet of fatty meats, processed carbohydrates, and sugars and start eating lean protein first thing in the morning with pure water. The Green Powders are a good source of alkalinization. They usually contain wheat grass, rye, barley, and blue-green algae. Also, alkaline water is now available to help raise pH.

Risk of colon cancer can be reduced by coffee enemas. Find a good colon therapist and get flushed.

Bottled-up emotions are not healthy, so get current with your emotions and tend to your emotional/psychological health as much as you do your physical health.

Candida

Candida Albicans / Thrush / Yeast Infection

See also Colon & Intestinal Health, Infection (Bacterial)

The fungi that cause Candida are present in almost everyone; in the mouth, intestines, and vagina. Normally, these fungi live harmoniously with the rest of the body's flora. However, when they are allowed to grow out of control, they can cause the condition known as Candida, or yeast infection. Vaginal candidiasis, or vaginal yeast infection, will affect three-fourths of all women in America—many of them several times. Symptoms include:

- Vaginal itching or irritation
- A thick, often milky and sour-smelling vaginal discharge
- Itching, burning, or irritation at the vaginal opening

Other types of Candida may cause rashes on the hands and moist, covered areas of the body, such as the feet, crease of the buttocks, folds of the breasts, underarms, and genitals. The rash usually manifests with redness, itching, and irritation.

Candida of the mouth, also known as Thrush, appears as soft, white patches on the tongue, lips, and cheeks. It is usually painless, but itching and irritation may be present.

What Causes Candida?

There is really only one cause of Candida: a lack of normal body flora (mainly intestinal, vaginal, and oral) that normally would keep the Candida yeast fungi in balance with the rest of the body's flora. Many things might cause this imbalance:

- Antibiotics and chemotherapy: Medication that eliminates healthy body flora is one of the principal causes of Candida. This includes common antibiotics, AIDS medications, and birth control pills.
- Diet: Poor nutrition may cause a deficiency in the immune system that can lead to the proliferation of Candida fungi.
- Blood sugar levels: High blood sugar levels can increase the risk of Candida infections.
- Thrush is common in diabetics and AIDS patients.

It should be noted that recurrent candidiasis signals the possibility of diabetes, chronic fatigue syndrome, or underlying immune deficiency syndromes.

Treatments

Two keys are needed to eradicate candidiasis. First, reduce the yeast in your diet (or exposure to yeast externally, if your yeast infection is topical). This means no more fermented foods like wine, beer, soy sauce, cheese, and pickled foods. Stop drinking and eating sugars and simple carbs like bread, since these cause blood sugar levels to rise, creating exactly the environment that yeast thrives in.

Second, increase your healthy body flora by taking probiotic cultures and eating yogurt with live cultures, kefir, or dahi. A variety of these foods is best. Your probiotic supplements should be taken 2 to 3 times per day for at least 30 days. For vaginal yeast infection, insert a probiotic capsule inter-vaginally once or twice per week in addition to the above daily oral doses. For intestinal yeast infection, causing diarrhea and food sensitivities, use a probiotic capsule as an enema once or twice per week in addition to the oral dosages.

For yeast infection on the hands or other external regions, apply garlic oil or oregano oil to the infected area 2 to 3 times per day. Dilute these oils 1:4 parts with mineral oil or sweet almond oil. Application of these oils should sting at first—that's just the antifungal oil doing its job.

Other Considerations

Additionally, taking colloidal silver orally can help cure yeast infections; it is an extremely powerful antibacterial that is effective even against Candida. The oral use of colloidal silver is somewhat controversial, as the U.S. Food and Drug Administration (FDA) has been trying to suppress and even ban its medicinal use since the 1940s, but many natural health experts agree that colloidal silver is perfectly safe if reputable brands are used in the appropriate dosages for the appropriate length of time.

Cardiovascular Health

Arterial Stenosis / Atherosclerosis

See also Blood Pressure, Cholesterol, Heart Disease, Weight (Over)

Cardio (meaning heart) vascular (referring to all the vessels throughout your body that carry blood, including arteries) health is generally the same basic idea: reducing the plaque, fatty deposits, and cholesterol that clog and narrow the arteries (called arterial stenosis) and restrict blood flow to the heart and brain. A healthy cardiovascular system includes normal blood pressure and circulation—especially during moments of exercise or exertion.

Cardiovascular disease is the number one cause of death in the United States and Europe—mainly due to the diet and lifestyle associated with these cultures. Over time, plaque and other deposits build up in the arteries until serious and life-threatening heart problems arise, including heart attacks and strokes. By this time, the cardiovascular system is usually quite unhealthy and treatment often must be invasive and radical.

The best treatment for cardiovascular disease is prevention. Maintaining cardiovascular health is about making the diet and lifestyle choices that promote a healthy heart and cardiovascular system.

Causes of Cardiovascular Disease

A number of factors may contribute to an unhealthy cardiovascular system—and most of them are food and lifestyle choices that are 100% preventable. Only genetic and age-related factors are not controllable. Here is a summary of possible causes:

- **Diet:** A diet high in cholesterol, sugar, starch, and saturated fat is the principal cause of cardiovascular disease in the United States.
- **Overweight:** Excess weight causes extra stress on the heart and arteries, and increases the fat that surrounds the heart.
- **High blood pressure:** Hypertension increases the chance of heart failure and other cardiovascular diseases. High blood pressure is caused by dietary considerations, stress, and metabolism (see Thyroid Imbalance and Adrenal Imbalance).

- **Sedentary lifestyle:** Often associated with excess weight, a lifestyle that does not include exercise increases the risk of cardiovascular disease and other related diseases.
- **Diabetes mellitus:** High blood sugar levels, such as those associated with diabetes, increase cardiovascular problems: weight gain, blood pressure, and plaque buildup in the arteries.
- **Genetics:** Studies show that there is often a genetic predisposition to heart and cardiovascular disease, although this usually works in combination with other causes discussed here.
- **Smoking and environmental toxins:** Smoking is well known to increase risk of heart attack due to its effect on blood oxygen, and the increase of harmful toxins that enter the blood from smoke.
- **Stress:** As it is related to hypertension, stress also plays a part in cardiovascular disease. It also causes hormonal imbalances and blood sugar synthesis problems that can damage the circulatory system.
- **Age:** The natural aging process brings about a stiffening of the arteries, which makes us more prone to cardiovascular problems. This can be minimized with vitamins and antioxidants.

Treatments to Strengthen Your Cardiovascular System

A healthy cardiovascular system starts and ends with good dietary choices. Whether you are taking preventative measures or treating cardiovascular problems, there are a few keys you should take to heart (no pun intended):

- Eat right, including plenty of antioxidant-rich foods and cholesterol-reducing foods like garlic, soy, fish oils, and raw cocoa.
- Switch from coffee to green tea or take a green tea extract.
- Take Co-Q10, B-complex, C and E vitamins, and minerals like zinc, calcium, and magnesium.
- Stop smoking, drinking, and prolonged drug use.
- Get omega-3 fatty acids from flaxseed oil or fish oils.

Garlic and garlic oil help promote healthy cholesterol and healthy blood pressure by decreasing levels of LDL (bad) cholesterol and triglycerides, increasing levels of HDL (good) cholesterol, and decreasing the risk of blood clots. Check with your health care provider before taking garlic supplements if you are on a blood-thinning drug such as Coumadin (warfarin sodium) because garlic also thins the blood.

Other Considerations

Red wine consumption for a healthier heart and to make blood platelets less sticky is not a hoax. Red wine contains powerful polyphenols that inhibit oxidation of LDL cholesterol. Red wine also has many antioxidants and bioflavonoids.

More helpful natural supplements include: eicosapentaenoic acid (EPA), ribose, beta-carotene; vitamins B3 (niacin), B6, B12, C, and E; folic acid; the minerals calcium, chromium, magnesium, potassium, and selenium; the amino acids L-arginine, L-taurine, and L-carnitine; Pycnogenol (pine bark extract); and curcumin, Bioperine (piperine, an extract of pepper), and hawthorn berry extract.

Get plenty of exercise, reduce or stop smoking, and engage in stress-reducing practices such as saunas, massage, and yoga.

Carpal Tunnel Syndrome

Cumulative Trauma Disorder (CTD) / Repetitive Motion Syndrome / Tendonitis

See also Inflammation

Do you spend your days typing or performing other repetitive motions? If so, then you may be at risk of acquiring carpal tunnel syndrome. This is especially true if you are a woman, because the hormonal changes associated with menstruation, pregnancy, and menopause are linked to the onset of carpal tunnel syndrome.

Although people afflicted with CTS appear to have normal use of their hands, they are, in fact, usually experiencing great pain and restricted movement. The primary symptoms of CTS include:

- Numbness in the fingers and palm, similar to restricted circulation in the hand or "falling asleep"
- Burning and tingling sensations in the hands
- Difficulty gripping or making a fist
- Reduced sensitivity to temperature.

What Causes CTS?

The carpal tunnel is a passageway between the wrist and hand through which the median nerve passes. This nerve controls sensations to the hand, particularly the palm and inner fingers (thumb, first, and middle fingers). The carpal tunnel passageway is lined with ligaments. When the median nerve gets pinched or squeezed at the wrist due to irritation of the tendons caused by overuse, carpal tunnel syndrome may result. Since not everyone who engages in repetitive motion of the hands and wrists contracts CTS, it is believed that a combination of factors are involved, including predisposition due to a physically smaller carpal tunnel, as well as hormonal influences.

Treatments for CTS

Treatment will depend on the cause in of each particular case. If repetitive movement caused your condition, for example, then you need to avoid the activity, or at least limit it if avoidance is not possible, until the symptoms subside. Here are some ideas to help reduce the effects of CTS:

- Give your hands and wrists a break. Stop repeating the same motion or change positions when performing them.
- Take frequent breaks from the stressful motion to stretch and shake out your hands and wrists. Give yourself a quick wrist massage. Do not underestimate what this type of stimulation can do to combat CTS.
- Take B vitamins for a healthy nervous system.
- Increase the anti-inflammatories in your diet, including tumeric, cayenne, curry, green tea, and vitamins C and E.
- Try acupuncture and yoga exercises.

Other Considerations

Since CTS is an irritation or inflammation of the tendons in the carpal tunnel, a regimen of anti-inflammatory herbs may relieve the symptoms. Some excellent anti-inflammatories include:

- Vitamins C and E
- Curry, cumin, tumeric, cinnamon
- White willow bark (precursor to aspirin)
- Skullcap
- Yarrow Root
- Aloe vera

Cataracts

More than half of all Americans over 50 have some form of cataracts, and nearly everyone over the age of 70 has them. Cataracts are the leading cause of vision loss. They are opaque, or blurry, spots on the eye lens. They don't improve and they don't go away. Depending on the severity of the cataract, vision loss can be significant.

Surgical procedures are available for repairing or replacing the lens, but the best medicine for cataracts is preventing them, or at least minimizing their severity. Diet and lifestyle treatments can help alleviate this problem.

What Causes Cataracts?

A cataract forms when proteins that form the lens of the eyeball begin to deteriorate. When this happens, a portion of the lens becomes opaque and hinders vision. Causes of lens protein deterioration include:

- **Genetics:** Some people are genetically predisposed to develop cataracts. These people should take precautionary measures to maintain eye health.
- **Age:** Deterioration from age is a common cause of cataracts. Again, this can be minimized by certain dietary influences, such as antioxidants and immune system support.
- **Radiation:** Ultraviolet radiation, usually from sun exposure, (and other forms of radiation) are a suspected cause of cataracts and other sight-related problems.
- **Hormonal imbalance:** imbalances caused by steroids, diabetes, and certain prescription drugs may play a part in causing cataracts.

Treatments

Ten years of vitamin C intake of 500 mg a day before the age of 60 helps reduce cataracts by 57%. Antioxidants such as Pycnogenol (pine bark extract) and beta-carotene also can be of help. Keep your eyes washed with carbon-activated water by spraying it into your eyes every morning. Don't worry about the overspray on your face: All it will do is preserve your skin and slow down wrinkle formation. Also, drink plenty of water for overall body hydration.

Don't forget to fill up your plate with lutein-rich vegetables: carrots, corn, kale, spinach, Swiss chard, collard, mustard greens, red peppers, dill, parsley, romaine lettuce, tomatoes, and potatoes, as well as red, blue, and purple fruits. Lutein and its associated carotenoid zeaxanthin help protect delicate eye tissues from free radical damage. In fact, according to a Harvard-based study, women with diets high in lutein reduce their risk of developing cataracts by 22%; men reduce their risk by 19%.

Besides lutein, other antioxidants are helpful for your eyes and overall health: bilberry, grape seed extract, Pycnogenol (pine bark extract), olive leaf extract, and dark red and purple fruits.

Exercise your eyes. Spend five minutes a day rolling your eyes in wide circles or focusing between near and far objects. Also, rest your eyes during the day for a couple of minutes—especially if you work in front of a computer or perform other tasks that create eye strain. Simply close your eyes for two or three minutes to give them a rest.

Cellulite

See also Cardiovascular Health, Liver & Gallbladder Health, Weight (Over),

The bane of many women's beauty programs, cellulite has become a national obsession. About 95% of all adult women have some cellulite on their body. It is responsible for a huge part of the billion-dollar cosmetic surgery industry and is the reason many women will not wear bathing suits or appear at beaches or swimming pools. So much grief caused by a single villain. How can we eradicate it? More important, how can we rid ourselves of cellulite without expensive and dangerous surgical techniques? And how do we prevent cellulite in the first place? Why do some overweight people have very little, while other people, only slightly plump, have a lot?

How is Cellulite Formed?

You don't have to be overweight to get cellulite, but it helps. Here's how cellulite is created: Weak blood vessels can't carry as many nutrients to the skin. When less blood and, consequently, fewer nutrients are circulated through fat cells on their way to the surface of the skin, bands of fibers surround fat cells and harden. These hardened bands contract around the fat cells, pushing them out toward the skin surface, creating cellulite's dimply appearance.

Good circulation equals less cellulite. Since the fat cells of women behave differently than those of men (being more rigid and prone to bulging toward the surface of the skin), women suffer from cellulite much more than men do. It has also been documented that Caucasian women are more prone to cellulite than women of other races.

There is likely a hormonal component to cellulite as well, because an increase in estrogen often leads to an increase in cellulite—even in men.

What's more, fat cells, once created, are not destroyed—even if the fat inside them is burned off. That's why it's so easy for dieters to gain their old weight back again. The cells are already there, ready to return to their previous state. So it's important to burn energy before it gets stored as fat. It's important to note that liposuction, which removes fat cells from under the skin, does not cure cellulite. Just because fat cells are removed, it does not follow that the remaining cells will stop pushing fat to the skin in their place.

Treatments to Reduce Cellulite

The process of eliminating cellulite is becoming less and less of a mystery. Today, we know much more about diet and the biochemical processes that result from our food choices. Here are the essentials:

- Rebalance your diet to include more proteins and amino acids and fewer fats, carbohydrates, and sugars.
- Exercise daily. Make sure your exercise is burning fat. You should be sweating and breathing hard at the peak of your exercise. Water-based exercise programs are not effective for fat burning. The best exercises are aerobic workouts, running, and bicycle riding.
- This is critical: Eat before you exercise, not after. Eating before stimulates the catabolic process of the body (to burn fat), while eating after stimulates the anabolic process (tissue building).
- Include vigorous massage or skin stimulation in your health program to physically break down cellulite structures.
- Increase your intake of bioflavonoids and vitamin C for healthy connective tissues. Mangoes, seahawthorn, and citrus fruit are good sources of bioflavonoids.
- Drink plenty of water for cell health.

Chapped Lips

Angular Cheilitis

Anyone who has spent time skiing, hiking, or just relaxing outdoors has probably experienced chapped lips at some point. This condition, which ranges from slightly annoying to extremely painful, is associated with drying of the lips from weather exposure. Lip salves and balms can help prevent and even heal chapped lips.

If you suffer from painful, even bleeding cracks and splits in your lips, especially at the corners of the mouth, then you may have developed angular cheilitis, a condition brought on not by weather or dryness, but by a virus or fungus.

What Causes Chapped Lips?

Your lips are prone to chapping because they are covered with epithelial tissue, the same sensitive material that lines your intestines. Exposure to cold, windy weather can cause chapping, as can excessive moisture (licking the lips) and allergenic lipstick.

Angular cheilitis is usually caused by a fungal, viral or bacterial infection. It also can be brought on by biting or excessive licking of the lips.

Treating Chapped Lips

Stop putting petroleum-based products on your lips. They feel slick but actually dry your lips, which is why you need to keep applying them—which is a good way for the manufacturer to get more of your money. Instead, use lip balms or gloss made from shea butter, beeswax, and vegetable or nut oils. Also use vitamin A, D, and E oils or ointments (preferably the concentrated 32,000 IU/ounce variety of vitamin E). Use a generous amount and your damaged lips will heal in nearly an instant. Also, B vitamins can help prevent chapping.

Tea tree oil is a natural antiseptic and antibacterial that can be an effective treatment against angular chelitis. It can be used in combination with vitamin E.

Cholesterol

Bad Cholesterol (LDL) / Fat / Fatty Acids / Good Cholesterol (HDL) / Lipoproteins

See also Blood Pressure, Cardiovascular Health, Heart Disease, Inflammation, Weight (Over)

There's a good and bad story with cholesterol. Cholesterol, in the right quantities, is vital for life. High-density lipoprotein (HDL) is good cholesterol. Low-density lipoprotein (LDL) is bad cholesterol. That's the easy part of the story. From there, and with the involvement of your liver, the cholesterol story becomes quite chemically complex. So, without going into a dissertation, here's the easy way to deal with cholesterol. Take the right nutrients (called lipotropics) and you can keep the bad cholesterol moving so it doesn't muck up your liver and stick to your arterial walls, thus greatly reducing your risk of coronary problems. Do not think about all the terms: triglycerides, VLDL cholesterol, saturated vs. unsaturated fats, and so on. Keep it simple!

What Causes High Cholesterol Levels?

Here's the culprit that creates too much bad cholesterol: The Standard American Diet (SAD), which is filled with fats, processed meats, and excess sugar and salt; smoking; caffeine; stress; birth control pills; environmental toxins; smog; and food additives. Though many of these elements are enjoyable, cutting back on them will make you thinner, healthier, and happier, while adding quality years to your life.

LDL (bad) cholesterol is like a Band-Aid in that it oxidizes and sticks to arterial walls whenever there is inflammation caused by foods such as refined white sugar and starches.

Treatments

Much is known about controlling cholesterol. The key is to form new eating and lifestyle habits and disciplines. Here is a summary of the foods, nutritional supplements, plants, herbal extracts, and lifestyle treatments that will do the trick:

- To keep LDL cholesterol under control, and thereby keep arterial walls clear, be sure to have a lot of garlic, soy, and lutein-rich vegetables in your diet. These include carrots, corn, kale, spinach, Swiss chard, collard greens, mustard greens, red peppers, dill, parsley, romaine lettuce, tomatoes, potatoes, and red, blue, and purple fruits.

- Research shows that the mushroom Cordyceps (tincture or pill form) reduces LDL and raises HDL cholesterol, while inhibiting the formation of plaque in cell walls and raising energy.
- Take potent lipotropics (to promote the utilization of fats) such as methionine, choline, and inositol.
- Also add vitamin B6, non-flush niacin, omega-3 fatty acids, chromium picolinate, pantothenic acid, red yeast, and tocotrienol vitamin E. Omega-3 fatty acids can be found in flaxseed oil, rapeseed oil, and some fish. You can also get omega-3 in chia seeds and salba seeds from the salvia plant.
- Reduce intake of saturated fats and omega-6 fatty acids. Sources of omega-6 include vegetable oils (canola, soybean, walnut, safflower, and sunflower oils).
- Drink a glass of red wine each night. Red wine contains powerful polyphenols that inhibit oxidation of LDL cholesterol. Red wine also has many antioxidants and bioflavonoids.

If you are on a blood-thinning drug such as Coumadin (warfarin sodium), consult your health care provider before taking garlic supplements because garlic also thins the blood.

Other Considerations

Soybean oil and walnut oil are rich in omega-3 and omega-6 fatty acids, with a leaning toward omega-6. Since our diets already tend to give us an excess of omega-6 and a shortage of omega-3, you should probably avoid these oils along with other omega-6 sources.

As you've probably already heard, eating foods high in fiber, like oatmeal, also helps lower the LDL cholesterol level, the cholesterol that free radicals oxidize and turn into plaque that sticks on arterial walls. Plus, eating whole grains (rather than refined grains) is better for your whole body, playing a role in the prevention of diabetes and obesity.

Chronic Fatigue

Epstein-Barr Syndrome / Post Viral Fatigue Syndrome (PVFS)

See also Adrenal Imbalance, Diabetes, Energy Enhancement, Fibromyalgia, Hypoglycemia, Thyroid Imbalance,

Chronic fatigue is commonly associated with overuse of the adrenal gland, known as adrenal exhaustion. Stress, the excess use of artificial stimulants (including caffeine), and viruses (including herpes virus 6 and Epstein-Barr virus) can all cause chronic fatigue. But chronic fatigue syndrome is not so simple. It may also be caused by other viruses, immune system disorders, or low blood pressure. In most instances, chronic fatigue is diagnosed when all of the above conditions are ruled out and no other explanation for the symptoms can be found. Typical symptoms include:

- constant fatigue, no matter how much sleep you get and lasting more than six months
- difficulty mustering energy for normal functions
- tenderness of the lymph nodes and muscles
- depression
- drowsiness
- light-headedness
- mental cloudiness and memory loss
- decreased libido

You may also experience disturbed sleep patterns, mood swings, headache, and loss of appetite.

What Causes Chronic Fatigue?

The exact cause of CFS remains unknown, making the condition difficult to treat. Following is a summary of the possible causes of CFS:

- **Adrenal Depletion:** Drink a lot of coffee? Have a stressful life? Then you may be at risk for adrenal exhaustion, also called adrenal depletion, which often manifests as chronic fatigue.
- **Viruses and Immune System Dysfunction:** Epstein-Barr virus and human herpes virus 6 have been linked to CFS, although some say these are not directly responsible for CFS. Excess Candida albicans (a yeast-

like fungus found normally in the body) is also often present in those who suffer from CFS.

- **Low Blood Pressure:** Studies show that low blood pressure is a common condition in CFS patients and that increasing blood pressure can improve energy in most cases.

Treatments for Chronic Fatigue

The most important thing you can do for chronic fatigue caused by adrenal exhaustion is to support your adrenal glands (see Adrenal Imbalance). If your condition is caused by a virus, then use antiviral herbs and food therapies:

- Maca root
- St. John's wort
- Garlic extract
- Green tea and green tea extract
- Una de Gato, or Cat's Claw, from the Amazon (scientific name, Uncaria tomentosa).
- Refer to Infection (Viral) for more information.

To augment and balance low blood pressure:

- Take an iron supplement.
- Eat Spirulina to aid in the body's absorption of minerals and help balance blood sugar levels.
- Eat foods rich in bioflavonoids, such as red grapes, green tea, bilberry, hawthorn root, and gotu kola.
- Eat antioxidant-rich foods.
- Refer to Blood Pressure (Low) for more details about treating low blood pressure.

Other Considerations

Some experts believe that Chronic Fatigue is as much a neuro-emotional-based problem as it is a physical or biochemical-based problem. When all the other possible explanations have been ruled out, and symptoms remain, then you are diagnosed with Chronic Fatigue, In other words, Chronic Fatigue is the medical establishment saying, "We don't know what's wrong with you." At this point, it would be wise to look into possible causes not associated with typical solutions, including (or maybe especially) emotional and psychological causes. Losing the will to continue, chronic hopelessness, depression, and shock or trauma can all cause the symptoms associated with CFS.

Chronic fatigue is often mistaken for Lyme disease; be sure you are tested for this if you are experiencing CFS symptoms.

Cirrhosis

See also Inflammation, Liver & Gallbladder Health

Cirrhosis refers to any organ that has chronic interstitial inflammation. It can be a leading cause of chronic liver disease, and is often found by the abnormal changes in liver cells that cause hardening and inflammation of the organ itself.

As a result of cirrhosis, the liver becomes damaged and cannot perform well. This can become a long-term problem before you even realize there is a problem, because there are sometimes no overt symptoms until it becomes chronic. Early symptoms include:

- Fatigue
- Rashes of unknown causes
- Constipation and diarrhea
- Alternating color of the stools
- Fever
- Indigestion
- Itching

Chronic levels of cirrhosis can lead to severe symptoms including:

- Abdominal swelling with fluid (ascites)
- Pain
- Vomiting blood
- Swelling or bloating of the body
- Jaundice (yellowing of the skin)
- Coma or death in the severe stages
- Easy bruising

What Causes Cirrhosis?

The liver is affected by any number of factors, and can become toxic because of toxic bowels or toxic blood. This may be caused by pharmaceutical drugs taken on a regular basis, alcohol consumption, and exposure to environmental chemicals.

Treatments for Cirrhosis

Diet is extremely important in preventing and reversing liver disease, and cirrhosis can be helped with detoxification and a steady, pure foods diet. Detoxification helps to reduce the symptoms of cirrhosis and cleanse the body's natural systems. Complete a colon and intestinal cleanse in your plans before you start a liver and other body cleanses.

Diets should be comprised of whole and organic foods that include seeds, nuts, whole grains, beans, nuts, green leafy vegetables, and goat, soy, or rice milk. Avoid alcohol and processed or saturated fats, including margarine and hydrogenated oils. Substitute with cold-processed oils such as olive oil and flaxseed oil.

Foods high in amino acids and potassium are helpful. These include nuts, seeds, bananas, raisins, rice, wheat bran, kelp, dulse, molasses, and brewer's yeast. Avoid animal protein, as well as raw or undercooked fish. Juice therapy can help eliminate toxins, especially apple juice. Also try beet and carrot juices and green drinks that contain Spirulina, Chlorella, and other green elements.

Herbs such as milk thistle can help treat and regulate liver cells, and help with cell regeneration. Other herbs, such as Picrorhiza kurroa, has a similar effect, and licorice root is often helpful. The Chinese herb bupleururn is another one to try.

Helpful nutritional supplements include vitamin C, vitamin E, lipoic acid, and raw liver tablets. Take regular doses of vitamin B complex, selenium, folic acid, digestive enzymes with hydrochloric acid, and the amino acides L-carnitine, L-cysteine, L-glutathione, and L-arginine.

Other Considerations

Other alternative therapies include acupuncture, detoxification therapy, natural hormone replacement therapy, and Traditional Chinese Medicine.

Cold Intolerance

Chills / Cold Sensitivity / Shivers

See also Energy Enhancement, Thyroid Imbalance

Tired of always having to wear an extra sweater or jacket wherever you go? Do you avoid movie theaters because you're always shivering in your seat from the freezing temperatures? Well, there's a cure and it's easy to come by.

If you are frequently cold or get cold easily, suffering from chills, shivering, and cold intolerance, natural therapies can be very effective. Extreme sensitivity to cold (getting cold even when others are warm) is a sign of possible dietary imbalances and should be treated. You will feel warmer and probably have more energy too.

What Causes Cold Intolerance?

Cold intolerance means a person may have difficulty staying warm or simply gets cold very easily. This can be a sign of poor health due to a variety of conditions, including

- Thyroid imbalance
- Adrenal imbalance
- Chronic respiratory conditions
- Low blood pressure
- Poor digestion
- Protein deficiency
- Nutritional deficiencies, particularly B vitamins and iron
- Anorexia

Chills are often associated with fever and may be caused by an infection.

Treatments for Cold Intolerance

Chills can be reduced or regulated in a variety of ways. For permanent increased body heat, try the following essential treatments:

- Substantially increase protein intake.
- Substantially increase exercise.
- Take liquid B-complex and C vitamins.
- Get plenty of amino acids.

- Add spices to your meals. Spices like cayenne, tumeric, curry and red pepper increase your heart rate and warm your body.

Herbs such as chamomile, ginger, boneset, and yarrow can help relieve chills. Adding cayenne pepper to food can boost the digestive fire and improve circulation. See Blood Pressure (Low) for more information about enhancing circulation.

Colds

See also Infection (Bacterial), Infection (Viral), Sore Throat

Colds come in two forms: viral (caused by any one of 200 different viruses) and bacterial. Either way, they are easily spread from person to person. A handshake, contact with a door knob, sneezes, and coughs are all potential transmitters of cold viruses. If you are often around kids, your chances of catching colds are higher than most. The infectious bacteria or virus usually enters through the nose or mouth and attacks your nasal passages or throat. From there, it spreads through the nasal cavity or down through the throat to the lungs to attack the mucus membranes there. At that point, there is little you can do to stop it. But some people manage to prevent colds before they spread and take over.

Treatments to Prevent Colds

The best way to prevent a cold is to boost the immune system with vitamin C, Spirulina, or olive leaf extract, and antioxidants from fruit and vegetable sources. During cold seasons, or when others around you have colds, you may also want to take extra vitamin C, Echinacea with goldenseal, and Lomatium. It's not always possible to know when cold viruses and bacteria are making the rounds, however, so it's important to have a cold-killing throat spray on hand. When you feel the first signs of itching or irritation in the throat, use the following ingredients together in an antiviral, antibacterial contact spray:

- Liquid St. John's wort (50 ml)
- Liquid Echinacea (50 ml)
- Tea tree oil or propolis (a few drops)
- Grapefruit seed extract (a few drops)

Mix these together and spray the solution onto your throat at the first sign of irritation. If you don't have a spray tincture bottle, use an eye dropper. Besides the above tinctures and extracts, pomegranate extract is a good topical antiviral for the throat. Some experts prefer to apply a few drops of 3% hydrogen peroxide into each ear upon first signs of a cold. You can apply drops two or three times per day until the symptoms disappear.

Treatments if you Already Have a Cold

If a cold is viral, accompanied by fever, vitamin C is very helpful, starting with 3 grams, then 1 gram every hour until the fever breaks. (Seasoned vitamin C veterans can increase the dosage but newcomers to high dosages of vitamin C may experience diarrhea.)

For a bacterial cold (the snotty kind), add 100,000 IU of vitamin A (beta-carotene) and 50 mg of picolinated zinc with a little food. (Do not take this amount of vitamin A if you are pregnant or may become pregnant.) Zinc is a potent remedy against the common cold because it boosts your immune system's T cells to help them kill the cold bacteria or virus quickly and efficiently. Though research on zinc and colds is inconclusive, a 2000 study found that taking 12.8 mg of zinc reduced the duration of cold symptoms in general by 50%, with cough reduced by 50% and mucus discharge reduced by 30%.

Traditional Chinese Medicine practitioners prescribe ginger for the common cold, and many Western alternative health practitioners today attest to its effectiveness. At the first sign of a cold, steep three to four pieces of ginger in hot water to make a tea. Then add some honey to taste. If you have chills and a fever, add some basil to the ginger tea.

Add three to four garlic capsules to speed up the results. Echinacea herb capsules (with goldenseal if possible), along with thymus glandular (builds T cells) will help. Olive leaf extract is a powerful antioxidant and boosts energy while decreasing recovery time from viral, bacterial, and fungal infestation.

If your cold has flu symptoms such as sore, achy muscles, mix one tablespoon of horseradish in one cup of olive oil. Let the mixture sit for 30 minutes, then apply it as a massage oil for instant relief for aching muscles.

If you're suffering from coughing bouts, licorice lozenges act as a natural cough suppressant and expectorant, so you'll cough less and cough up more mucus when you do. Cayenne pepper in 3 to 4 capsules spread through the day helps break up congestion.

Colon & Intestinal Health

Bowel Health / Colon Cleanse / Colonics / Colon Therapy / Enema

See also Candida, Constipation, Diarrhea, Digestion, Irritable Bowel Syndrome, Liver & Gallbladder Health

The colon and bowels are probably among the worst cared for parts of the body by most Americans. Our dietary habits create a host of intestinal problems, including the presence of more than a hundred different kinds of worms and parasites, clogged and sluggish plumbing, and colon cancer and other serious intestinal diseases. Want more possibilities? Here's the short list on what poor colon health can mean:

- Increased allergies and food sensitivities
- Increased risk of parasites
- Foul-smelling flatulence and bad breath
- Constipation and slow bowels
- Irritable Bowel Syndrome (IBS) and colon diseases
- Increased risk of illness from bacteria and viruses
- Lack of energy, sluggishness, chronic fatigue
- More intense PMS pain and cramping
- Headaches
- Back pain
- Liver disease

Treatments for a Healthy Colon

Since the causes of poor colon health are fairly straightforward (mostly stemming from dietary habits), the cures are also fairly straightforward. The key is to eliminate or greatly reduce unhealthy foods from the diet, including: saturated fats, dairy products, excess starches and sugars, and red meat. Here are some of the keys to getting your colon back into shape:

- **Enemas and Colonics:** Colons are like massive honeycombs, with pockets that can harbor years-old waste. In fact, several pounds of bacteria-laden fecal matter can become attached to the walls of the colon, causing chronic fatigue, flatulence, bloating, skin disorders, breathing difficulties, arthritis, and constipation. Colonic cleanses help remove this waste and restore the youth to your intestines and bowels. Colonics can help eliminate some intestinal parasites,

too. Flatulence often can be cured by hydro colon therapy and a good diet.

- **Probiotics:** The opposite of antibiotics, probiotics work to restore the healthy bacteria in your body, including your intestinal flora. Two of the most common probiotic flora are acidophilus and bifidophilus. It is essential to take probiotics after taking antibiotics, doing a colon cleanse, or chemotherapy, so as to regenerate the friendly fauna and flora that live in your colon and intestines and help you digest and absorb your food. Remember, antibiotic means anti (against) bio (life). Antibiotics kill everything in the bacterial realm, including the good bacteria in your body. Candida yeast infections are caused by a lack of healthy body flora.
- **Fiber and raw foods:** It is widely known that fiber from raw foods helps clean your intestines, especially raw or lightly cooked broccoli, Brussels sprouts, and cabbage (all in the cabbage family). Fiber from grains and seeds is also beneficial.
- **The cholesterol connection:** Too much cholesterol in the diet forms gallstones in the liver and gallbladder, leading to poor digestion and processing of fats and proteins. These poorly digested fats and proteins end up in the intestines and colon, mucking up the works.

One of the most widely used agents for enemas or colonics is coffee. Coffee stimulates the lining of the colon and causes it to excrete more proficiently. It also cleans up the bile ducts between the colon and the liver / gallbladder. Coffee gets the deep peristalsis (the natural movement through your entire digestive tract) going again.

After your enema or colonic cleansing is complete, you can reintroduce liquid chlorophyll, which is very healing, energizing, and soothing, back into your colon. Chlorophyll is molecularly the closest substance to the hemoglobin in your red blood cells, so you can imagine the regenerative and healing benefits it has.

Colon cleanse supplement programs are also widely available. Most of these are multi-day programs that use herbs and supplements to help remove waste from the intestines. Some key ingredients used in these programs include: ground black walnut shell / husk, garlic extract, psyllium husk, bentonite clay (or liquid), pau d'arco, wormwood, yellow dock, citric acid from lemon or grapefruit, cayenne pepper, and slippery elm.

Other Considerations

The best way to instantly lose five pounds is an enema, which you can do yourself in case you're embarrassed by a technician putting a hose in your tailpipe. Colon work seems to be the most embarrassing and secretive thing for most people, but if you were initially embarrassed by the idea, once you've done it to yourself, hydro colon therapy done by a practitioner will be no problem for you. Hydro colon therapists are very gentle and professional in what they do.

Though colon therapy is great for most people, those with intestinal tumors, Crohn's disease, ulcerative colitis, diverticulitis, or severe hemorrhoids should not do colon therapy because it may worsen these conditions.

Conjunctivitis

See also **Cataracts, Macular Degeneration**

Conjunctivitis is also called pink eye, and is easily identified by the characteristic pink on the cornea of the eye. It is due to an irritation of the mucus membrane that lines the eyes and eyelids. Symptoms include:

- Pain, irritation, and itching in the eye
- Discharge and watery eyes
- Swelling around the eyes
- Sensitivity to light

In addition, the eyelids can sometimes stick together, especially after sleeping or napping.

What Causes Conjunctivitis?

The leading causes of conjunctivitis include allergies, infection, stress, and nutritional deficiencies. If you rub your eyes often, bacteria and viruses may be carried to the area from your hands. Some pharmaceutical drugs can also cause conjunctivitis, including antihistamines, oral contraceptives, steroids, Chlorpromazine, Digoxin, and Tetracycline. These drugs can also lead to additional vision problems.

Treatments for Conjunctivitis

Diet is important in treating conjunctivitis, and a diet rich in organic, whole foods, and fresh fruit is recommended. Vegetables high in antioxidants can help cleanse the system and reduce or remove the appearance of conjunctivitis. Antioxidant-rich foods include dark-green leafy vegetables, dark rich-colored berries, cherries, mangos, citrus fruit, melons, and purple or red grapes. Organic egg yolks are also recommended for their high carotenoid content; they are best eaten soft, rather than hard cooked. Organic raw eggs may be eaten after a thorough washing. Avoid processed and fried foods, excess sugar, and alcohol.

Nutritional supplementation includes vitamin A, vitamin B complex, beta-carotene, vitamin E, flavonoids, N-acetyl-cysteine (NAC), selenium, zinc, zeaxthanin, and taurine. Juice supplementation with a combination of carrot and beet juice, cucumber, parsley, and spinach is also recommended.

Traditional Chinese Medicine can improve vision problems by enhancing liver function with herbs like ginseng and Ginkgo biloba.

Other Considerations

Exercise your eyes on a regular basis to prevent or reverse vision problems. Relax your eyes, then focus, then relax. Blink regularly to reduce eyestrain and roll your eyes in a circular motion at least three times a day.

Costipation

Irregularity / Laxatives / Lazy Bowel Syndrome / Slow Bowels

See also Colon & Intestinal Health, Digestion, Irritable Bowel Syndrome

Constipation, in a strict medical sense, refers to an inability to completely evacuate the rectum. In practical terms, however, constipation quite likely is an indication that the colon is clogged, sluggish, loaded with poison, and malfunctioning. Cleansing your colon is the most critical step in improving your health! Purging accumulated toxins and waste from your body and restoring normal waste removal function is often the quickest way to cure disease and restore health.

A clogged bowel impedes the assimilation of nutrients by the body, since it affects the entire digestive system. The major drawback to being constipated is the resulting lack of nutrition you receive from your food. The list of diseases and ailments that could be avoided or cured with a quality colon cleansing program is practically endless: problems with weight gain, prostate, kidneys, heart, fertility, blood sugar, blood pressure, hormonal balance, liver, cholesterol, immune function, energy are just a few linked to constipation and inactive bowels.

The colon is very large and positioned within the body in such a way that it comes into direct contact or is in the vicinity of every major organ in the body, with the exception of the brain. It is also in direct contact with most major blood vessels and nerves in the abdominal area. Constipation causes the colon to swell and in some cases even herniate. When this occurs, the colon will compress and crush the major organs nearby—the reason a constipated, swollen colon can be the underlying cause of a long list of diseases and ailments that may seem completely unrelated.

What Causes Constipation?

Quite simply, constipation and other colon-related problems are primarily a result of dietary habits. The Standard American Diet is high in dairy products, fats, red meat, and starches, while lacking enough dietary fiber, vegetables, and fruit. As a result, the average American adult stores from six to 10 pounds of toxic waste in the colon—an extremely unhealthy state. Other possible causes of constipation include:

- **Medications:** Many prescription medications cause constipation, as do plenty of over-the-counter treatments. Avoid products that contain aluminum (you should avoid these anyway) and try to avoid excess calcium and iron. Other common offenders include antidepressants, antihistamines, beta blockers, muscle relaxants, and most of all analgesics.
- **Thyroid Imbalance:** Imbalance in the thyroid can cause a biochemical chain reaction that, for some, results in constipation. This will usually be accompanied by other symptoms related to hypothyroidism. See Thyroid Imbalance for more information.
- **Radical change in diet:** People commonly experience constipation when vacationing in a foreign country or whenever they make a radical change of diet.

Usually, regularity is restored upon returning to the normal routine.

- **Intestinal disorders:** Tumors, hernia, muscle disorders, and other damage to the intestine may be a cause of constipation. Also, absence of friendly flora such as acidophilus can cause constipation and other disorders, like Candida.
- **Sedentary lifestyle:** Contributing to many disorders, a lack of movement and exercise may also be making your constipation worse.

Treatment

In people without medical problems, the main treatment for constipation is to increase your intake of fluids (preferably pure water) and dietary fiber. A good herbal laxative is psyllium seed. You can also try folic acid and vitamin C supplements. Avoiding animal products and consuming more fresh organic vegetables and fruit is vital. Healthy dietary changes will go further in getting your colon back on track than anything.

If you are suffering from constipation or lazy bowels, avoid using over-the-counter laxatives that contain such poisons as strychnine, belladonna, and aloin.

Many effective natural supplements can relieve constipation. Perhaps topping the list is cascara sagrada, a bark from a tree in the Amazon, which is gentle but powerful for restoring regularity. You should stop taking cascara sagrada once regularity is restored. Other good natural products include curacao and cape aloe leaf, barberry root bark, senna leaves and pods, ginger rhizomes, and habeero pepper.

Colonics are amazingly effective for helping to clean the colon and restoring normal bowel function. Natural products great for removing toxins from the colon include pharmaceutical-grade bentonite clay (absorbs and draws poisons from the walls of the colon and intestines), slippery elm bark, marshmallow root, psyllium seed, and peppermint leaf. More information on colon cleanse can be found under Colon & Intestinal Health. Check with your healthcare professional for a qualified referral.

Other Considerations

Regardless of how little your problem may seem to relate to the colon, cleansing the bowel first is often a good bet. The best way to restore and maintain health is to detoxify the body and remove accumulated waste. In order to detox properly, the colon must be clear and operating smoothly. When you detox to purge accumulated waste and toxins, all this waste is finally processed through the colon. If the colon is constipated and not functioning properly, all of the poisons and toxins that were being flushed from your body will not be efficiently eliminated and could even be reabsorbed. This is why many people feel so ill during a detoxification program and often quit shortly after starting. By cleaning your colon first, the program will work much better and you will actually feel great throughout the process.

Corns

Calluses

Corns are painful growths on the outside of the foot. They look like wart-like bumps or hard fleshy knots on and around the toes. Corns can resemble infected calluses and warts and can become painful when pressure is applied to them. They also can swell up and become irritated. The usual treatment is to cut them away with a sharp instrument.

What Causes Corns?

Corns can result from poorly fitting shoes or infected calluses or warts. Soft corns often occur between the toes, while harder corns are usually found on the tops of the toes. Corns can also be the result of poor walking or gait problems.

Treatments for Corns

Aromatherapy treatments include rubbing lemon or verucas essential oil on the infected area to help relieve pain. Apply flower essences topically, including Rescue Remedy Cream, arnica, and herbs such as calendula petals. These can be applied two to three times a day. These treatments help soften the tissue and act as anti-inflammatory agents.

You can also try hydrotherapy with an application of hot and cold temperatures (hot water and ice).

Consult your podiatrist, osteopath, or chiropractor, who can evaluate your natural gait to determine if you are walking in an irregular manner, thus causing the rubbing and irritation that results in corns.

Other Considerations

Nutritional supplementation includes vitamin A and vitamin E; both can be applied topically or taken orally. Well-fitting shoes and clean socks are also recommended.

Cough

See also Colds

Coughing is a natural reaction to obstruction in the trachea or air passages. When a cough is associated with other cold symptoms, this obstruction is usually excess phlegm or mucus from the lungs or nasal passages. The mucus buildup results from bacteria or viruses in the body that have attacked the mucus membranes in an insidious effort to spread themselves to other humans (through contact, coughing, and sneezing).

Chronic coughing (ongoing and not associated with a temporary illness) is usually caused by smoking, nasal problems, or asthma. In some cases, chronic coughing could indicate disease.

Treatments

Since coughs have so many possible and divergent causes, it's difficult to offer a few, simple keys to cure them. Nevertheless, here are some possibilities to help with cough symptoms, whatever the cause:

- Use essential oils of eucalyptus, myrrh, peppermint, chamomile, pine, or rosemary in steam diffusions or room diffusers.
- Avoid foods that cause mucus, including dairy products, wheat, sugar, and starchy foods.
- Eat more nutrient-rich, health-forming foods, including Spirulina, bee pollen, spinach, dandelion greens, kale, and other super foods. This will help your immune system fight off pathogens that are causing the cough.
- Reduce mucus with ginger, cayenne, cinnamon, tumeric, and clove. Use as a gargle or take these spices in capsule form or combine them with honey to soothe the throat.
- For coughs associated with cold or allergy, gargle with sea salt water as hot as you can stand.

Other Considerations

Combine ground perilla seed, ground apricot seed, slippery elm, and licorice and take orally. Take vitamin A (100,000 IU) until the cough dissipates (pregnant women should not take this much vitamin A). A research study published in 2000 demonstrated that 12.8 mg of zinc reduces the length of time you suffer from a cough by 50%.

Cysts

See also Antibacterial, Anti-Inflammatory, Antiviral

There are many types of cysts and many locations where they may form on (or in) the body. In general, cysts are benign, non-cancerous, and harmless. But some can be irritating and unattractive, and some internal cysts can grow dangerously large. Cysts can form on the neck and upper part of the back; near joints, such as the wrists and knees, and in the ovaries, vagina, and breasts.

Cysts are usually caused by fluid that gets trapped and collects under the skin, often near joints or glands. They can cause swelling and irritation and, if they break, can be quite painful. Ovarian cysts may cause irregular menstruation and abdominal pain, and vaginal cysts can be irritated by sexual activity and can quickly become infected.

Cysts often have few symptoms and go away naturally over time. However, you can help them go away more quickly. Large cysts should probably be drained by your doctor so they do not continue to grow or rupture.

Treatments

High dosages (800-1600 IU) of succinate (dry) vitamin E for periods of six months will greatly reduce cysts of all kinds. Tocotrienols are best, but try rotating them, so your body doesn't get used to the same product. Vitamin E thins your blood, so don't be alarmed if any cuts bleed a little more during this time. After the cyst shrinks away, reduce your dosage to 200 to 400 IU/day.

If you have cysts in your breasts, do not drink caffeine. Caffeine is known to cause painful breast cysts and lumps, especially after menopause.

If joint-related or vaginal cysts become irritated, ice packs can reduce the pain and slow growth. Any infection should be treated with topical antiviral and antibacterial extracts. Ovarian and cervical cysts usually go away on their own. However, if they become very large, consult a health care practitioner.

Dandruff

Dry Scalp / Psoriasis / Seborrheic Dermatitis

See also Skin Health

Dandruff is not life threatening or even a serious health concern, but it can cause damage to your self-esteem. Skin cells on the scalp generally die and fall off every month or so, which rejuvenates the scalp. But in cases of dandruff, the skin cells turn-over at an accelerated rate, resulting in the unsightly white flakes in your hair and on your shoulders. Certain types of dandruff itch and the scalp can be irritated.

What Causes Dandruff?

Dandruff is usually caused by a fungus or bacteria. But different types of dandruff have different causes:

- **Fungus:** The fungus known as Pityrosporum ovale is the principal cause of most cases of dandruff. This fungus is present in most people, and can grow out of control, causing dandruff. If you have dandruff but your scalp does not itch, it is most likely caused by this fungus.
- **Seborrheic dermatitis:** When your scalp is itchy, red, flaky, or when you have rashes or redness around your nose and eyebrows, you may have seborrheic dermatitis. This condition can be aggravated by cold air and stress.
- **Dry scalp:** Contrary to popular belief, dry scalp is not the cause of dandruff. In fact, most dandruff sufferers have oily scalps, along with topical fungal infections. Drying out the scalp can actually help reduce dandruff flakes by helping to kill the fungus, which thrives on moist environments.
- **Psoriasis:** Most likely a mild type of autoimmune disorder, psoriasis is difficult to diagnose and more difficult to cure, and it can be the cause of dandruff and other skin problems. See Autoimmune Disorders for more information.

- **Anxiety:** Stress and emotional anxiety have been linked to skin and scalp problems, and are known to make dandruff worse.

Treatments for Dandruff

A great herbal cure for dandruff: Mix equal amounts of the dried herbs, dandelion root, chamomile, burdock root, horsetail, chaparral, rosemary, coltsfoot, and lavender, and two parts nettle. Boil sufficient water for a hair rinse in a saucepan, then remove the pan from the heat. Sprinkle the mixture of herbs over the top and let cool. (Do not add the herbs while the water is boiling.) Strain the herbs and pour the decoction over your hair after shampooing. Many people don't wash their hair with shampoo at all (it causes dryness) and exclusively use the hair tea daily. Bye, bye dandruff!

Here are some other things you can try:

- **Supplements:** Zinc has been found to reduce dandruff in some people. Vitamin A (2500 IU) and B complex are also effective against dermatitis. Also, take selenium and vitamin E for better overall skin health. Selenium can also be used topically.
- **Herbs:** You can combat fungal and bacterial infections that cause dermatitis and yeast infections with apple cider vinegar, oregano oil, and tea tree oil (all topical). St. Johns wort is also an antifungal and antibacterial. Some people claim to have cured their dandruff and dermatitis using apple cider vinegar baths and rinses.
- **Reduce antihistamines:** Antihistamines can exacerbate dandruff problems, especially in cases of seborrheic dermatitis.

Dehydration

Dehydration can be a factor in many health conditions, such as Alzheimer's Disease, kidney stones and failure, failing vision, prostate problems, and ulcers. Many health experts believe that most Americans are in a constant state of being partially dehydrated. In simple terms, we don't drink enough pure water.

What Causes Dehydration?

Classic dehydration can be caused by overexertion, excessive sweating, and just plain lack of drinking enough liquids. You can also get dehydrated from drinking too much caffeine and alcohol. If you do consume large amounts of these, be sure to drink extra water. Also, drink plenty of water if you are overweight and exerting yourself. Remember that you can get dehydrated in wet, humid heat just as easily as in dry heat.

If you are constantly thirsty, check for diabetes. Symptoms of dehydration include:

- Dizziness
- Headache
- Dry skin and mouth
- Dark urine, and not voiding often enough
- Constipation
- Poor digestion, as enzymes don't function as well without enough water in the system
- Overweight
- Eczema
- Premature aging and wrinkles, sags, dark circles under the eyes, listless skin tone
- Low blood pressure, causing dizziness upon standing
- Being overly acidic
- Urinary infections
- Aching joints, particularly in the big toe
- Nausea
- Lethargy
- Skin that doesn't snap back upon being pinched, particularly on the back of the hands (known as turgor)
- Edema
- Toxemia
- Hunger and stomach pain

Cures & Treatments

To avoid dehydration, you should drink around eight to ten eight-ounce glasses of pure water per day. Other liquids can contribute to hydration, but water is the best to rehydrate your body.

The simplest thing to do for dehydration or dehydration sickness is to drink plenty of water. If you need to sleep, then sleep. Carbon Activated Water (CAW) and coconut water can give you better hydration. Another common remedy is a simple saline solution which you can make by adding a tablespoon of sugar and a few pinches of salt to a quart of water. Your body will absorb this more quickly than plain water. Severe dehydration may require intravenous hydration.

Depression

Bipolar Disorder / Manic Depression / Post Partum Depression / SAD

Most of us will suffer from depression at some point in our lives. In most cases, it's a passing malaise, associated with a particular event or cause. But for some, depression is a long-term visitor. Women suffer from depression twice as often as men do. It can affect your ability to function and cope in society and lead to illness, substance abuse, and other problems. Some common symptoms of depression include:

- Constant feelings of low self image, guilt, failure, hopelessness, or shame
- Difficulty concentrating and focusing, lack of motivation, indecisive
- Lack of energy, lethargy, excess sleeping
- Nervous energy, buzzing without direction or focus
- Unusual weight gain or loss
- Lack of perspective, making things larger or more important than they are
- Thoughts of suicide
- Alcohol or other substance abuse
- Lack of interest in sex

Types of Depression

Although the symptoms are similar, depression comes in several different forms. Here's a quick review:

- **Transitory Depression:** Depression related to a specific event, such as a death or broken relationship, can be intense, but usually passes within a few months.
- **Chronic Depression:** Long-term depression, lasting four months or more, is a chronic condition. Chronic depression may be intense or mild.
- **Manic Depression / Bipolar disorder:** Alternating mood swings between depressed and overly positive moods

- **Seasonal Affective Disorder:** Depression that occurs primarily during winter months
- **Post-Partum Depression:** Depression that occurs after childbirth
- **Post Traumatic Stress Disorder:** Depression that occurs after a traumatic event, such as an auto accident. This can also occur after a "positive" but traumatic event, such as a major performance.

Causes of Depression

While many factors can trigger depression (events, memories, repressed emotions, etc.), there are really only a couple of possible causes:

- **Mental & Emotional Causes:** Abuse, both emotional and physical, is a common cause of depression (often latent) in adults and children. Emotional trauma may also cause depression, as in the death of loved ones, relationship issues, bankruptcy or financial troubles, or other traumatic events. Repression of emotions can also result in depression.
- **Chemical Causes:** Recent studies have shown the chemical imbalances in the body are associated with depression, including faulty neurotransmitters, hormonal imbalances, and other chemical secretions in the body. No one is yet sure if these imbalances are the causes or the symptoms of depression.

Treatments for Depression

Here are the keys to treating depression naturally:

- **Foods:** Dark chocolate or pure cocoa contains nutrients (theabroma, a methyl-xanthine) that are beneficial for depression, and the less sweetened darks have nice antioxidizing properties as a bonus. Consume plenty of fruit (it's difficult to be depressed while eating an apple or mango), as these supply the body with antioxidants and vitamins. Foods to avoid include dairy products, starchy foods, excessive sugar and fructose, and processed foods. Also minimize alcohol (stay off the booze, bye-bye blues). Research suggests that alcohol robs the brain of precious omega-3 fatty acids.
- **Vitamins & Supplements:** You likely won't need pharmaceutical antidepressants if you take this simple

nutritional formula for depression: dehydroepiandrosterone (DHEA), phosphatidylserine, choline, inositol, St. Johns wort, glutamic acid (or glutamine powder), phenylalanine, theanine, S-adenosyl-methionine (SAMe), 5HTP and tyrosine. Play with the combinations of these supplements for best results. Many people feel incredible in days.

- **Herbs & Essential Oils:** Some good antidepressant herbs include bergamot, mint, rose, geranium, pine, and rosemary oils. You can also use geranium and rosemary oils on your body (diluted with a splash of water or with almond oil).
- **Lifestyle:** Exercise! Body movement helps stimulate circulation and the lymphatic system, which reduce depression. It also helps the brain produce more serotonin and endorphins, two "feel-good" brain chemicals. Treat yourself to relaxing saunas or baths with healing herbs and aromas. Use those listed above, or other essential oil scents that make you feel more energized and happy.

Other Considerations

DHEA, an omega-3 fatty acid, may be one of the most important supplements to relieve your depression. DHEA determines the fluidity of brain cell membranes, making it extremely important for both thought processes and mood control. Studies show that omega-3 fatty acid supplements improve depression and may even stabilize mood fluctuations associated with bipolar disorder, making DHEA much like lithium, but without the side effects. Try taking 1,000 mg of omega-3 in supplement form per day with breakfast.

Caution: If you are taking or have taken an antidepressant MAOI (monoamine oxidase inhibitor), DO NOT take nutritional supplement formulas until six weeks after you stop taking the MAOI. It takes that long for the drug to get out of your system. Additionally, certain foods and drinks contain tyramine, an amino acid that reacts adversely with MAOI drugs. Do not eat or drink any of the following if you are on an MAOI drug: Chianti and vermouth (other red wines, white wines, and port wines may be tolerated at an amount less than 120 ml), beer and ale, whiskey and liqueurs, nonalcoholic beers and wines (may contain tyramine, so it's best to avoid them), bananas and their peels.

Diabetes

Diabetes Mellitus / High Blood Sugar

See also Cardiovascular Health, High Blood Pressure, Hypoglycemia, Thyroid Imbalance

Diabetes is all too common in the United States. The American diet is high in sugars, carbohydrates, and fats that cause or contribute to high blood sugar. Excess caffeine can, indirectly by way of the thyroid, contribute to hormonal imbalances that cause diabetes. Some of the symptoms include:

- Frequent urination
- Thirst
- Blurred vision
- Weight loss accompanied by increased appetite
- Fatigue
- Erectile dysfunction
- Headaches

What Causes Diabetes?

Simply put, diabetes is caused by high blood sugar, or "too much glucose in the blood." This is a problem with insulin, whose job is to carry blood sugar into the cells of the body. A lack of insulin or faulty insulin response by the cells results in too much glucose in the blood. Another cause of diabetes is simply too much sugar intake—especially fructose. Here is a summary of the causes of diabetes:

- **Diet:** Too much sugar. Too much fat. Too much caffeine.
- **Obesity:** Often resulting from dietary problems, obesity can cause a loop of insulin and hormonal problems that can cause or worsen diabetes.
- **Thyroid imbalance**: Hormonal imbalances from thyroid and adrenal problems can affect insulin response and cause or contribute to diabetes.
- **Poor liver health:** If the liver cannot cleanse the blood and process excess blood sugar, the result is diabetes.
- **Chronic use of steroids**: These drugs can change your body chemistry and cause or worsen diabetes.

Treatments

A new set of dietary habits is the first line of defense against diabetes. Here is a summary of these dietary strategies, along with some other natural treatments:

- **Avoid sugars:** Sugars come in the form of sucrose (cane sugar and maple syrup), lactose (dairy products), fructose (fruit and corn syrup), corn starch, dextrose, glucose (usually glucose is converted by the body from other sugars), sorbitol, and malt.
- **Reduce carbohydrates and starches:** The body converts starches from carbohydrates into glucose. Avoid simple carbs, which include fruit, fruit juice, dairy products, honey, and sugars. Also avoid peanut butter, soybean oil, cheese, and processed meat. Keep complex carbohydrate consumption under control, including breads, pasta, beans, grains and fibrous vegetables (squash and eggplant, for example). Remember that whole wheat products are better than refined products. Better yet, replace wheat with other grains, such as oats, bran, rye, and barley.
- **Eat more low-glycemic food:** Healthy foods for maintaining good blood sugar levels include green leafy vegetables, potatoes, yams, whole grain breads, nuts, legumes, chicken, and fish. Raw foods have a lower glycemic level than cooked foods.
- **Take herbs to help control blood sugar:** Herbs that help include fenugreek, garlic, bilberry, ginseng, and olive leaves (or extract). Other helpful supplements for diabetes include chromium, vanadium, cinnamon, and bitter melon.
- **Strengthen your immune system:** If you have diabetes, you should definitely take a multivitamin. Concentrate especially on getting enough antioxidants, as they help prevent free radical damage that causes many common diabetes complications (blindness and the necessity of limb amputation). Spirulina provides vitamins and minerals, while helping to balance blood sugar.

- **Cleanse:** If you crave sweets, you may be suffering from a lack of protein or you might have parasites in your system. Cleansing your liver and colon cannot only help with these cravings, but can help reduce your blood sugar levels by providing better nutrient absorption.

For 1,000 years, Japanese culture has used flour made from a plant called konjac-mannan (glucomannan). An extract of konjac-mannan helps provide protection from diabetes by lowering blood sugar.

Lipoic acid, known as LA, or alpha-lipoic acid (ALA) are both excellent antioxidants and blood purifiers. What's more, LA enhances your body's insulin sensitivity and the glucose response to insulin. This is good news for diabetes patients. You can get LA supplements without prescription and should take them on an empty stomach. Food sources of LA include spinach, broccoli, tomatoes and Brussels sprouts.

Gymnema sylvestre (gurmar leaf) is called the poor mans insulin in India, and if chewed, will block the receptors on your taste buds that register sweetness on your tongue. Sweets will taste like cardboard and this will take away your desire for sweets. When Gymnema sylvestre is taken orally for six weeks, the desire for sweets will be eliminated.

Aloe vera juice (get the pure filet of aloe, not products that use the whole spike because the outer skin of the aloe vera plant has a toxin in it) controls blood sugar. Aloe has more oxygen in it than any other plant. Colloidal silver is also beneficial for diabetes.

Other Considerations

Diabetics are prone to heart disease, so either have a lot of garlic in your diet or take garlic supplements, as garlic provides many cardiovascular health benefits. Use sesame oil to reduce hypertension and B-complex vitamins to help prevent both heart disease and diabetic neuropathy, which is a precursor to limb amputation. Diabetics are also prone to yeast infection, so include a healthy dose of vitamin E in your supplement regimen.

Diarrhea

See also Colon & Intestinal Health

If you're suffer from diarrhea, the first question is, what's causing it? Sometimes diarrhea is a symptom of a larger problem. In most cases, diarrhea passes through the system in a few days at most, or is related to specific illnesses, such as flu or food allergy. If diarrhea continues for more than ten days, or if there is severe weight loss accompanying the symptoms, you should probably seek medical attention.

Causes of Diarrhea

Diarrhea occurs when the colon cannot function properly, due to inflammation, irritation, infection, or disease. Here are some details:

- **Food Reaction:** Reactions or allergies to certain foods may cause diarrhea. Some people cannot drink beer, for example, while others cannot eat spicy foods. This type of diarrhea is the body ridding itself of toxic or unwanted substances. The message is: don't eat or drink these things anymore.
- **Dairy products:** An allergy to milk and other dairy products, for example, often manifests in diarrhea rather than hives or other common allergy symptoms. If you're suffering from chronic diarrhea, try eliminating all dairy products from your diet for a few weeks. If the diarrhea doesn't stop, a dairy allergy is not to blame.
- **Viral Infection:** Many types of viral infections can cause diarrhea, including both mild and serious infections.
- **Parasites:** Parasites from traveling, undercooked meats, or contact with animals or their stool can cause severe diarrhea that requires medical attention. If antibiotics are prescribed, be sure to take probiotics when your treatment is over.
- **Vitamin C:** Too much vitamin C results in diarrhea in most people. If you are mega-dosing vitamin C, cut back when you start getting diarrhea. Too much magnesium will also cause diarrhea.
- **Disease:** Diarrhea is a symptom in some serious illnesses, including dysentery, food poisoning (botulism), AIDS, Crohn's disease, and radiation sickness. All of these require medical attention.

Treatments for Diarrhea

Diarrhea should be treated according to its cause. But you should do some things no matter what the cause. Here are some suggestions:

- Avoid dairy, caffeine, processed foods, alcohol, and fermented foods and beverages.

- Take antifungal, antibacterial and antiviral herbs, such as green tea extract, garlic extract, oregano extract, barberry root and St. John's wort.
- Take probiotic cultures, which are helpful even if your diarrhea is not caused by fungal infection.
- Take a nutrient-rich food supplement to restore the vitamins and minerals your body has lost from the diarrhea.

Other considerations

If an infection is causing your diarrhea, colloidal silver (a solution) helps kill all the bad bacteria in the colon. It even kills Cryptosporidium parasites, which cause only minor diarrhea in people with healthy immune systems, but can cause severe, life-threatening diarrhea in people with compromised immune systems, such as people with AIDS.

If you don't have colloidal silver, barberry root is effective for treating diarrhea, especially when caused by virus. It has been shown to inhibit the E. coli virus's ability to flourish within the cells. Some herbalists suggest that grapefruit seed extract and goldenseal are also good diarrhea remedies.

If diarrhea is severe, watch out for dehydration. Drink plenty of pure water. You can also drink green tea, which has antibacterial qualities.

Diarrhea in children should not last more than one or two days. To help it go away quickly, try a diet of bananas, fiber in the form of wheat germ or bran, and plain yogurt (no sugar or flavoring, except for the bananas). Add a teaspoon of bee pollen to restore lost vitamins and minerals.

Digestion

Digestive Cramps / Indigestion

See also Flatulence, Heartburn, Liver & Gallbladder Health

All animals digest other organisms (plant, animal, or microorganisms) to convert them into the nutrients needed for life. Digestion usually begins with some kind of physical breakdown of the food. Humans, for example, chew food as the first stage of digestion. The food is then broken down further through chemical processes in the stomach and intestines.

The entire multi-phase process takes about 24 hours for humans, which puts us in the category of herbivores, animals that eat only plants and that have slow digestive systems. Carnivores, by contrast, usually process their food quickly—from twenty minutes to a few hours—and have short digestive tracts to help expel waste quickly. Carnivores rarely chew their food. In this way, nature does not let meat sit around in the digestive tracts of animals. Humans are the only exceptions to this natural law, as we are the only herbivores that also eat meat on a regular basis.

Poor digestion plays a role in a number of disorders. These include acne, oily skin, and other skin problems; chronic fatigue; and breathing difficulty.

What Causes Digestive Problems?

Good digestion is the first step to good nutrition. For many, however, digestion is compromised along with other health problems. Digestion can be compromised from chemical imbalances, accumulated toxins and waste, and from physical damage to the stomach or intestines. Here are some possibilities:

- **Too much fat:** The digestive system can process only so much fat. Excess fat that is not secreted out through the bowels is stored and can interfere with the proper functioning of the liver and gallbladder.
- **Too much meat:** The human body does not metabolize red meat well, and eating too much of it can cause blocks in the intestines and bowels, triggering all kinds of illness.
- **Too much sugar:** Sugar that is not metabolized into blood glucose and used by the cells may be stored as fat and clog up the digestive system. This may also cause an imbalance in the thyroid, which slows metabolism and digestion.
- **Too much protein:** Protein from red meat and dairy products is not well metabolized by the human digestive system, so it can sit in the digestive tract, blocking the metabolism of other nutrients.
- **Too much caffeine:** Excess caffeine causes an adrenal secretion, which shuts down the digestive system.
- **Food toxins:** Preservatives and other food toxins can damage the liver, which directly undermines the digestive system.
- **Food Reactions:** Your body may react to certain foods with cramping, nausea, or indigestion. Foods known to be hard on the stomach and intestines include

broccoli and Brussels sprouts. Other foods, such as oily, acidic, or highly processed foods may cause nausea or cramps.

- **Environmental toxins:** Heavy metals and other environmental toxins can damage cells, resulting in poor metabolism of blood glucose, which then causes a slowing of the digestive system.

Treatments to Aid Digestion

As you might imagine, diet plays a large role in digestion. A healthy diet equals healthy digestion, while an unhealthy diet equals poor digestion. For good digestion, avoid eating fatty foods such as butter, fried food, and cheese. Instead, choose high-fiber foods such as whole grains, rice, and raw or lightly cooked vegetables. Excellent foods for digestion include apples, avocados, and oranges. Here are some other ideas:

- Don't drink water with your meals, as this dilutes your stomach acids right when you need them most. Also, chew your food thoroughly to help your digestion.
- Avoid greasy, oily foods.
- Don't mix coffee or alcohol with food. Wait at least 30 minutes after eating before drinking these things.
- Be careful with food combinations. Avoid eating fruit with carbohydrates or animal proteins. Also avoid mixing hot and cold foods.
- Avoid foods or drinks containing chocolate, soft drinks and tomato sauces.

Aloe vera juice aids digestion. Chewing licorice or fennel seeds after a meal is an East Indian tradition that freshens garlic and onion breath and lowers the incidence of flatulence. Fennel, ginger, and catnip all contain oils that absorb intestinal gas, calm your stomach, stop diarrhea, prevent constipation, aid digestion, and stop heartburn. One of the best cures for these maladies (especially heartburn, acid indigestion, and nausea) is carbon in the form of activated carbon supplements. You can also try a cup of hot green tea or yerba mate to help digestion after eating greasy food.

There are a host of digestive enzymes. Look for papain, bromelain, and protease. Pepsin is also helpful. These will help improve your digestion while eradicating your pain. Take a double dose of enzymes for a week if you want an easy way to cleanse five to ten pounds away quickly. Probiotics work well, too. They contain Bifidobacteria longum, Bifidobacteria bifidum, Lactobacillus acidophilus, and Lactobacillus bulgaricus. Stomach acid destroys acidophilus taken alone, so take this combination.

Ginger enhances digestion and circulation as well as promotes healthy lungs. A glass of pure apple juice during your evening meal will often prevent the symptoms of gastroesophageal reflux disease (GERD).

Diverticulitis

Diverticulosis

See also Colon & Intestinal Health, Constipation, Diarrhea, Irritated Bowel Syndrome

Diverticulitis, the result of the standard American diet, is a condition where balloon-like sacs or pouches form outward from the intestinal walls. The sacs can become inflamed, causing pain and other medical conditions. This condition is virtually nonexistent when a diet of whole foods, fruits, and vegetables is followed. Symptoms include:

- Abdominal pain (usually in the left lower quadrant)
- Excessive gas
- Poor elimination
- Constipation
- Diarrhea and mucus in stools
- Symptoms similar to appendicitis and IBS
- Dark blood in stools

What Causes Diverticulitis?

The primary cause of diverticulitis is poor diet. Over time, lacking a diet in fresh fruits, vegetables, and fiber-rich foods can lead to many health problems, including diverticulitis. Other causes include food allergies, reactions to various pharmaceutical drugs, lack of exercise, and 'leaky gut' syndrome. A 'leaky gut' is a condition where damage to the intestinal lining causes undigested food particles to move through the gastrointestinal tract. An unhealthy diet can be dramatically improved with the inclusion of organic, whole foods, fresh leafy vegetables and foods low in hydrogenated and trans fats.

Many pharmaceutical drugs can cause and irritate gastrointestinal disorders. Some offenders include aspirin, analgesic tablets, cuprimine, Ecotrin, Prokine, and Voltaren, and nearly all antibiotics.

Treatments for Diverticulitis

Improving the diet is the best treatment for diverticulitis, and a diet high in organic, whole foods, and fiber is essential for reversing and preventing the condition. Avoid all commercially processed foods, sugars, and refined carbohydrates. Avoid foods that cause allergies, such as soy, milk and dairy, wheat, and shell fish. Nuts are also difficult for some people. Eat more:

- Easily digestible antioxidant fruits and vegetables
- Free-range organic meats and poultry (or better, cut out meat completely for awhile)
- Fresh green vegetables and green vegetable drinks, fresh juices
- Steamed vegetables
- Olive oil and flax seed oil
- Cooked whole grains

The primary herbal remedy is known as Robert's Formula, a combination of comfrey, Echinacea, geranium, goldenseal, marshmallow root, poke root, slippery elm, and wild indigo. It is best taken in combination with licorice root tea.

Smoking will worsen your condition, so try to cut down or quit. Likewise, coffee and alcohol are not recommended. Regular exercise can improve circulation and overall bowel function.

Homeopathic remedies include Belladonna, Bryonia, and Colocynthis. Nutritional supplementation includes B-complex vitamins and vitamin C, and probiotics such as acidophilus and Bifidobacteria.

Other Considerations

You can do an at-home hyperthermia treatment to induce sweat and effectively eliminate toxins. This is a good way to reduce the presence of bacteria and viruses as well, as they cannot survive elevated body temperatures.

Traditional Chinese Medicine techniques, including acupuncture, have been helpful in reducing symptoms of diverticulitis.

Dizziness

Disequilibrium / Vertigo

See also Anemia, Anxiety, Motion Sickness

Dizziness is a feeling of being off balance or of disequilibrium, which could be described as spinning or a sense of falling. Vertigo is a specific form of dizziness often associated with heights or stressful situations. There are two types of vertigo. Subjective vertigo is when the person feels that he or she is spinning. Objective vertigo is when the person feels that objects are spinning around the individual.

True vertigo is an internal problem, usually associated with the inner ear, middle ear, one of the cranial nerves, brain stem, and eyes. Unlike dizziness, vertigo is often accompanied by nausea, vomiting, and severe sweating, and can be caused by a viral infection. Severe bouts can cause ringing in the ears (tinnitus) or hearing loss.

What Causes Dizziness?

A sudden drop of blood pressure in the brain is a key cause of dizziness. This can be caused by:

- Fatigue
- Stress
- Low blood sugar
- Temporary blockage of blood to the brain
- Low blood oxygenation
- Iron deficiency
- Drug reactions
- Adrenal exhaustion from overuse of stimulants
- Inadequate or incorrect breathing patterns
- Head trauma and cerebellar tumors

Depression or anxiety can also lead to dizziness.

Treatments for Dizziness

Eating healthy, pure foods can help your overall health and minimize the effects of vertigo. Eat smaller meals throughout the day to maintain your blood sugar levels, and reduce sugars, caffeinated beverages, and alcohol. Iron supplements or iron-rich foods (spinach, kale, bee pollen, raw seeds, and dark leafy-green vegetables) can help with anemia, which may cause dizziness.

Homeopathic remedies include Gelsemium, Phosphorus, Cocculus, Convallaria, and Granataum. Also try the herbs ginger and Gingko leaf extract.

Nutritional supplementation includes vitamin B complex, niacin, vitamin E, and iron. Vitamins C and B5 can help with adrenal exhaustion. You may also try acupuncture and different forms of bodywork to help with energy flows in the body.

Ear Infection

For the most part, ear infections occur as a reaction to blowing the nose incorrectly, a reaction to an infusion of water from outside the ear, or an allergic response to milk or other allergenic agents. (The exception to this rule is if the person has a congenital-constitutional defect or a surgery-related injury).

Our nose, eyes, mouth, throat, and ears are connected. Each ear has a tiny tube called the Eustachian tube, which is connected to the nasal passages. These delicate tubes are a one-way street and can easily get clogged with mucus when you blow your nose incorrectly. Always keep your mouth open when blowing your nose and blow through both nostrils at the same time. NEVER block one nostril to force a strong gust through the open nostril.

When water gets into your ear, it usually drains out and the ear dries. Sometimes, however, water remains trapped in the ear canal. When this happens, bacteria and fungi can grow and infect the outer ear. Resulting symptoms include:

- Chronic Itching of the ear canal
- Pain in the outer, middle, or inner part of the ear
- Yellow secretion from the ear
- Hearing loss

Causes of Ear Infection

Some of the most common causes of ear infections include:

- **Virus or bacteria**: Swimming in polluted water or acquiring bacteria from humid conditions can infect the outer, middle, or inner portion of the ear.

- **Congestion from colds and flu:** Congestion usually affects the middle ear and can cause inflammation and loss of hearing.
- **Swelling and inflammation:** Caused by infection and blockage, inflammation accompanies most ear infections.
- Trapped water or earwax: Inner ear infections are usually caused by water trapped inside the ear canal. This moisture can become infected with fungi or bacteria and cause hearing loss and other problems.

Treatments and Prevention

A buildup of cerumen (earwax) can lead to and complicate these infections. The most effective way of extricating the buildup of earwax is not with cotton swabs! Cotton swabs can push the wax farther into the ear canal and irritate or damage the sensitive skin of the outer ear. Earwax is best removed by gently flushing the ear canal with a 50-50 solution of hydrogen peroxide (3% solute) and water. Warm the water first, then add the peroxide to cool it. Put this solution into an ear bulb syringe (you can get one at the drugstore) and gently squirt the solution into your ear. Have a bowl and/or towel under the ear to catch all of the material that comes out. This same solution also combats the infection.

Other natural products that are effective in treating ear infections include: apple cider vinegar, grapefruit seed extract (diluted), and unscented, warmed garlic oil. All are best eye-dropped gently into the ear canal.

Treatments for Children

Research suggests that probiotics may help children beat chronic ear infections. Some children are prone to ear infections, and may require surgery to enable ear drainage. Experts now are beginning to realize that the antibiotics usually prescribed to treat these infections may actually prolong the problems (this is a situation that we are hearing more and more regarding traditional medical treatments in general). By destroying the friendly bacteria that keep harmful bacteria in check, antibiotics may actually promote painful, chronic ear infections. If your child suffers from chronic ear infections, opt for probiotics instead of antibiotics. Probiotics will help your child's body fight the infection for good.

Eczema

Dermatitis / Skin Rash

See also Dandruff, Liver & Gallbladder Health, Stress

Eczema is a type of skin rash, or dermatitis, with some notable characteristics, including difficulty in eradicating it and its tendency to flare up somewhat violently, with

- Redness and itching
- Blistering
- Dry, flakey, or cracking skin

Eczema can appear anywhere on the body, but common locations include the chest; skin folds, such as the breasts and buttocks, and the face.

What Causes Eczema?

Eczema has many possible causes, but most tend to narrow it down to a few major factors, including:

- **Poor liver and blood health:** Diet and environmental toxins, as well as viruses, can compromise the liver and blood and result in eczema.
- **Stress:** There appears to be a connection between eczema and stress and between eczema and excess caffeine.
- **Iron deficiency:** Low iron levels have been linked to eczema, along with low levels of trace minerals.
- **Allergies:** Food and environmental allergies can cause the skin rashes associated with eczema. Clothing and airborne allergens are two possibilities that are often overlooked.

Treatments

Apply Listerine (an antifungal) or a methylsulfonylmethane (MSM) preparation to the affected area and do not wash off (use original Listerine, not the flavored variety that contain sweeteners). Continue applying daily until the eczema patches are gone.

Take B vitamins, vitamin A, inositol, copper, iodine (seaweeds), dry vitamin E, MSM, picolinated zinc, and probiotics (for example, acidophilus and bifidophilus).

As is the case with dandruff, herbalists believe that eczema is a disorder of the liver and blood, so they recommend burdock root to detoxify the blood and liver. Along this line, eczema may be a symptom of iron deficiency, so try taking iron supplements to see if they help.

Specifically for skin problems such as eczema, consider mixing burdock with red clover or cleavers, as they help the lymph system clean toxins from the blood.

Since stress triggers eczema, find out what triggers your stress and you'll help alleviate your eczema. If you have stress-triggered eczema, mix burdock with nettles and figwort. Also see Stress for more ideas.

Wear only cotton clothes and don't use perfumes. Use only hypoallergenic lotions and moisturize the patches with those lotions. Stay away from alpha hydroxy creams or creams with urea; they burn.

Edema

Ascites / Swelling

See also Cardiovascular Health, Liver & Gallbladder Health

Edema is the buildup of excessive amounts of fluid in the body, usually in the cells themselves. The fluid is generally water and salt, and is often associated with allergic reactions to food or environmental toxins. It can occur in the face, hands, feet, knees and other extremities, but can also cause brain swelling that leads to headaches, behavioral changes, and memory problems. Symptoms include:

- Bloating and swelling of the face, fingers, hands, and legs
- Bloating of the abdomen (known as ascites)
- Overall weight gain
- Lung fluid buildup with shortness of breath

What Causes Edema?

Edema is associated with the cardiovascular system and the kidneys, and is usually caused by heart failure, kidney failure, or liver failure. It can sometimes be caused a reaction to low air pressure in airplanes, especially on long flights. Likewise, climate changes can cause edema in certain people. Other causes include:

- Poor kidney health and problems related to protein absorption
- Vitamin B deficiencies
- Tumors in the groin or pelvis
- Hypothyroidism
- Heredity (especially with edema of the legs)

Treatments for Edema

Edema often can be reduced or minimized by dietary changes. Eat foods high in water content, such as cucumbers, apples, potatoes, grapes, beets, onion, cabbage, citrus fruits, and watermelon. Avoid caffeine, alcohol, salt, fried foods, milk, and dairy products. Also reduce meat, sugar, processed grains, white flour, and pickled foods. Hydrate yourself with a Carbon Activated Water (CAW).

Herbal remedies include dandelion leaf, which is rich in potassium, and horse-chestnut seed extract. Supplement with a good vitamin B complex, vitamin C, vitamin B6, pantothetic acid, and potassium. Free-form amino acids and alfalfa tablets may also be helpful. Here are the keys:

- Eat healthy, nutrient-rich foods or find a good nutrient-dense super supplement.
- Keep your body hydrated with high water-content foods and liquids.
- Take B-complex and C vitamins, potassium and omega-3 fatty acids.
- Consider a regular body detoxification practice, such as hydrotherapy or massage.

Energy Enhancement

Energy Drinks / Lethargy / Low Energy / Stimulants / Vitality

See also Adrenal Imbalance, Chronic Fatigue Syndrome, Hypoglycemia, Thyroid Imbalance,

High energy makes us feel better and younger, helps us get more done, and even stimulates creativity and will. Energy is the currency of our very life force. So how do we get more energy for the body and mind? How do food and other fuel sources translate into energy? And how do we increase the "octane" of our fuel for the energy efficiency of our bodies?

The answers to those questions are both simple and complex. On a physical level, our bodies use one primary type of fuel for energy: glucose. It's that simple. Glucose that enters the bloodstream is converted by the body into glycogen, which is then burned as fuel in the cells.

What Causes Low Energy?

The chemical energy our body uses for fuel comes from blood sugar. Different forms of sugar enter the bloodstream through our normal digestion and food conversion processes. When we need energy for physical activity, the hormone insulin transports blood sugar into the cells, where it can be used for fuel or stored as glycogen. The liver also converts much of this glucose into energy or glycogen. Excess sugar is excreted from the body through urine or converted into fat. This process can break down in many places, causing low energy, nervous high energy, and energy "crash" (rapid energy loss). Low insulin levels (diabetes), low blood sugar (hypoglycemia), low blood pressure, and poor cell health can all affect the production of energy.

Other conditions that can affect energy levels include poor liver health, adrenal imbalance, thyroid imbalance, and even insufficient muscle mass (not enough muscle to fat ratio).

Energy Enhancements

So how do we get more energy? What are the safest and most effective ways to increase energy and get more of life's sweet nectar? Well, let's start with a few basic principals. Here are the essential concepts for increasing body energy:

- **Improve the quality of your fuel:** Find the optimal mixture of proteins, carbohydrates, and fats for your body, so it can more effectively convert these elements into fuel. The optimal mixture is not the same for everyone.
- **Reduce the quantity of your fuel intake:** Generally, eating less food results in more energy efficiency. Oxidation from overeating causes the body to slow down, as does the excess stored fat that overeating causes.
- **Clean your engine:** Clean out your liver and purify your blood for increased energy. This will support the chemical processes that carry glucose into the cells, where it is used as energy. It also wouldn't hurt to clean your intestines, as this is where sugars get extracted from foods and passed to the bloodstream.
- **Streamline your body:** Losing excess fat and increasing muscle mass will give you more energy and improve energy conversion from the food you eat.
- **Attend to "other" energies:** Steer clear of high frequency wires, unnecessary x-rays, and other foreign energies. Keep your emotional archives clean, your heart light, and your self-image positive.

Other Considerations

Glucose is the most important and most used source of energy for our tissues and muscles. Most of this glucose should come from complex carbohydrates (grains, vegetables, beans) for best energy conversion. People with higher metabolisms or those on a muscle-building program can increase their intake of carbohydrates. Sucrose (sugar) is a combination of glucose and fructose; the glucose is quickly and easily converted into energy by our liver and muscle tissues. Note that energy from fructose (fruit and corn syrup) is converted into energy only by the liver, and any excess will be converted into fat and stored as body tissue. It's best to stay away from excess fructose, especially high-fructose corn syrup, commonly added to juices. For long-term energy, it also helps to boost your protein levels.

Pure cocoa is an excellent antioxidant and helps normalize your circulation, not to mention improve your mood. Eat dark, bittersweet chocolate for a hit of cocoa and sucrose, but keep this in check as you can easily consume too much sucrose. Energy without caffeine is built by taking a regimen of Co-Q10, ginseng, suma (South American root sometimes called Brazilian ginseng), maca (Peruvian root called Amazon ginseng), and organic minerals from seaweeds. Spirulina is an excellent energy source for its vitamin, mineral, and protein content, not to mention the chlorophyll.

In Traditional Chinese Medicine, the Schizandra berry is a well-known adaptogenic herb. Due to its ability to increase strength and balance body systems, Chinese herbalists recommend the dried berry for relief from exhaustion and fatigue, and they believe that it can increase both your energy level and your life expectancy.

Erectile Dysfunction

ED / Impotence

See also Prostate Health, Sexual Dysfunction

One of the most fashionable (and profitable) issues of the day, erectile dysfunction (ED) has led our society into a complicated game of biochemical manipulation. Using prescription medications to resolve a performance problem will almost certainly cause a biochemical tipping of the scales, resulting in other, possibly dangerous, problems down the road. Most of these medications concentrate on chemically increasing nitric oxide in your system, which is the main factor in creating erections. Nitric oxide, however, also causes inflammation in your joints, skin, and other body tissues.

If nothing else, the new explosion of ED medications should teach us that we can manipulate our sex drive and performance. But be careful of traditional medicine's answer. Here are some suggestions for natural alternatives.

What Causes ED?

ED has many possible causes, ranging from physical to biochemical, to emotional issues. What's important is that you don't go right out and get a prescription drug to eradicate the symptoms. This will do nothing to cure the problem behind the ED. Instead, use natural stamina enhancers while digging into the root of the problem. Some possible causes include:

- Diabetes
- Thyroid and Adrenal imbalance (including stress)
- Other hormone imbalance, including pituitary issues
- Low energy or Chronic Fatigue Syndrome
- Prostate disorders
- Psychological and neuro-emotional issues (even relatively mild ones)

- Depression
- Use of anti-hypertensive agents, anti-depressants, analgesics and anti-psychotics
- Use of anti-inflammatories, especially anti-inflammatory pharmaceutical medications
- Food and drug toxins
- Sedentary lifestyle and circulation problems
- Peripheral arterial disease

Treatments

First make sure your prostate is healthy (see Prostate Health), then check possible causes one by one to see what's truly ailing you. Hypothyroidism, often caused by insufficient intake of iodine, can sometimes cause impotence. Poor circulation may also be a contributing factor. Diabetes and the vascular problems associated with diabetes account for a large percentage of impotency in middle-aged men. In fact, Viagra was first used to treat diabetic vascular disease. Each of these causes has a representative entry in this book. When you're ready and have begun a plan of attack on the true cause of the problem, follow the plan associated with that issue. Here are a few herbal treatments you can add:

- Take picolinated zinc (50-75 mg/day) with succinate vitamin E (400 IU) or vitamin E complex with tocotrienols. For men, this combination puts lead in your pencil. For women, it builds testosterone naturally and will increase your arousal potential.
- One of the most potent plant-based performance enhancers is the mushroom Cordyceps, which is considered an aphrodisiac as well as stimulating erection in men. Athletes often use it to increase energy levels.
- Many have reported that the following supplements work like Viagra: tongkat ali, Rhodiola rosea, yohimbe, maca and L-arginine (poor man's Viagra). L-arginine helps stimulate blood flow to the penis and helps create nitric oxide. Viagra, by contrast, inhibits the PDE5 enzyme that blocks nitric oxide. Either way, you end up with more nitric oxide in the right place. L-arginine should be taken regularly for best results.
- Foods like peanuts, bananas, and mangoes are reputed to be sexual stimulants and performance enhancers. And spices like clove, cinnamon, cumin, coriander, and cayenne are circulation enhancers, therefore possibly directing increased blood flow toward the groin.

- The tantric tradition builds sexual potency through awareness and control of energies—sexual and others. Through certain practices and beliefs, practitioners and adepts can control the flow of energy to (and from) the sex organs, resulting in total control over orgasm, arousal, and performance.

Fainting

Blacking Out / Passing Out

See also Dizziness

Fainting is a sudden and brief loss of consciousness, sometimes accompanied by sweating, anxiety, and heart palpitations. It can happen abruptly, without an apparent cause, and can progress to fainting spells over time. In the movies, fainting seems to be quite common, falling upon anyone who is shocked by sudden, surprising news. In fact, a combination of low blood sugar (or poor nutrition) and anxiety or a sudden drop in blood pressure (which can be caused by strong emotion) can cause it.

What Causes Fainting?

Fainting is usually caused by decreased blood flow to the brain. This can be a result of:

- Low blood sugar
- Arrhythmia (abnormal change in the beating of the heart)
- Heat exhaustion or dehydration
- Low blood pressure (hypotension)
- Allergies
- Anemia
- Nutritional deficiencies, including magnesium and iron

It's also important to rule out more serious conditions, such has slow heart rate, mild strokes (TIA's), blockages and brain tumors.

Treatments for Fainting

The best recommendation for reducing fainting spells is to improve nutrition and body hydration. Eat whole foods with an emphasis on vegetables and high-protein foods (fish, bee pollen, chicken, beans). Drink plenty of spring or filtered water. Supplement with vitamin B, pantothetic acid, iron, and magnesium. Eat small meals throughout the day.

Herbs that help regulate blood pressure include shepherds purse, unsweetened cocoa, Una de Gato (Cat's Claw), and olive leaf extract. Traditional Chinese Medicine also uses many herbs to help stimulate circulation and blood pressure along with energy flows in the body. Homeopathic remedies include Ignatia, Aconite, and Arsenicum album.

Other Considerations

To help gently revive someone who has fainted, try aromatherapy treatments such as rubbing an essential oil such as peppermint, neroli, basil, lavender, rosemary, or black pepper under the nose.

Acupuncture and bodywork have been found to help reduce fainting spells and increase energy and blood circulation.

Farsightedness & Nearsightedness

Hyperopia

Farsightedness is the inability to see objects up close, while the ability to see far away is unaffected. It is also known as hyperopia, and most common symptoms include:

- Difficulty seeing and working up close
- Blurred vision
- Eyestrain
- Headaches
- Inability to read for a long period of time

Nearsightedness is, of course, the opposite. But both are caused by similar deficiencies in the eye muscles.

What Causes Farsightedness & Nearsightedness?

Farsightedness and nearsightedness occur because light rays containing visual images focus behind or in front of the retina instead of on it, making it difficulty to see up close or far away (respectively). Often this is caused when the eyes become shorter than normal and the cornea flattens out, the result of insufficient muscle tone in the ciliary muscles that control the lenses of the eyes.

Treatments for Farsightedness

Traditional Treatment and Their Risks

Both corrective prescription lenses and surgery are used to correct farsightedness. Corrective lenses (glasses and contact lenses) may cause:

- Inflammation of the cornea, a condition known as microbial keratitis
- Decreased sensitivity of the eye muscles (which causes the condition to worsen)
- Increased sensitivity to artificial light
- Loss of depth perception

Surgical procedures can correct nearsightedness and farsightedness. Lasik and photorefractive keratomy (PRK) are the leading procedures, but may have some side effects, including:

- Halos around lights
- Loss of detail
- Chronic dry eye due to a diminished capacity to produce tears
- Retinal tears and detachment
- Damage to the optic nerve
- Holes in the macula, leading to macular degeneration

Alternative Therapies

There are several schools of natural vision restoration, most of which focus on eye muscle exercises. Since nearsightedness and farsightedness are primarily muscular problems, these alternative therapies can, indeed, be effective treatments. The drawback is that most of them take some time to start working.

Dietary measures can help improve eyesight, including a diet rich in antioxidants and minerals:

- Red, orange, and purple bell peppers
- Carrots
- Celery
- Dark-green leafy vegetables such as chard, kale, collard, spinach, and green leaf lettuces
- Parsley, tomatoes, and yellow squash
- Purple berries, purple and red grapes, plums, cherries, mangos, melons, and citrus fruits

- Unsweetened cacoa, mixed with raw honey or agave syrup
- Organic egg yolks for their high carotenoid content

Nutritional supplementation includes vitamin A, vitamin B complex, vitamin C, vitamin E, beta-carotene, lutein, flavonoids, N-acetyl-cysteine (NAC), riboflavin, taurine, selenium, zeaxthanin, and zinc.

Fertility

Impotence / Sperm Count

See also Sexual Dysfunction

Almost 10 million couples in the united states suffer from fertility challenges, and about 40% of those are related to male sperm count issues. The remaining 60% has to do with female fertility issues. Either way, fertility enhancement is a big issue in the United States. Thankfully, almost half of all couples will eventually conceive, although not necessarily those who seek fertility treatments. About half of the couples who eventually conceive never seek medical intervention. In many cases, they simple keep trying until it works. Here are some natural ways to increase the odds.

Causes of Infertility

First, let's take a look at some causes of diminished fertility in men and women:

- **Pesticides & other environmental toxins:** Toxins from household or industrial poisons, especially pesticides, can damage the reproductive system in both men and women. Other harmful toxins include automobile exhaust and smoke.
- **Low sperm count:** Sperm counts lessen as men get older, but counts can also be negatively affected by prostate problems and some medications.
- **Tight underwear:** Constrictive underwear for men does not in itself lower sperm count. Rather, it interferes with the body's ability to regulate the temperature of the testicles and, therefore, the sperm. A delicate temperature balance is required for successful fertilization to occur. Similarly, there is some evidence to suggest that cooler climates produce more male offspring, whereas warmer climates produce more females.

- **Food toxins:** MSG, caffeine, sulfates, and nitrates are some of the food toxins that can interfere with the reproductive system in both men and women. Women should be especially careful to avoid such additives when pregnant to assure a successful pregnancy and birth.
- **Alcohol and tobacco:** Too much alcohol can reduce sperm counts in men, while smoking reduces sperm counts by around 15%.
- **Bad timing:** Sometimes, just knowing when to make love has a large effect on fertility. For some couples, honing in on the ovulation period is essential for success.

Treatments to Increase Fertility

Studies show that standardized fertility treatments do very little to increase the chances of a successful pregnancy. But you can increase your chances of pregnancy. Here are some natural ways that might be helpful:

- Women—track your menstrual cycles, so you know when you are ovulating. Making love just before and during ovulation increases your chances of getting pregnant.
- Take red raspberry leaf tea before, during, and after pregnancy. This herb is shown to fortify the female reproductive system. Other herbs include blessed thistle, black cohosh, maca, and ginseng. Maca root has been used as a fertility tonic for centuries by the people of the Andes, who suffer from difficulties conceiving due to the high altitudes.

- Men should take zinc supplements, and stop smoking and drinking alcohol.
- Men should ejaculate less often, as time between ejaculations increases the density of sperm and ejaculate. Try having sex only during your partner's ovulation.
- Care for your prostate. Don't sit for long periods, get plenty of exercise, and reduce toxins that harm your prostate. See Prostate Health for details.
- Both men and women should avoid food toxins and environmental toxins and consider a blood, liver and colon cleanse. See Liver & Gallbladder Health and Colon & Intestinal Health for more information.

Fibromyalgia

See also Backache, Infection (Viral), Muscle Cramps,

Fibromyalgia is best defined as chronic muscle pain throughout the body. Many conventional physicians and physical therapists fail to realize that fibromyalgia is not due to physical inactivity, which can cause muscles to atrophy and weaken. Instead, it is most common in highly physically active people.

There are two types of fibromyalgia: primary fibromyalgia, which occurs for no foreseeable reason, and post-traumatic fibromyalgia, which occurs as a result of physical trauma, such as an accident or injury. Symptoms include:

- Headaches
- Pain in the upper back, hips, knees, and rib cage
- Increased allergies or sensitivities
- Anxiety and depression
- General body stiffness and fatigue
- Dizziness
- Irritable bowel syndrome
- Insomnia
- Irritability and mood swings
- Heightened sensitivity to cold, light, smells, and sounds
- Painful menstruation in women

What Causes Fibromyalgia?

Causes of fibromyalgia are largely unknown, but specific conditions can contribute to the problem. These can include:

- Heavy metal poisoning and environmental toxins
- Hormone imbalances, especially low levels of human growth hormone
- Infections such as influenza type A, or Candida
- Low levels of serotonin
- Sleep disorders
- Thalamus dysfunction

Fibromyalgia is often associated with Chronic Fatigue Syndrome (see related entry in this book).

Treatments for Fibromyalgia

Acupuncture can significantly reduce the pain associated with fibromyalgia, as it increases blood flow into the affected joints and muscles. This can increase levels of oxygen and nutrients to the affected area, and also help regulate the brain's production of neurotransmitters.

Bodywork is highly recommended for fibromyalgia patients, because it can improve nerve function, restore muscle balance, shut off pain trigger points, and eliminate stored cellular waste that can worsen pain.

Diet is very important in treating fibromyalgia. Eat foods that support the immune system and do not impair healthy digestion. An organic, vegetarian diet is ideal, with an emphasis on organic fruits, vegetables, dark leafy greens, organic free-range eggs, and small quantities of tofu, beans, and quinoa. Use more extra virgin olive oil, flaxseed oil, and coconut butter or oil.

Herbal treatments can reduce, prevent, or eliminate pain. These include:

- Cayenne and cinnamon to improve circulation and enhance digestion
- Capsaicin cream, applied topically, to ease and relieve pain
- Chamomile to reduce anxiety and tension, and induce deep sleep
- Pure, raw cocoa to increase serotonin levels in the brain
- Fish oil supplements to reduce inflammation and support immune function, and evening primrose oil to help balance your system
- Tinctures of black cohosh, olive leaf, dandelion, devil's claw, Echinacea, and licorice taken three times a day to reduce inflammation and boost the immune system
- Bentonite clay taken orally to leech out the harmful toxins in your digestive system

Nutritional supplementation can help reduce fibromyalgia symptoms and pain. These include vitamin C, vitamin, E, niacinimide (vitamin B3), eicosapentaenoic acid (EPA), magnesium, selenium, zinc, and lipotrophic factors.

Fibrocystic Disease

Fibrosis

See also Cysts, Scarring

Fibrosis is the formation of fibrous (fiber-containing) tissues. Scar tissue is one kind of fibrous tissue. Enzymes digest scar tissue and reduce the buildup of fibrin (a protein that is deposited as filaments). Fibrin reduces the function and size of our organs as we age.

More than 50% of women between the ages of 35 and 50 are prone to fibrocystic breast disease. In this form of fibrosis, the connective tissue that supports the breast's milk ducts thickens into scar tissue. Some experts believe that this occurs as a result of too much estrogen in the body. There is also a genetic relationship. Some of the symptoms include:

- Lumpy breasts in upper and outer quadrants
- Painful breasts during pre-menses and during menses

What Causes Fibrosis?

Caffeine and birth control pills are major factors in developing fibrosis, along with genetics and hyperestrogenism.

Treatments

Fibrocystic Breast Disease is often difficult to cure and medical treatments mainly focus on slowing it down. However, this condition may be treated with success, especially if treatment is started early. Here are some things you can do to help:

- If your fibrocystic breast disease causes you pain or discomfort, start taking 400 IU of vitamin E per day, increasing the dose to 500 IU per day if the vitamin E doesn't raise your blood pressure. Vitamin E will reduce the quantity of painful cysts in your breasts, while helping with cellular health.
- Take plenty of antioxidants, including those found in berries, pure cocoa, and pine bark extract.
- Use only low-dose birth control pills.
- Increase your intake of bioflavonoids and vitamin C for healthy connective tissues. Mangoes, seahawthorn, and citrus fruit are good sources of bioflavonoids.

- Drink lots of water. In fact, switch to a carbon activated water for best hydration and mineral retention. Another excellent source of hydration is from coconut water (the juice from young coconuts), which has the same sugar and salt makeup as blood plasma. See Dehydration for more information.

Flatulence

Gas

See also Colon & Intestinal Health, Digestion

You don't have to make up elaborate excuses (like blaming the dog) for flatulence after meals. And you don't have to avoid eating those foods known for their musical properties. Beans can be giant culprit when it comes to flatulence (gas) because they are broken down into a certain sugar in your intestines that bacteria love to eat. When certain bacteria feast on this bean sugar, the waste is methane (sulfur dioxide gas) and nitrogen gas. Other culprits include veggies like cabbage and Brussels sprouts. The natural sulfur in eggs can also be an offender, as can milk and dairy products.

But many natural remedies can minimize that volatile combustion of nitrogen and sulfur dioxide gas in your system.

What Causes Gas?

Flatulence comes from a combination of ingested air (from eating and swallowing) and gas produced in the digestive tract. Intestinal gases arise from an overabundance of bad bacteria in your gut. This overabundance and lack of bacterial balance is usually caused by poor eating habits or eating certain foods. When not enough good bacteria are present in your gut, the waste in your system becomes a gas feeding ground for the bad bacteria. What creates bad bacteria or kills off the good bacteria?

- Tap water, full of chlorine and fluoride
- Antibiotics and certain medications
- A diet rich in fermented foods and beverages (wine, beer, cheese, vinegar, dried fruit, risen breads, baking powder, and pickled foods)
- Too much blood sugar, which can give rise to bacteria that cause constipation and gas

Chronic gas may also be a symptom of a larger problem, such as diabetes, thyroid imbalance, poor liver health, or intestinal disorders.

Treatments

For quick relief, try acidophilus, bifidophilus and the probiotics cited in Digestion. Antibiotics are known for killing good bacteria, so if you've taken them, be sure to take probiotics for one month to reintroduce your system to the good bacteria.

In the Eastern Indian culture, people eat a yogurt-cucumber dish and other yogurt recipes, which are high in acidophilus and other exotic probiotic cultures. Another piece of Ayurvedic advice is to eat fennel and anise seeds after a meal to stop flatulence. They are chewy, taste great, and also freshen your breath. Besides probiotic cultures, you can also try these cures:

- Take digestive enzymes such as papain, bromelain, and protease.
- Gas associated with acid indigestion can be minimized or cured with carbon tablets.
- Put a couple of drops of peppermint or anise oil in a glass of water and drink before meals.
- Naturopaths also recommend kelp for flatulence. Along with relieving gas and bloating, the iodine in kelp can help you maintain a healthy weight by keeping your thyroid gland functioning normally.

Glaucoma

See also Cataracts, Macular Degeneration

Glaucoma is one of the two most common cause of blindness in the United States, second only to cataracts. It is caused by a buildup of fluid pressure inside the eyeball, which can damage or completely destroy the retina and optic nerve. This first leads to a loss of peripheral vision, and then gradual blindness. Symptoms are usually gradual and progress slowly. These include:

- Narrowing of peripheral vision
- Headaches
- Tunnel vision
- Sensation of seeing halos around lights
- Difficulty adapting to darkness
- Swollen eyelids
- Nausea and vomiting
- General vision loss

Open-angle glaucoma is the most common type. In this type, the fluid produced each day by the eye is slow to drain off. This causes a buildup of the drainage channels in the eye itself. Closed-angle glaucoma is usually caused by a rapid buildup of fluid pressure, causing the eyeballs to feel hard to the touch.

What Causes Glaucoma?

Glaucoma can be a result of various influences, including:

- Aging and premature aging
- Accumulation of debris and waste products in the eye drainage channels
- Allergies
- Eye injuries and tumors
- Nutritional deficiencies
- High blood pressure, diabetes, and macular degeneration
- Use of pharmaceutical drugs such as antidepressants, antihistamines, blood pressure medication, diuretics, steroids, and tetracycline

Treatments for Glaucoma

Eat plenty of antioxidant-rich foods, including bell peppers, carrots, parsley, spinach, tomatoes, dark-green leafy vegetables, purple berries, mangos, melons, and citrus fruit. Organic egg yolks are also recommended because they are rich in carotenoids. Avoid all processed and fried foods, sugar, caffeine, and alcohol.

Eye exercises can help reduce tension in the eye area and face. You may also want to avoid eyestrain from watching too much TV or sitting for extended periods in front of the computer. Use sunglasses with polarized lenses.

Nutritional supplements to add to your diet include vitamin A, vitamin B complex, vitamin C, vitamin E, alpha-lipoic acid, beta-carotene, chromium, lutien, magnesium, N-acetyl-cysteine (NAC), riboflavin and taurine.

Other Considerations

Some alternative therapies that can help with glaucoma include acupuncture and craniosacral work.

Gout

*See also **Arthritis***

Gout is a form of arthritis caused by the accumulation of uric acid crystals in the joints. It is an intensely painful disease, and in most cases affects only one joint. In 75% of cases, gout will attack the big toe; however, it can also affect other joints such as the ankle, heel, instep, knee, wrist, elbow, fingers, and spine.

What Causes Gout?

Although the exact cause of gout is unknown, it is thought to be linked to defects in purine metabolism. Purine is an organic compound commonly found in the body and is metabolized by the body to create uric acid. People with primary gout have either an increased production of uric acid or an impaired excretion of uric acid, or a combination of both. Certain types of chemotherapy can promote gout due to rapid tumor breakdown.

The classic picture is of excruciating and sudden pain, swelling, redness, warmness, and stiffness in the joint. Low-grade fever may also be present. The patient usually suffers from two sources of pain: the crystals inside the joint cause intense pain whenever the affected area is moved, and the inflammation of the tissues around the joint causes the skin to be swollen, tender, and sore if it is even slightly touched.

Treatments

Dietary change can make a contribution by lowering the plasma urate level if a diet low in purines is maintained because the body metabolizes purines into uric acid. Gout sufferers should avoid high-purine foods such as meat, fish, dry beans, lentils, peas, mushrooms, spinach, asparagus, cauliflower, shellfish, white flour, yeast, and sugar. Alcohol, aspirin, and high-sodium foods should also be eliminated from the diet.

Consuming purine-neutralizing foods, such as fresh fruits (especially cherries and strawberries) and most fresh vegetables, diluted celery juice, and distilled water. B-complex and C vitamins can also help.

Here is an old English cure for gout: Black cherry juice, apple cider vinegar, and horsetail herb (organic silica is a natural diuretic). It is a little raspy on the palate, so add some honey and water before chugging it down.

Additional gout remedies include bilberry, which is great for arthritis and has a collagen-stabilizing affect; enzymes, especially bromelain, which is prevalent in pineapple; burdock root, which helps reduce swelling; and quercetin and bioflavonoids, which counteract the effects of xanthine oxidase, an enzyme that promotes uric acid production.

Make a tea of bilberry, burdock root, and sarsaparilla (a natural diuretic). This decoction will help get and keep the swelling down. Take vitamin C (3 grams a day) and niacin (50 mg) with food.

Adios gout!

Hair (Graying)

See also Hair Loss

Why is it that some people have healthy hair color well into their advanced years, while others go prematurely gray? Are there ways to prevent premature graying? How about natural graying that we tend to accept as a part of aging; is there a way to prevent that?

Everyone wants to look young and coloring your hair might help you look and feel younger. But signs of graying may be an indication that our bodies need some rejuvenation too. Stress and the depletion of the kidneys, spleen, and pancreas may play a part in the graying process. Reducing stress and supporting these important organs may not only help your hair look younger, but may also help your body feel younger.

What Causes Gray Hair?

Gray hair, like wrinkling and other aging processes, is largely caused by the waning of testosterone and estrogen. This reduction in hormones can be prematurely advanced by the production of too much cortisol, which in turn is caused by stress and excess caffeine. Chinese herbs such as ginseng and supplements such as dehydroepiandrosterone (DHEA) help to build the reserves from which testosterone and estrogen are created.

Treatments

If you want to avoid using harsh chemicals on your hair, try a few natural alternatives to keep your color going strong:

- Bump up your hormone levels by taking B vitamin supplements. According to animal-based research studies, pantothenic acid (vitamin B5) deficiency causes hair to gray prematurely. DHEA supplements assist in the creation of hormones, which help to prevent hair loss and graying.

- Increase circulation with cat's claw, pure cocoa, and green tea extract. Chinese medicine uses ginseng in the treatment of hair loss and graying.
- Reduce stress. Stress causes increased cortisol, which reduces the hormones in your body needed for healthy hair.

Hair Loss

Alopecia / Female Hair Loss / Male Pattern Baldness

See also Hair (Graying)

Many men feel that hair loss is unavoidable, since it predominantly a genetic condition. But while the pattern associated with male pattern baldness may be predetermined, the rate of hair loss itself can be slowed down significantly. In fact, studies show that hair loss can be reversed in some cases. And while you may not experience a complete reversal with a full head of new hair, you may be able to restore 5 or 10 years to your thinning hair.

What Causes Hair Loss?

A number of factors influence hair loss. Genetics, hormonal imbalances, nutritional deficiencies, and external influences may all play a part in thinning or loss of hair.

- **Genetics:** The foremost cause of hair loss, known as alopecia or male pattern baldness, is genetic and it affects both men and women, following the maternal grandparent.
- **Hormones:** Balding and thinning hair is often caused by hormonal imbalances, specifically, an over-abundance of the male hormone androgen. This is why female hair loss often occurs after menopause and childbirth, resulting from a decrease in estrogen and a resulting androgen overload. Hypothyroidism may also be a factor.
- **Stress:** We also know that stress affects the production of hormones in the body and, as a result, can increase hair loss. Stress can be caused by excess

stimulants (coffee and other caffeinated products), mental and emotional chaos, traumatic experiences, and severe illness or medical treatment. Often, when these stress factors are eliminated, hair growth returns.

- **Nutrition:** Lack of nutrients for healthy hair also may cause hair loss. This can result from a low protein diet or one that is vitamin and mineral deficient.
- **Circulation:** Nutrients must be able to reach the top surface of the scalp, so excellent blood circulation is required for healthy hair. Changes in the scalp itself may also make it more difficult for nutrients to get into the follicles.

Treatments for Hair Loss

If we had a proven, sure-fire natural treatment for hair loss prevention, the hair transplant clinics would be out of business tomorrow. But that's not to say that herbs and lifestyle treatments cannot be effective. They work for some and not for others. More study is required to give us conclusive evidence as to the results of these natural treatments. Most natural treatments center on stimulating blood circulation to the scalp. Here are the highlights:

- Stimulate circulation in the scalp area with massage, exercise, herbs, and topical applications.
- Reduce or stop smoking and excess alcohol consumption. Smoking causes damage to the DNA of the hair follicle and inhibits tissue remolding during hair growth.
- Reduce protein and starch consumption and increase fruit and vegetable consumption.
- Try acupuncture treatments.

Other Considerations

For starters, start eating a healthier diet. High-fat, high-carbohydrate diets increase male and female pattern baldness, while diets abundant in fruits and vegetables but low in starch slow down the process. Take B vitamins with biotin, add organic silica (horsetail herb), and alpha-lipoic acid. Also increase vitamin E.

If you're already experiencing hair loss, a number of herbs and supplements can help you. The moss called golden maidenhair and inositol found in beans, nuts, grains, and fruits may help prevent further hair loss. The silicon in the herbs horsetail and oatstraw reportedly stop the process of hair loss completely. Furthermore, red sage and castor oil topical treatments supposedly encourage the growth of new hair, according to Eastern medicine.

The Amazon herb Una de Gato (cat's claw) is a known stimulant and circulation booster. It is used throughout South America for circulation disorders and weight loss programs.

Get plenty of rigorous exercise for better blood circulation and stress reduction.

Hangover

The "day after" often makes us wonder if the "night before" was worth it. Hangovers can be miserable experiences, and worse still, they can weaken our immune systems, digestive systems, and organ functions, making us vulnerable to disease and infections. Classic hangover symptoms include headache, fatigue, fogginess, nausea, vomiting, and sensitivity to light and noise.

What Causes Hangovers?

A hangover is caused by excess consumption of alcohol, which lowers your blood sugar, dehydrates the body, and pollutes the liver and kidneys with toxic chemicals. Repeated excess drinking can result in serious liver, kidney, and/or stomach damage, not to mention increased skin aging and weight gain.

Treatments for Hangover

Prevention is the best treatment for hangover, as it is difficult to counteract the dehydration and fatigue when you begin treatment the "day after." Some possible remedies include:

- Eat plenty of food before drinking, especially greasy food that helps block or slow down the digestion of alcohol.
- Drink a glass of tomato juice in the morning, with added cayenne pepper, sugar, and lime juice.
- Drink several glasses of pure, filtered water before going to bed and upon waking up. Also, drink plenty of water between alcoholic drinks. Better than water, make a simple saline solution with a pinch of salt and a teaspoon of sugar in a large glass of water.
- Try a mixture of digestive bitter herbs: gentian, mugwort, and dandelion root before going to bed and upon waking. Bitter herbs of special note include

boldo, olive leaf extract, and milk thistle extract. Take these before going to bed if you can. Otherwise, take them upon waking up.
- Support your kidneys by drinking diuretic teas.

Other Considerations

Some people claim that hot steam baths can help eliminate toxins. Even a hot shower will help by washing off the toxins and alcohol that are captured in the pores of your skin.

Headaches

Migraine Headaches

See also Allergies, Congestion, Stress

Probably the most common medical complaint in the Western world, just about everyone suffers from headaches at some point in their lives. Most believe their choices for curing themselves of this painful malady are limited to aspirin and non-aspirin pain relievers. But you have many alternatives in treating and preventing headaches that do not require traditional medicine.

Migraine headaches are particularly disruptive. They are characterized by a slow-growing throb in the head that often produces nausea and localized vision loss. Often the nausea and vision loss appear before the headache actually become acute. They can last for days.

What Causes Headaches?

Headaches have a variety of causes, including food allergies, environmental toxins, stress, eye strain, and sinus congestion. Premenstrual headaches are often related to hormonal imbalances. Each of these has its own entry in this guide, so be sure to check these cross-references for additional information.

Headache Treatments

Keep in mind that most non-aspirin pain relievers are immunosuppressant. That is, they weaken the immune system. Taking them once in a while may be okay, but prolonged and repeated use is definitely costly to your health. For a natural alternative, try white willow bark extract, the plant from which aspirin was originally discovered and made.

Allergy expert Dr. James Braly believes that 90% of all migraines are caused by either food allergies or allergic reactions to food additives. But it's possible that any headache can be traced back to a food or substance allergy. Allergenic substances include food preservatives and colorings, caffeine, and chocolate. Try removing foods and drinks containing these products from your diet, one by one, for three to four weeks at a time, and notice if your migraine attacks lessen or disappear completely during that time. This process can take time, but is likely to produce results. Start with the typical offenders:

- Coffee, soda and caffeinated beverages
- Wine, beer, and alcohol products
- Cheese and dairy products
- Wheat and refined wheat products with gluten
- Other fermented products, including vinegar and any pickled products
- Sugar and high fructose corn syrup
- Food additives, dyes, and preservatives (particularly those in processed and dried meat), MSG, and sulfites
- Peanut butter and peanuts
- Soy products
- Shell fish

The other 10% of headaches are probably caused by a variety of things, but you can bet that environmental toxins are among the most likely culprit. Check your home and work environment for chemical out-gassing from carpets and wall coverings. Consider sleeping with a device that oxygenates the air in your room.

If you suffer from migraine headaches, products containing the artificial sweetener aspartame may be to blame. Aspartame triggers migraines in many sufferers.

Many headaches are caused by dehydration, and dehydration is as prevalent in winter as in summer. Drinking two large glasses of pure water will relieve the pain of these headaches almost immediately, without the unpleasant side effects caused by traditional pain relievers.

Other Considerations

Massage under the two ridges on either side of the back of the skull until you can feel the contracted muscles relax. The two nerves there can be pressured by tight muscles in the region, causing headaches, including migraines. Once the headache subsides with this therapy, use your thumbs to stroke gently in opposite directions across the brow with lavender essential oil. This will put you or the person you're massaging in a relaxed state.

Lavender has been used since the time of Cleopatra for stress reduction, headache relief, lessening of scars, and faster healing of burns. Some herbalists believe that quinine bark, feverfew, butterbur and magnesium are also an effective headache remedies. Other natural herbs that help control blood pressure and relax the vascular system include pure cocoa, olive leaf extract, mint extract, chamomile, passion fruit extract, bay leaves, chamomile, coriander, skullcap, turmeric, valerian root, and wild yam.

Finally, acupuncture and different forms of bodywork can be effective cures for headaches. Acupuncture may be able to move or change the energies in the body that are accumulating to cause headaches, and bodywork such as massage may be able to release the stress that causes some headaches.

Heart Disease

See Anti-inflammatories, Blood Pressure, Cardiovascular Health, Cholesterol,

Heart disease remains the number one killer of adults in developed countries. When we think of heart disease, most people think of high blood pressure, arterial plaque, obesity, cholesterol, and all of the elements and conditions related to atherosclerosis. But coronary heart disease, while the most common form of heart failure, is only one of many different heart conditions. More than 25 million Americans are diagnosed with heart disease and they maintain a sixty billion dollar industry. In most cases, heart disease can be prevented with natural treatments and lifestyle changes.

What Causes Heart Disease?

Today the following facts might seem controversial, but in ten years they will be looked back on as the norm. We'll be saying, "How stupid could people have been?" Sound familiar?

Cholesterol is NOT the main culprit in heart attacks. More than 13 million people in the United States have been saddled with lifetime prescriptions to statins (cholesterol-lowering drugs) while heart disease statistics continue to soar! And many experts agree that statins can cause liver problems and muscle aches.

The majority of people who suffer heart attacks have normal cholesterol levels. The majority of people with high cholesterol never suffer heart attacks. Half of all heart attack victims have none of the standard risk factors, that is, smoking, obesity, genetics, or high cholesterol. Statin drugs can rob your heart of Co-Q10, the nutrient that powers your heartbeat.

The real culprit in heart disease is not just cholesterol; it is also inflammation. Conditions that cause or increase inflammation include: age, smoking, toxins, high blood sugar, lack of nutrients, and a sedentary lifestyle.

Treatments and Prevention

Anti-inflammatory foods and herbs include calendula, catuaba, cat's claw, hawthorn, milk thistle, vitamin C, wormwood, black cohosh, garlic, motherwort, pine bark extract, white willow, and wild yam. You can use these as tinctures, infusions (tea), powders (capsules), or extracts. The spices tumeric, ginger, and cayenne also have anti-inflammatory properties as do fish oils.

Herbs and foods with antispasmodic and hypotensive qualities for calming the heart, nervous system, and blood pressure include leonuri, valerian root, haw, eucalyptus, St. John's wort, and spearmint.

Vitamin C, vitamin B6, niacin, a consistent enzymes program, colloidal silver, primrose oil, and red algae help get rid of arterial plaque and coronary and arterial inflammation. A major component of arterial plaque is a substance called lipoprotein-a, which serves to strengthen blood vessel walls in the absence of adequate amounts of vitamin C in the body. The only problem is that lipoprotein-a also clogs your arteries.

EDTA and vitamin C help get rid of this arterial plaque and the condition caused by the Standard American Diet (SAD). This condition is elevated levels of homocysteine, an amino acid metabolite that is highly damaging to arterial walls. To help reduce homocysteine levels, add 800 mcg of folic acid, 1 mg of B12 (methylcobalamine), and 500 to 1,000 mg of trimethylglycine (TMG) to your meals, at least twice a day.

Add 100 mg of coenzyme Q10 (Co-Q10) and 20 mg of potassium. Potassium cell salts are also helpful in strengthening the heart muscles. Hawthorn berry and magnesium help regulate the heart's electrical activity.

Dehydroepiandrosterone (DHEA) supplements may prevent heart disease, as studies show that declining DHEA levels due to age are linked to heart disease, as well as to obesity, diabetes, and arthritis. In fact, according to a groundbreaking, 12-year research study of 242 men ranging in age from 50 to 79 years old, only 100 mcg of DHEA reduced death from heart disease by 48% and the death rate in general by 36% (excluding accidents). Selenium has been reported to improve cardiomyopathies (flabby hearts).

Other Considerations

Avoid licorice if you have heart disease. Though licorice has many health benefits, it can cause sodium retention and excess potassium depletion, causing high blood pressure and electrolyte imbalance. For people with heart disease, licorice's cons far outweigh its pros.

Heart Palpitations

Arrhythmia / Ectopia

See Adrenal Imbalance, Anxiety, Hypoglycemia, Thyroid Imbalance,

Have you heard the romantic notion that upon seeing a lover, one's heart will "skip a beat?" This may not be far from the truth, as heart palpitations are quite common and can be brought on by strong emotion, fear, shock, panic, and the like—perhaps even the awe of seeing something beautiful. If your heart occasionally skips a beat, thumps, or races, it's probably nothing to be concerned about. However, if you frequently sense heart palpitations, or if racing or pounding continues for prolonged periods, your heart could be functioning abnormally. Here's what to look out for:

- Frequent racing or pounding of the heart
- Prolonged racing or pounding, lasting for several minutes or even an hour
- Pain or acute discomfort in the chest during or just after palpitations
- Dizziness, lightheadedness, or sweating during or just after palpitations

What Causes Heart Palpitations?

The electric impulses that cause the heart to beat may be interrupted or affected by external influences, making the heart change its rhythm or pound heavily. Most commonly, this is brought on by exertion and goes away after your body receives more oxygen from the blood. Excess adrenaline may also cause palpitations. Adrenaline is produced by panic, shock, fear, and similar emotions. It may also be caused by excess caffeine intake (or intake of other stimulants, such as guaraná and ephedra). Adrenal imbalance also may be caused by a weak thyroid. An overactive thyroid and/or Grave's Disease or too much thyroid medication is a common cause of ectopia.

Heart palpitations can also be a symptom of anxiety or panic attacks. A rare cause of palpitations is carcinoid syndrome (too much serotonin).

Treatments

If you notice unusual or frequent palpitations, you can help protect yourself from heart dysfunction, including:

- Reduce caffeine and other stimulants.
- Take black haw bark along with relaxing herbs such as motherwort, hawthorn berries, Chinese skullcap, mint, and chamomile.
- Check for thyroid imbalances, including thyroid disease (Graves disease) or if you are taking too much thyroid medication.

Eating grapes has been linked to a reduction in heart palpitations, especially those related to hot flashes. Eat fresh grapes or drink organic grape juice. Also, the potassium found in fruit, vegetables, and fish helps reduce blood pressure. Bananas and nectarines are an excellent source of potassium. If you cannot get enough potassium from foods, try a potassium supplement. Also, take a calcium-magnesium supplement; magnesium is effective in preventing palpitations by relaxing the chest area, including the heart and lungs.

Replenish your body after shock, trauma, or stress by taking B, C, and E vitamins.

Heartburn

Acid Indigestion / Gastroesophageal Reflux Disease (GERD)

See also Digestion

Although heartburn has nothing to do with the heart, the primary symptom is a burning sensation around the heart area, or just below the breast plate. It can rise into the esophagus and even affect the throat. For some, heartburn is an uncomfortable sensation. For others, it causes acute pain and damage to the esophagus, and it can last for days.

Avoid using over-the-counter antacids. Prolonged use of these products can cause severe kidney damage and other problems resulting from aluminum and sodium bicarbonate.

What Causes Heartburn?

Most people believe too much stomach (hydrochloric) acid causes heartburn. Usually, however, the problem is too little acid. Eating only small meals after 3 p.m. and avoiding all caffeine, fried foods, spicy foods, and tomato sauces in the evening can eliminate many of your serious gastroesophageal reflux disease (GERD) problems.

Additionally, some behaviors cause heartburn and, in these cases, the only way to prevent and relieve heartburn is to change those behaviors. Overeating, for example, is a major cause of heartburn, as the excess food causes pressure changes in the stomach that push food up into the lower part of the esophagus.

Natural Treatment and Prevention

Let's start with some ways to treat heartburn. Here are some ways to quickly recover and restore your normal stomach pH. Try different ideas from this list until you find a solution that works for you:

- Drink a cup of cold milk. The milk will coat your stomach and esophagus, providing quick relief from the burning acid.
- Take a teaspoon of apple cider vinegar (acetic acid) to aid digestion and stop the heartburn.
- If you need a little more help, take a teaspoon of baking soda (not baking powder, which is full of deadly aluminum) in half a glass of warm water and drink. This will cut down gas and heartburn.

- Try carbon tablets for reducing acid and gas.

Here are some keys for preventing heartburn:

- Don't stuff yourself when you eat; remember that your body will consider even small amounts of food late at night (or after exercising) as overeating.
- Chew your food well. Your digestive enzymes simply can't handle large chunks of food, so heartburn often will develop from improper chewing.
- Avoid eating caffeinated foods and drinks (chocolate, coffee, tea) and foods containing refined carbohydrates (white bread, refined white sugar, pasta). These foods and drinks can all cause heartburn, as can fried foods, tomato sauce and drinking two or more glasses of beer or wine at night.
- Avoid combining sugars with other foods. Wait before eating dessert. Also, avoid combining fruit and fresh salads with other foods, so wait after eating them as well. Coffee and wine should also be drunk by themselves.
- Take a daily enzyme or probiotic—friendly bacteria to help with digestion.
- Don't smoke. In addition to creating a myriad other health disorders, smoking, especially before meals, can lead to heartburn.

Hemorrhoids

See also Colon & Intestinal Health, Constipation

Approximately half of everyone older than 50 is afflicted to some degree by hemorrhoids, and almost 25% of those patients seek surgical treatments. A mild case usually only causes itching and irritation in the anal area, generally on the outside of the body. In many cases, blood may be visible on stools, coming from lesions in the anal tissues. Constipation or difficult bowel movements can worsen the condition and make it difficult to heal. Advanced cases can have painful and swollen tissues that can interfere with normal life functions.

What Causes Hemorrhoids?

Improper diet (low water intake), lack of exercise, chronic constipation, and straining when passing stool (low-fiber and other dietary influences) are strong contributing factors to the development of hemorrhoids. Childbirth causes hemorrhoids in many women, since they are essentially swollen or inflamed veins often caused by strain. The sudden appearance of hemorrhoids in the over-50 age group may be a sign of rectal cancer.

Treatments

Eat raw vegetables, drink more pure water, and take vitamin C. Large doses of digestive enzymes will shrink the swelling. Drink plenty of liquids to ensure softer stool. Other natural stool softeners include coffee, vitamin C, and pure olive oil.

Natural hemorrhoid treatments include quinine bark and chlorophyll. Putting some chlorophyll in your diet may help your hemorrhoids heal. Spirulina, alfalfa, Chlorella, wheatgrass, and barley are all high in chlorophyll (and a number of other nutrients, too).

Immediate pain relief requires putting a balm directly on the hemorrhoids. Witch hazel extract soothes and cools hemorrhoid pain; in fact, it is the active ingredient in many commercial, over-the-counter (OTC) hemorrhoid treatments. For a less expensive, natural alternative to these OTC remedies, simply use a cotton ball to apply witch hazel extract directly on your hemorrhoids. You can find witch hazel extract in drugstores anywhere. You can also apply aloe vera gel, which is also widely available, to your hemorrhoids for soothing pain relief.

For prevention, avoid dairy products (especially fibrous cheeses), hot spices, and alcohol. And get plenty of exercise.

Hepatitis

See also Liver & Gallbladder Health

Hepatitis is a potentially serious condition that affects the liver and causes yellowing of the eyes and skin, fatigue, joint pain, stomach pain, nausea and vomiting, fever, and dark or discolored urine. Hepatitis can lead to cirrhosis of the liver and can be life threatening.

What Causes Hepatitis?

The most common cause of hepatitis is a viral infection. The hepatitis A virus is contagious and is found in human feces. Hepatitis B, C and D are blood borne. It is important to sanitize your surroundings and take anti-viral herbs if you have been exposed to someone with the virus. Other causes include:

- Alcohol or drug abuse
- Food toxins
- Prescription medications

Treatments

Antivirals such as olive leaf extract will give your liver a chance. Of course, stop drinking alcohol, stop smoking, and stop eating sugar.

Glutathione (glutamine) strengthens the liver. High doses of enzymes taken between meals support the liver in its work of processing toxins. Milk thistle herb helps cleanse the liver. A potent liver-strengthening combination and viral killer is drinking licorice tea twice daily and taking milk thistle, selenium, N-acetylcysteine (NAC), alpha-lipoic acid, S-adenosylmethionine (SAMe), vitamin B12 (methylcobalamine variety), green tea extract, and garlic.

A Chinese herbal blend commonly called Liver Tea consists of bupleurum, citrus peel, cyperus, ligusticum, white peony, auratium fruit, and licorice. This will thoroughly cleanse the liver and, if used over a two-week period, will help dissolve gallstones and kidney stones. Fill a large pan with purified water and bring it to a boil. Add a handful of this herbal combination (available in health food stores, online, or where Chinese herbs are sold) to cover the top of the water completely. Boil for 20 minutes, then turn off the flame, and steep for two hours. Drink at least two 12 ounces glasses per day without food. The more the merrier and the faster it acts.

Traditional Chinese Medicine practitioners also prescribe burdock tea for liver problems, as it is believed to improve liver function and cleanse the blood. To make burdock tea, use 12 teaspoons of dried burdock root powder per cup of hot water, or add 23 drops of burdock extract to hot, distilled water.

High-quality colloidal (microscopic particles) silver is a powerful antiviral. Intravenous vitamin C can be useful in strengthening the immune system against the hepatitis virus.

Other Considerations

Avoid a high-protein or high-sugar diet and acetaminophen-containing analgesics (like Tylenol) when hepatitis is present. You may also want to work with a healthcare practitioner who does UV (ultraviolet) blood cleansing or ozone therapy.

Herniated Disc

Spinal discs cushion the vertebrae, but if a disk's outer shell weakens, part of the soft, inner core can bulge out. If the herniated disk presses on any of the many nerves that run along the spine, it can cause numbness, pain, weakness, incontinence, and loss of bowel control. Symptoms include pain in the general region of the herniated disc, sometimes with numbness, tingling, or weakness in the extremities, frequent urination, sciatica, and headaches.

To avoid herniating a spinal disc, be careful with heavy lifting, stay in shape, do yoga, exercise, keep your bones mineralized, get plenty of sunshine, avoid fluoride and coffee, acid foods, and dairy, and stand up straight.

Causes of Herniated Discs

The common causes of herniated disks include:

- Age
- Heavy lifting and unusual positions
- Weak muscles and inflexibility
- Poor bone quality
- Genes

This is advice for herniated discs only, not for ruptured discs. The difference between the two is that the pain of a rupture is completely debilitating. Get X-rays or a magnetic resonance imaging (MRI) scan as fast as possible. If you have a rupture, seek out a good spinal surgeon and get it repaired, then follow the nutritional advice below.

Treatments for Herniated Discs

- High doses of digestive enzymes taken between meals will reduce the inflammation.
- In addition to digestive enzymes, you may want to try nettle leaf, prickly ash bark, marshmallow root, and rose hips.
- Try hyaluronic acid, collagen, MSM, and chondroitin.
- Magnets applied to the affected area help relieve pain, as do magnetic beds. Some medical facilities

have had excellent results using highly focused magnetic tubes, much like an MRI tube, that focus directly on the hernia site.

- Rest at first, but exercise when you can.
- Get an inversion table and hang (start slowly) partially upside down at first. Don't go completely upside down immediately without building up to it. Being upside down will cause dizziness as the blood rushes to your head.
- Place heat, such as sun lamps, sunshine, heating pads and warm baths, and ultrasound, on the affected spot.
- If your doctor has suggested surgery, try acupuncture before agreeing to go under the knife. Dr. Eugene Kozhevnikov of St. Petersburg, Russia, uses electro-acupuncture, physical manipulation, and various energy medicine devices to help ease back pain and muscle contractions. In fact, he believes that 90% of all herniated discs should be treated by acupuncture rather than surgery.

"I'm at an age where my back goes out more than I do."
Phyllis Diller

Herpes

Cold Sore / Fever Blister / HHV-6 / HSV

The herpes virus comes in several forms, and all are epidemic, easily transferable, and leave the body more vulnerable to other diseases. Herpes is a virus family to avoid if possible, though this is difficult in today's society. One of the most promising new treatment developments comes from India, in the form of Neem oil.

Types of Herpes

Herpes simplex is a virus that creates blisters on the mouth or on the genitals. It is contagious, particularly during an outbreak, but also during periods of shedding, which is unpredictable and usually asymptomatic.

Genital herpes appears anywhere on the pelvic region, so to avoid contagion, this entire region should not be in contact with another "danger zone" when the virus is active. It causes sores that itch when an outbreak begins, then break open and form scabs. The initial outbreak is often accompanied by fever and nausea, but later outbreaks often have no symptoms. It is contagious as soon as an episode begins, and particularly throughout the time of the outbreak. Often, the viruses are passed along during times when people think it is safe. It is important to remember that the virus goes through shedding phases, which are seemingly random. The disease is contagious during that time; however, there are no symptoms at that point to warn of its contagious state..

Epstein Barr Virus is a form of Herpes responsible for mononucleosis, causing long-term fatigue.

Less known is **Type 6 herpes**. About 95% of the world has been exposed to this virus and developed antibodies. Most infants have this form of herpes, which is called roseola, a feverish rash. It can lead to bone marrow or brain infection in a small number of cases, but usually leaves little trace. However, the virus reactivates in some adults whose immune systems are weakened by hormonal imbalances, stress, and toxins. Herpes Virus Type 6 has been implicated in Chronic Fatigue Syndrome.

Prevention and Treatment of Herpes

Herpes is activated by four things: sunburn; an excess of the amino acid arginine, which is present in orange juice and other fruit juices; malic acid, which is also concentrated in fruit juices; and the worst culprit, stress.

- Lysine, another amino acid, which is like poison to herpes, looks like arginine to the herpes virus. When lysine is present, the herpes virus eats the lysine, thinking it is arginine, and dies. The herb lorea can help if you can find it, but do NOT take lorea if you have a liver condition. Eat lean animal protein in the morning and evening and significantly reduce carbohydrates such as sugar and bread.
- Garlic is better known as a remedy for fungal infections, but research indicates that it is also effective against viruses such as genital herpes and herpes simplex. In the case of herpes simplex, but not necessarily genital herpes, zinc supplements may help stop the virus from spreading throughout the body. Also, chewing folic acid tablets and taking L-lysine and zinc may clear up herpes simplex as quickly as overnight.

- Sarsaparilla, taken as a tea boiled for twenty minutes, or as an extract or capsule, can help prevent contracting oral and genital herpes if you are exposed. It also helps keep outbreaks under control.
- Neem also prevents and controls oral and genital herpes. It has a challenging taste and smell and stains whatever it touches. It can be added to massage oil and rubbed on the genitals and used intervaginally, and it helps prevent pregnancy as well as herpes. (Be sure to study this subject closely before using it.) This has been used traditionally in India and now is available commercially.
- Vitamin C is an antioxidant, antihistamine, immune system booster, and antiviral. Zinc lowers the frequency and severity of herpes outbreaks and can be taken internally and applied in ointment.
- HSV replication requires arginine, so a diet high in lysine may block arginine and prevent it from activating the virus. Chocolate, nuts, and grains are high in arginine and low in lysine. Legumes, including peanuts, are high in lysine and low in arginine.
- Lemon balm extract oils or creams can be applied to the herpes sores, as can aloe vera.
- Licorice is similar to steroids but without the side effects, and can reduce pain and aid healing of lesions. It can be applied topically and ingested. Make tea by boiling the roots for twenty minutes. Drink four to five cups of licorice a per day and put a bandage soaked in licorice on the ulcer.

Hiccups

Mostly, hiccups are considered a cute body function that goes away in its own time. Symptoms of hiccups are rarely serious, but hiccup attacks have been known to require medication, as prolonged attacks can lead to exhaustion and fatigue. Everyone knows at least a few of the numerous home remedies for hiccups, including holding the breath, drinking water upside-down, and holding onto your tongue until they go away.

What Causes Hiccups?

Hiccups are caused by the sudden closing of the vocal chords, either from obstruction or a sudden contraction of the diaphragm. Too much oxygen and improper breathing may also cause hiccups. This results in a sudden contraction of the diaphragm.

Treatments for Hiccups

Hiccups are easily treated with a few simple techniques. Remedies can include:

- Take as deep a breath as possible, then hold it. After a moment or two, try adding more air to fill your lungs to absolute capacity. When you've held it for a moment, let it out and repeat this process two more times.
- Repeat for several minutes (four or five times). You may even try sipping water while holding your breath.
- Consume two parts honey and one part castor oil during an attack.
- Slowly sip a warm chamomile or pau d'arco tea.
- Take charcoal tablets or chewable papaya enzymes.
- Breathe the essential oils of peppermint, rosemary, pine, sesame and/or anis. One technique is to drip the oils onto a warm, dry cloth and hold it over your nose and mouth to breathe in the energies.

Other Considerations

Alternative professional care therapies can include acupressure, massage, chiropractic medicine, and hypnosis.

Hives

Dermographia / Heat Rash / Urticaria / Wheals

See also Allergies

Hives normally appear as raised bumps on the skin, usually white with red patches around them, like welts or insect bites. However, different forms of this condition can appear as red streaks or lines on the skin. They usually appear in the upper body area, the chest, back, and arms, but they can occur anywhere on the body, including the hands and feet. With some people, they last only a few minutes, but many people experience them for several hours or even several days.

This condition is also called urticaria, from the scientific name of the stinging nettle plant. This plant is associated with skin irritation because direct contact with the live plant often produces the same type of skin rash, itching, and redness.

Causes of Urticaria (Hives)

Urticaria is a histamine response in the body, where the body produces histamines in an attempt to combat allergens or other influences. With urticaria, the histamine response is excessive and causes redness and itching. Urticaria is brought on by several possible factors:

- **Heat**: Exposure to hot air, humidity, or hot water can bring on this rash.
- **Pressure**: Also known as dermographia, pressure urticaria occurs around the beltline from the pressure of a belt, around bra straps on women, and even on parts of the body that have been leaning against a table or wall. The area experiencing the extra pressure turns red and itchy and often clears up within an hour. For some, however, the reaction can be intense and last hours.
- **Allergies**: Food allergies, especially those related to red meat and dairy, can cause the histamine reaction of urticaria. Also, strawberries, tropical fruit, citrus fruit, shellfish, and some nuts can cause the reaction.
- **Environmental Toxins**: Household toxins in cleansers, paints, and bug sprays can cause a histamine reaction.
- **Emotion**: International experts believe there may be an emotional component to urticaria, or that stress and depression can at least exacerbate the symptoms.

Treatments

The most common prescription for Urticaria is an antihistamine. For some, a simple, over-the-counter allergy medicine works to remove the symptoms. For others, the dosage of 10 mg of active antihistamine (the highest dosage available over the counter) is not nearly enough. Formulas of up to 25 mg are often required. Urticaria has no known cures, and there are no good plant substitutes for antihistamines. However, you can lessen the intensity of urticaria and consequently the dosage or frequency of your antihistamine. Here are a few tips

- Use arnica cream topically or apply chamomile oil on hives to help ease redness and itching.
- Drink peppermint tea or take peppermint oil.

- Homeopathic remedies for hives include Apis mel and Urtica Urens.
- Cold baths and body brushing can reduce the symptoms.
- Hydrochloric acid (HCL) supplements can be effective to aid digestion in people who suffer from urticaria caused by food allergies.
- Vitamin B can help reduce symptoms and even prevent attacks, as can vitamin C and bromalain.
- Avoid scratching the hives or red areas, as this only worsens the reaction.

The Truth About Antihistamines

Antihistamines are broken down by the liver and eliminated through the kidneys. Over time, they can damage the liver. Be sure to take plenty of liver-strengthening remedies (including milk thistle) if you are taking antihistamines. The best natural alternatives to chemical antihistamines are vitamin C and green tea extract. Combine these with extra iron and B-complex vitamins.

Human Papilloma Virus

HPV / Cervical Cancer / Genital Warts / Plantar Warts / Vaginal Warts

See also Infection (Virus)

Since its discovery in recent years, HPV has become a hot topic. It is the only known cause of cervical cancer in women. As a sexually transmitted infection (STI), the HPV virus is more common among younger and more sexually active adults. An estimated 20 million people have HPV in the United States. Since there are very few symptoms, it is often undetected for a long time. This is the greatest threat from HPV, so women should be tested from time to time with a Pap smear analysis.

Don't be fooled by compelling advertising for HPV vaccinations! They do not cure HPV infections and they are not proven effective in preventing HPV. They are simply an unnecessary chemical vaccine administered on a public frightened by pharmaceutical company advertising, designed to promote and sell products. These chemicals have numerous side effects that can compromise your health.

What Causes HPV?

HPV is a virus and, as such, it is transmitted through contact with other humans. Sexual intercourse is not necessary for HPV transmission, as it lives on the skin around the genitals and can come into contact through almost any sexual contact (not necessarily penetration).

Treatments

HPV is usually not dangerous or problematic for either partner. Of course, for women, it should be treated early so it does not develop into a larger problem, such as cervical cancer. If treated early, HPV is not serious or health threatening. Traditional treatments for women are not necessarily more effective than natural treatments. It's a virus that affects the skin and can be treated quite well with natural antiviral topicals. These include:

- Tea tree oil (the best and most expensive)
- Artemisia
- St John's wort liquid extract
- Liquid Echinacea

These will work just as well as topical antiviral medications from the doctor. Put these into an aloe vera gel for best results. Use them every day for several weeks. Oral treatments to supplement these topical treatments include:

- Take olive leaf extract and nutrient-rich, health-forming foods to support your immune system.
- Take Echinacea, St. John's wort, and skullcap herbs for antiviral protection. Oregano oil also works well.
- Take pine bark extract (Pycnogenol), pure cocoa, green tea extract, and flaxseed oil for antioxidant support, which helps protect your cells from viral attack.
- Stop smoking, excess drinking, and remove processed foods and excess sugar from your diet during your antiviral treatment.

For HIM

At the moment, there is no trustworthy test that detects HPV in men. However, genital warts can be detected in men, which is the most common symptom of HPV. Generally, visual inspection is used to determine if the man has genital warts from HPV. However, these inspections are not always 100% reliable. For men, HPV is not a high-risk STI (sexually transmitted infection). It affects only the skin and often goes away on its own.

A burning sensation while urinating is not a symptom of HPV in men, so if you have this symptom, you might have a bacterial infection or allergic reaction—not a viral infection. Bacteria can be eliminated with:

- Garlic extract
- Oregano extract
- Cranberry juice (12 oz at morning and night while symptoms last)
- Getting your body pH more alkaline and less acidic by eating lots of green foods like Spirulina, spinach, kale, Echinacea, devil's claw
- Avoiding soda, sugar, cheese, beer, wine, vinegar, pickled foods, too much bread or yeast
- Some men are allergic to spermicidal creams used in contraceptive devices and reactions can be harsh. Usually, the reaction subsides within 48 hours.

Other Considerations

Condoms may provide some protection against HPV, but are not a total solution, since HPV-infected areas could come into contact with any exposed skin.

Hypoglycemia

Low Blood Sugar

See also Adrenal Imbalance, Blood Pressure (Low), Candida

Hypoglycemia can make a person feel he is losing his mind, causing confusion, mental imbalance, emotional outbursts, and sudden changes, low moods appearing when blood sugar dips, fears, and forgetfulness. It causes the shakes, general lack of energy, heart palpitations, and the constant need to lie down—but often causing insomnia. Other symptoms include blurry vision and the sudden desire for food (especially sweets) to bring the blood sugar back up. Then, for awhile, a person can feel normal until it starts up again.

Causes of Hypoglycemia

There are two types of hypoglycemia: conditioned hypoglycemia and reactive hypoglycemia. When a person with conditioned hypoglycemia eats foods high in refined sugar or starch, the resulting spike in blood sugar causes the pancreas to produce too much insulin, which converts sugar into energy. This pulls too much blood sugar out of circulation and results in that tired, out-of-it feeling that accompanies low blood sugar. A person with reactive hypoglycemia initially experiences an extremely high spike in blood sugar before it plummets. For someone with reactive hypoglycemia, the unpleasant symptoms of muscle cramps, nausea, sweating, dizziness, and even fainting, are a result of the rapid change in blood sugar levels, rather than the low level itself. Reactive hypoglycemia is, unfortunately, often a precursor to Type 2 diabetes.

Low cortisol levels when the adrenal glands have been pushed too far over a long period of time can lead to low blood sugar. This can be caused by too much stress or caffeine.

Treatments for Hypoglycemia

Hypoglycemia is an easy condition to lick when you start your day with protein the size of your fist and two 12-ounce glasses of purified water, preferably drunk at least 20 minutes before your meal. Stay away from the simple carbohydrates and sugar. Once the protein is on board in the morning, the desire for sweets will dissipate. Sugar craving is usually a protein deficiency.

Take care of any Candida infection, as this will also cause a strong sugar and simple carbohydrate craving in order to feed the yeast/fungus. Many people think they have hypoglycemia and then find their blood sugars levels are fine. Avoiding sugary foods to kill off Candida can cause false hypoglycemia, as the Candida causes the same symptoms in order to nudge a person towards consuming more sugar for it to survive.

- Add 150 mg of adrenal cortex extract, 500 mg of pantothenic acid, and 1,000 mg of vitamin C in the morning, and 500 mg of pantothenic acid and 1,000 mg of vitamin C just before bed with a glass of water. Follow this regimen for six weeks and the stars and lightheadedness that occurs when you get up quickly from a sitting position (caused when your orthostatic, or standing, blood pressure drops) will be gone, along with difficulty concentrating, and the other assorted symptoms. (If you experience dizziness upon standing but your blood sugar is normal, drink more water, add salt for low blood pressure, and try an iron supplement for possible anemia.)

- Chromium picolinate (200 mcg with food) helps stabilize blood sugar, since it helps transport glucose from the bloodstream to the cells that need it for energy.
- If you have hypoglycemia, you should, of course, avoid refined white sugar and refined starches, alcohol, and fruit, as well as caffeine. Even decaffeinated coffee, tea, and soft drinks may have too much caffeine (trace amounts) for hypoglycemics.

Immune System Health

Recovery from Illness / Viral Immunity

See also Autoimmune Disorders, Infection (Bacterial), Infection (Viral), Stress

In a strict medical sense, the immune system is not actually one of the body's systems, like the cardiovascular system or the nervous system. The immune system is a set of byproducts produced by the proper and balanced functioning of the organs and body systems—perhaps even the proper functioning of the whole person: mentally, emotionally, and physically.

There is a lot we don't know about the immune system, but we do know that it is the body's principal line of defense against viruses, parasites, bacteria, fungi, and toxins that cause decay and damage to the body. It is the body's major defense mechanism against cancer formation. It is as if the organs and body systems joined together to create a defense system to protect themselves.

In many ways, good health boils down to a healthy immune system. Just about all of the body's defenses against sickness and disease are now seen to be part of its great interconnected network of chemical processes. And while the components of the immune system are intricate and complicated, the pathways to a healthy immune system are easy to understand and follow.

What are the Symptoms of a Weak Immune System?

Since the immune system is linked to our overall health, it has at least some responsibility for just about every ailment that can afflict us. Still, there are a few signs you can watch for that point to an immune system in need of support:

- Recurring infections
- Chronic fatigue, sleep disorders, never feeling rested
- Chronic diarrhea
- Slow healing
- Allergies, especially the onset of several new allergies
- Inflammation
- Frequent colds or flu (more than 3 times per year or one that never seems to go away)

What Causes Damage to the Immune System?

The immune system is amazingly versatile and flexible. It responds to foreign substances, viruses, and other threats with speed and intelligence. Nevertheless, certain antigens may prove too strong for the immune system to fight off completely, and some may even damage the immune system. We often add to the problem by increasing our exposure to toxic substances—from our environment, our foods, and through our behaviors. We may also neglect to fortify our immune systems with proper diet, supplements, and lifestyle habits. In short, damage to the immune system falls into two simple categories: damage from toxins and damage from neglect.

Boosting the Immune System

Science has identified a number of foods and supplements proven to enhance the various elements and processes of the immune system. Most likely, a combination of these therapies is necessary to cover all the bases: combat toxins, improve chemical and hormonal imbalances, and stimulate the thymus. The details on these immune enhancers could fill several books, but here is a quick hit on the essentials:

- Eat an antioxidant-rich diet. Reduce smoking and excess drinking.
- Balance your hormones and thyroid/adrenal activity (for many, this means taking DHEA supplements, reducing stress, and lowering caffeine intake).

- Take a green drink that includes maca, Chlorella, and Spirulina.
- Take vitamin C supplements.
- Include one or more herbal supplements in your diet (Echinacea, goldenseal, olive leaf extract, Astragalus , Panax ginseng, or mistletoe extract).
- Get plenty of active enzymes from fermented foods and many tropical fruits.
- Increase your sense of well-being by adding plenty of sleep, laughter, and love.

The best thing you can do to maintain a healthy immune system is to eat well. That means getting a healthy balance of proteins, carbohydrates, fats, fiber, and nutrients. Although no single dietary formula works for everyone, a few nutritional principles are generally accepted for good health. No matter who you are, your diet should be:

- Low in saturated fats
- Low in cholesterol
- Low in starch and carbohydrates *
- Low in salt and sugar
- Low in processed foods and artificial ingredients (dyes, preservatives, and chemical additives)
- High in plant nutrients, such as those from fruits and vegetables
- High in antioxidants
- High in fiber

Other Considerations

An excellent way to get plenty of nutrients from food is to include one or more super foods in your diet. These are foods that are super high in nutrients and offer these nutrients in well-balanced ratios. Some of these include bee pollen, Spirulina, olive leaf extract, maca, and kale. Also, refined natural proteins, including thymic protein-A are useful in rebuilding your immunity. It's important to remember that cooked foods do not contain active enzymes. Heating foods destroys both microorganisms and enzymes.

From Japan, we have maitake mushroom extract. This amazing mushroom has been shown to have immune-enhancing and cancer-fighting properties in the form of beta-glucans, a sugar/protein complex that stimulates the white blood cells into action. It is especially useful for chemotherapy patients. Baker's yeast is another potent source of beta glucans.

Infection (Bacterial)

See also Infection (Viral), Urinary Infections

Bacteria are single-celled microorganisms that reproduce by dividing. Commonly treated by antibiotics (which don't work against viral infections, by the way), they constantly mutate into new forms that are not responsive to antibiotics, called MRSD. It is more important now than ever to keep our bodies in infection-fighting condition. Bacteria enter a body to break down cells when they are dying, taking advantage of a weak and dying system. Make your body more "alive," more alkaline, and strengthen its immune system as a general strategy to fight against infection.

Many people confuse bacteria with viruses. Bacteria are living organisms that reproduce in your body. Viruses are not living organisms and they do their damage by entering the cells of the body and changing them. They can even change DNA. We have many different kinds of bacteria in our body, including some that are good for us because they balance out other forms of bacteria by cleaning or otherwise helping the body's processes.

What Causes Bacterial Infection?

The simple answer to this question is that a weak immune system, combined with exposure to bacteria, creates an environment for infection to take hold. It's possible to be exposed to bacteria without becoming infected, depending on your body's immune response and the type of bacteria. But don't tempt fate; be sure to keep your hands and environment clean and free of germs. Here are some specific problems that encourage bacteria growth:

- A diet high in sugars lowers the immune system and allows the proliferation of infection.
- An overly acid condition of the body is a home for bacteria.
- An alkali stomach, however, with too few digestive enzymes allows the bacteria to take over. Eating cooked foods uses up your own digestive enzymes. You have only so many.
- The immune system is at a disadvantage if you are deficient in nutrients, have high stress, or don't sleep regularly, making you more prone to catching infections.

- Women are vulnerable to vaginal and urinary bacterial infections, because of diet and exposure to germs from sexual contact, bathing, and even soiled clothing.
- Improper hygiene—washing your hands reduces the rate of bacterial and viral infections by up to 50%, and gastrointestinal infections by 80%.

Treatments for Bacterial Infection

Bacterial infection is often localized. If it appears on the skin, it can easily be treated topically with antibacterial and antifungal extracts, including:

- Oregano oil
- Garlic oil
- Tea tree oil

Internal infections, such as yeast bacteria, can be treated with the following supplements:

- Probiotic cultures
- Oregano oil
- Garlic oil
- Echinacea
- Pau d'arco tea
- Devil's claw

Other Considerations

Use large amounts of vitamin C and zinc, though be careful with zinc if you have symptoms of adrenal exhaustion. Grapefruit seed extract can be applied or ingested. The liquid form tastes very bitter, which is helpful for liver health, but for those who can't stomach it, it is also available in pills.

Bovine colostrum may be effective against infections that are otherwise difficult for the immune system to defeat. Available in supplement form, colostrum is rich in IgG-type immunoglobulins, which are effective against Cryptosporidium (a genus of protozoa that can cause life-threatening diarrhea in AIDS patients), some strains of E. coli, Shigella flexneri, Clostridium difficile, and rotavirus, which is the most common cause of severe diarrhea in young children.

Colloidal silver can effectively fight infections deemed undefeatable, and it is amazingly effective against about 650 infectious agents, including E. coli and Candida (which causes yeast infections). It can even quickly clear up potentially deadly AIDS-related pneumonia caused by streptococcal, staphylococcal, klebsiella, and fungal infections. Use the non-chemical type, in glass containers, with golden-colored silver, and make sure you purchase from a reputable source. It should not be used for extended periods.

Avoid sugar in any form, as it immediately shuts down the immune system and attracts bacteria.

Natural Antibiotics

Overuse of antibiotics has produced many drug-resistant bacterial strains of "super bugs," and they also kill the beneficial bacteria in the gut, leading to digestive problems and systemic yeast overgrowth. The only time to take a commercial antibiotic is when you absolutely must, and if you do, take anti-fungal supplements such as caprylic acid. Use goldenseal as a natural antibiotic, but treat it in the same way, staying on a schedule and continuing until it is gone. Then, give it a break. Echinacea should also only be used sporadically, as it stresses the immune system if used over a long time period.

Infection (Viral)

See also Colds, Infection (Bacterial)

Some say that there are two types of organisms on this planet—productive, self-sufficient organisms, and the parasites that live off them. Viruses are like the parasites. They live off of other organisms, taking advantage their weaknesses. The weaker and more vulnerable an organism, the more prone it is to picking up viruses as long-term passengers. In many ways, a weak immune system is an invitation to viral infection, since viruses cannot thrive in a healthy system.

In the animal kingdom, those free of parasites are the ones with the brightest colors, the longest feathers, the shiniest fur, and all of the features that attract their mates. The bottom line is that good health can be defined as the absence of viruses.

What Are Viruses?

Unlike bacteria, viruses are not living organisms. They are particles or molecules that reproduce inside the cells of other (host) organisms, causing damage to the host. They are difficult to remove once they take hold, so the best treatment against viruses is preventative treatment.

Antiviral Treatments

Viruses live and thrive in unhealthy systems, so the most effective way to remain virus-free is to keep your system strong and healthy. This means fortifying your immune system and taking antiviral supplements. Besides adding these positive substances, your antiviral treatment should include the removal of negative substances, such as tobacco smoke, excess alcohol, food toxins and additives, environmental toxins, stress. Here is a summary of the essentials:

- Take olive leaf extract and nutrient-rich, health-forming foods to support your immune system.
- Take Echinacea, St. John's wort, and skullcap herbs for antiviral protection.
- Get exercise and sunlight every day, and take antioxidant supplements.
- Stop smoking and excessive drinking, and remove processed foods and excess sugar from your diet.

Other Considerations

Research indicates that the mineral zinc is also an effective antiviral agent. For example, a double-blind study published in 2000 demonstrated that zinc significantly reduces the length of overall common cold symptoms by 50%, including cough by 50% and nasal discharge by 30%. Other antiviral supplements include:

- N-acetylcysteine (NAC)
- Lysine
- Colloidal silver (be sure to find a reputable source, don't make your own)
- Vitamin C and Citricidal grapefruit seed extract

High doses of enzymes will also make your body a hostile environment for viruses, while assisting digestion and cleaning out pockets of waste in your lower bowel, a place where viruses breed. These natural viral reagents will cause the weaker viruses to die and the stronger, more virulent ones to retreat into a small, safe place they can burrow in, somewhere in your body, depending on the type of virus. They'll only awaken if you feed them something that wakes them from their dormant state (e.g., poor diet, smoking, drinking, drugging, a negative mind-set, stress, and poor sleep patterns).

In some studies, chronic hepatitis B and hepatitis C have responded to selenium, milk thistle, and alpha-lipoic acid (see Hepatitis).

Inflammation

Anti-Inflammatories

See Arthritis, Joint Pain

Inflammation is implicated in many illnesses. Where the inflammation occurs is what gives an illness a particular label, from Alzheimer's, arthritis, Lou Gehrig's disease (ALS), multiple sclerosis, and Parkinson's disease to heart and arterial disease.

Causes of Inflammation

A wound can become inflamed without adequate hygiene, so it's best to keep them clean, with a goldenseal paste and a bandage. Any part of the body can become inflamed. Inflammation is now understood as an autoimmune reaction doing its work, bringing circulation and protection to an injury in the form of swelling and heat. The white blood cells travel to the site to fight the infection.

For some, inflammation becomes a chronic state and many experts believe this is caused by digestive problems. Bloating may indicate that your intestines are inflamed as the immune system fights parasites, viruses, and bacteria, as well as foods you are allergic to. Sugar, simple carbs, trans fatty acids, polyunsaturated oils, wheat, and dairy cause inflammation in the intestines, which cause reflex pain throughout the body. Insulin levels cause inflammation when they rise too high. Inflammation is regulated by hormones, which are made from omega-3 fatty acids found in such foods as wild salmon, tuna, walnuts, and almonds. Eating the wrong balance of oils, carbohydrates, and proteins overwhelms the body's response, and it has a hard time healing other inflammation. Prescription drugs may also cause inflammation.

Treatments for Inflammation

The best thing you can take to reduce inflammation is large, consistent doses of enzymes. Enzymes sustain life. Enzymes are proteins. They are biocatalysts, which means they either begin a chemical reaction or cause a chemical reaction in the body to speed up. Enzymes cause the chemical reactions responsible for breathing, digestion, growth, nerve health, reproduction, and all other body functions. They are critical in warding off all forms of disease and support injury repair and food metabolism. As you age, your enzyme levels decrease. Stress, injuries, and poor diet cause even more enzymes depletion.

Physicians in Europe and Asia have long prescribed enzyme supplementation to restore a multitude of bodily functions and promote natural healing in their patients. Most arthritis is caused by the loss of a certain enzyme in the body. Taking enzymes on an empty stomach breaks down the products of inflammation, reducing pain. As such, they are a perfect substitute for aspirin and ibuprofen, which are known to have ill effects on the liver, kidneys, and stomach. Dehydroepiandrosterone (DHEA) can help remove the waste in the circulatory system caused by the Standard American Diet (SAD) high in the wrong kind of fats, carbs, and proteins. Curcumin, the yellow pigment in the turmeric herb, promotes healthy circulation and lowers inflammation. More ideas include:

- Avoid sugar and simple starches, as they can make inflammation worse.
- Boost your antioxidant levels to keep your joints healthy. Vitamins A, C, and E prevent inflammation and protect your joints from free radical damage.
- Hydrate. When you do not drink enough water, inflammation worsens. Avoid caffeine and alcohol, as they are harsh diuretics.
- Food sensitivities are common, and some have a delayed reaction that confuses the issue. Food sensitivities increase inflammation. The most common culprits are milk and dairy, wheat, corn, eggs, beef, yeast, and soy.
- Devil's Claw, white willow bark (natural aspirin, containing the same active ingredient), ginger, and tumeric are all good inflammation-reducing herbs.
- Quercetin, an anti-inflammatory, can be taken in supplement form, and it is also found in garlic, red grapes, and onions.
- Many berries are rich in polyphenols, which help fight inflammation.

Other Considerations

You don't need dangerous anti-inflammatory pharmaceuticals. Use the alga Chlorella and foods rich in omega-3 fatty acids. If you don't like the taste of fish, you can also fulfill your omega-3 needs with fish oil supplements. However, even if you are a vegetarian, you can find plenty of omega-3 essential fatty acid sources for your diet, such as walnuts, flaxseed oil, and pumpkin seeds

Homeopathic physicians swear by Arnica for minor inflammatory wounds. This can be used internally or topically.

Insomnia

Sleep Disorders

See also Restless Leg Syndrome

Insomnia is a type of sleep disorder with a variety of causes. Our bodies need an average of 8 hours of sleep a night; without it, our minds and bodies do not function at full capacity. Also, lack of sleep affects our muscle tone, immunity, and mood. If it progresses, it can lead to adrenal depletion and a viscous cycle of sleeplessness and hormone imbalances.

Biochemical Causes of Insomnia

- Medicines
- Hormonal imbalances, periodic or chronic
- Deficiencies in magnesium, calcium, and other nutrients
- Many believe that body parasites can keep a person awake and that they are especially restless during the full moon. Sleeplessness during the full or new moon cycles can also be caused by your body rhythms.
- Chronic Fatigue Syndrome (CFS) and fibromyalgia make it difficult to get restful sleep.
- A disrupted sleep schedule can throw off sleep, but can usually be restored when the schedule returns to normal.
- Inadequate exercise can cause sleeplessness.
- Eating too close to bedtime. Also, an over-acidic body composition can make you lose sleep.

Neuro-Emotional Causes of Insomnia

- Emotionally caused stress and anxiety
- Excessive mental activity, too much going on in your head. Ayurvedic medicine associates this with a particular body type called the vata dosha.
- TMJ and dental stress from improper bite are common causes of insomnia.

- Post traumatic stress disorder after an overwhelming event or series of events can cause insomnia.
- Depression and grief

Treatments for Insomnia

- Use melatonin (35 mg) supplements in the late afternoon to help you sleep at night. You can take one every night over extended periods.
- Drink a strong decoction (tea) of valerian root, skullcap, kava kava herb, and chamomile.
- Most insomnia is caused by caffeine, including caffeine in soft drinks, coffee, dark chocolate, and many over-the-counter drugs.
- Some experts believe that aspartame causes insomnia, so that diet cola you're drinking may pose a double risk for insomnia (and myriad other health problems).
- Make non-caffeinated teas your new drink of choice. If you need an afternoon pick-me-up drink while at work, drink a cup of ginseng tea rather than coffee. In the evening, drink relaxing teas such as chamomile, valerian, hops, wild lettuce (contains opiates), and catnip.
- Taking power naps; 15 to 30 minutes in the midday is very helpful if your schedule allows. This is particularly helpful for individuals with porphyria.
- Try hypnosis to help you enter a state of sleepiness at a certain time of the evening.
- Acupressure, acupuncture, and reflexology, and especially Jin Shin Do, can release habit patterns, imbalances, and set your body back in alignment. You can try some acupressure on yourself before you go to sleep: press the inside of the wrist crease with your palm up, at the base of the hand and in line with the little finger.
- Instead of letting your mind think for too long, start focusing on trying to have a dream.
- Go to a chiropractor or deep tissue body worker to help you release deep-seated tension stored in your body. If you suffer from TMJ or teeth grinding, you might seek out a dentist or practitioner who can help realign your jaw and relax your TJM stress.
- Do a long herbal parasite cleanse that includes black walnut hulls and wormwood, and cloves to kill the eggs. Put your pets on herbal parasite maintenance as well. You can take powder from capsules and

spread it over their food in the proportionate amount to human weight.

- Consider natural anti-depressants such as St. John's wort, kava kava, 5-HTP or SAMe.

Jet Lag

Dysrhythmia

You may land at your faraway destination in a startlingly different mood than when you left home, feeling ill or out of sorts, tired, ready to go to bed, but unable to sleep. You may experience uncharacteristic irritability and mental processes, brain fog, and difficulty with orientation. You may feel the varied sensations of dehydration such as muscle aches, confusion, and heavy headedness. Your appetite may be poor, you may even feel nauseous, and you may have headaches, often with sinus involvement. The sensations may be hard to pin down and explain, even if people are telling you to snap out of it and get with the program. There is actually a physical reason for your discomfort and you can minimize or eliminate it with proper precautions.

What Causes Jet Lag?

The popular perception is that jet lag is only lack of proper sleep, but it's not that simple.

When you jump time zones, it disrupts more than 100 essential body functions, including hormone, heart rate, and temperature regulation. For example, if you fly west across six time zones, it can take up to six days for your reaction time to return to normal, according to Dr. Robert M. Giller, author of Natural Prescriptions. Traveling east makes jet lag even worse, although experts don't understand why. Each person handles the disruption differently, but passing through many time zones disrupts the internal clock we all have that tells us when to sleep and eat. The unfamiliar light/dark cycle disrupts the circadian rhythms, especially under certain conditions that you often cannot control. Being in a plane is dehydrating, especially if you drink alcohol and are stressed.

Treatments

Jet lag prevention should start before your trip. Drink several glasses of water. else is processed like water, so although you may gain some additional Nothing benefit from drinking juices or decaffeinated tea, pure water is most advantageous by far, and is best drunk when you are not eating a meal.

- Go to bed at a regular time for a few days before your trip. Then, two days before you leave, go to bed 15 to 30 minutes before your actual bedtime to give your body the extra rest it needs.
- About five to ten minutes before you board the plane, take one ginger tablet and a 6C dose of homeopathic Cocculus.
- Drink until you urinate on the flight, then drink a glass of pure water every 30 minutes, preferably water without ice (cold drinks pull blood from your extremities so as to warm the icy drink in your stomach; Traditional Chinese Medicine practitioners believe that icy drinks cause you to age faster).
- Avoid drinking alcohol, carbonated beverages, or coffee before or during long flights, as these will only make jet lag worse.
- For a natural remedy, the best cure for jet lag is to take a maximum of 1 mg of melatonin as a sublingual tablet before bedtime. Melatonin naturally controls your body's circadian rhythm. When you awaken, you'll be in your new time zone.
- Valerian root and ginseng can also help you acclimate quickly to your new environment.

Kidney Stones

Gravel / Renal Calculi

The pain caused by passing a kidney stone is infamous. But worse things can happen. Kidney stones are crystallized minerals formed from deposits in urine and can be as small as a grain of salt. The larger ones, however, can become lodged in the urinary tract, backing up the flow of urine in the system and causing a great deal of pain. There may also be nausea, bloody urine, and fever. There is almost always some degree of lower back pain and kidney pain.

What Causes Kidney Stones?

Kidney stones are usually caused by cholesterol binding with inorganic calcium (from dairy products, drinking water, and other inorganic sources). If your tap water is high in calcium deposits, drinking it can increase the risk of your body's forming these painful stones. Other causes include:

- Eating foods and drinks containing oxalic acid, such as spinach, rhubarb, beets, nuts, tea, wheat bran, strawberries, rhubarb, chocolate, and coffee. The oxalic acid reduces calcium absorption.
- Eating too much sugar or salt
- Dehydration
- Consuming too much phosphoric acid, found primarily in soft drinks
- Eating too many acid forming foods, such as an overabundance of proteins
- Gout

Treatments for Kidney Stones

You probably throw away one of the best natural remedies for kidney stones and kidney problems in general each time you eat corn on the cob. Numerous natural health experts recommend corn silk, the long, silky strings linked to the ripe kernels of corn, for kidney problems such as kidney stones. You can make this into a tea by boiling it for a few minutes. Add to a green tea base, if desired. Corn silk helps relieve kidney stones both by acting as a natural diuretic and by soothing the urinary tract, which can become irritated by the stones. It and other emollient diuretics, such as marshmallow root and couch grass, protect the kidneys' sensitive nephrons (structural and functional units of the kidney) from inflammation and irritation. Besides corn silk tea, you can make kidney-friendly teas from Watermelon seed, celery seed, and parsley leaves and seeds. Here's more:

- Taking 1,500 mg of vitamin C and 50 mg of vitamin B6 daily can help break up these stones. Magnesium supplements may also help.
- Liver Tea (see Hepatitis) and Cordyceps mushroom extract will complete the break-down of the stones and help transport the residue out of your body. In Brazil, a common weed, called quebra pedra (stone breaker) is used to dissolve kidney stones, as is cerveja do campo (beer of the field).
- Gravel root, uva ursi, horsetail, and dandelion root are all kidney tonics, along with water, water, water. You cannot drink too much water.
- Eat black cherries and drink a glass of organic apple juice in the morning, and one at night. Take vitamin C supplements and eat plenty of citrus fruit.
- Avoid alcohol, animal products, and black pepper. Avoid chocolate, coffee, and other foods containing

oxalic acid. Many people report that drinking apple cider vinegar helps with kidney stones.

Other Considerations

Along with corn silk, some experts believe that the kombucha mushroom can help dissolve kidney stones. When kombucha is mixed with a sweet tea, it forms a sweet, fermented brew.

If you have gout or a family history of gout, you likely will be prone to develop uric acid stones (a type of kidney stone). Black cherry juice and adequate hydration are important natural treatments. If you have gout, avoid foods high in purines, such as sardines and dried beans.

Gout

If you have gout or a family history of gout, you likely will be prone to develop uric acid stones (a type of kidney stone), gallstone, or gouty formation. Black cherry juice and adequate hydration are important natural treatments. If you have gout, avoid foods high in purines, such as sardines and dried beans.

Laryngitis

Hoarse Voice

See also Candida, Colds, Infection (Bacteria), Infection (Viral),

Some people get laryngitis every couple of years, while others almost never get it. It's characterized by a hoarseness in the voice or, in serious cases, complete lack of ability to speak. It is often associated with colds, flu, bronchitis, pneumonia, and other conditions.

What Causes Laryngitis?

Usually caused by bacteria or viral infection, laryngitis can be triggered by exposure to viruses and bacteria, overuse of the voice (screaming, regular singing, or speaking, etc.), allergies, or other illnesses.

Avoiding Laryngitis

The best medicine for laryngitis is prevention. If you are susceptible to this condition, then arm yourself with an antibacterial throat spray and soothing lozenges. Good antibacterial agents to use in a natural and homemade spray include St. John's wort, liquid Echinacea, propolis, and grapefruit seed extract.

Treating Laryngitis

If you have picked up a case of laryngitis, use the antibacterial formula above, and add some other treatments to help sooth your throat, such as peppermint, honey, ginger, chamomile, sage, bayberry, and licorice. The best idea is to use these ingredients in different combinations for tea. You can also try making a juice with one or more of these ingredients: apple, carrot, pineapple, celery, and beet. Some excellent combinations are peppermint with pineapple and carrot with celery.

Liver & Gallbladder Health

Fatty Liver / Gallstones / Liver Cleanse

See also Candida Albicans, Colon & Intestinal Health, Hepatitis, Obesity

The liver is one of the body's most important organs. It is responsible for cleaning the blood of impurities, aiding in digestion, and is essential in the process of waste elimination. Toxins build up in the liver and gallbladder and are eliminated into the colon. That is, if everything is functioning normally. You can imagine that a damaged liver can result in an excess accumulation of toxins and waste in your blood, intestines, and your entire system.

Gallstones are the result of years of blockages and calcification of bile that clog the liver and gallbladder, and even the bile ducts through which they release their wastes. Just about every adult has gallstones. They range in size from smaller than a pea to as big as a golf ball. They vary in number from a few to several thousand. Gallbladder operations are one of the most common surgical procedures in the United States.

What does that tell us? If nothing else, it tells us that liver and gallbladder health is essential to our overall health and well-being. In fact, liver detoxification can help our digestion, increase our ability to remove harmful toxins (which cause all sorts of maladies from premature aging to chronic fatigue), and give us more energy and vitality.

Symptoms of Poor Liver Health

Symptoms of poor liver health include chronic fatigue, nausea, loss of appetite, yellowing of the skin and eyes (jaundice), fever, and dark-colored urine. Other symptoms include rapid weight gain (poor bile production means poor fat elimination), obesity, and increased allergies. In a reaction to an overload of toxins and lack of nutritional support, the liver often expands and becomes "fat." Fatty liver is often associated with obesity, starvation, and alcohol abuse. If the liver continues to decline, diseases such as Crohn's disease, irritable bowel syndrome (IBS), colitis, and even cancer may result.

What Causes Poor Liver Health

The most common enemy of the liver is excess alcohol consumption. The liver can only keep up with a certain amount of toxins entering the body, and alcohol has a tendency to go straight to the blood—therefore heavily taxing the liver in its effort to clean the blood. If the liver is overloaded with toxins from alcohol, then it can't perform its duties very well in removing heavy metals from our blood.

Poor diet is also a cause of poor liver health. Too much fat in our diet interferes with the proper bile-related functions of the liver and gallbladder. This causes the system to ineffectively eliminate the fats, which puts more pressure on the liver, and so on. The cycle continues until obesity and other problems occur.

Not only the type of food, but the quality of the foods you eat affects the liver. Foods that are laced with toxins from preservatives or artificial additives will force the liver to work harder. Toxicity from extended use of drugs (pharmaceutical or otherwise) takes a heavy toll on the liver.

Treatments to Support the Liver

While eating good foods and avoiding bad ones is certainly important in liver health, most people want more specific detail about how to clean their liver and get it back to normal working order.

- To best support the liver, your diet should be high in antioxidants. Eat plenty of deep-colored berries, fruits, and vegetables. Foods with carotenoids, such as carrots, papaya, and peaches, are especially good for the liver, as are apples and apple juice.

- The antioxidant selenium is recommended for liver support. Sources include Brazil nuts, kelp, garlic, onions, and brewer's yeast.
- Avoid saturated fats and be sure to get plenty of essential fatty acids from olive oil, flaxseed oil, and sesame oil. Other great sources include fish oils, such as cod liver oil.
- Studies show that B vitamins strengthen the liver, especially riboflavin and niacin.
- Take milk thistle extract, olive leaf extract, and dandelion root. Another excellent herb for blood cleansing is burdock root. Artichokes also help support the liver.
- Eat plenty of alfalfa, known for its positive effects on blood cholesterol levels and bile functions of the liver.
- Stop excessive drinking, smoking and drug use (including pharmaceutical drugs).

Other Considerations

Lipoic acid, known as LA or alpha-lipoic acid (ALA), is shown to have chelating qualities, blood and liver purification characteristics, and is high in antioxidants. It also can help stimulate other antioxidants in the system. It enhances insulin sensitivity and glucose response to insulin, and may be an aid to diabetes mellitus patients. You can get LA supplements without prescription and should take them on an empty stomach. Food sources of LA include spinach, broccoli, tomatoes and Brussels sprouts.

The synthetic chemical SAM-e is said to have curative effects on the liver, including detoxification, which may help explain its anti-depressant effects (clean your liver, clean your mood). SAM-e is a synthetic form of a chemical produced naturally in our bodies (mostly in our intestines) and therefore not a natural cure. However, it is presently sold as a dietary supplement. Although promising, much more information is needed on this substance.

Finally, the chemical compound EDTA is a known chelating agent, binding to heavy metal ions in the blood and liver and removing them through the urine and feces. It binds to metals like lead, mercury, aluminum, silver, calcium, manganese, copper, iron, and zirconium. This is a powerful and effective chelating agent, known and used for more than 50 years, that your doctor will never tell you about!

Macular Degeneration

See also Antioxidants, Cataracts

One of the most common eye and sight degenerative problems, macular degeneration is associated with age, particularly with those over 55. In macular degeneration, the retina is slowly destroyed, leading to first a lack of focus and eventually blindness. There are two types of macular degeneration:

- Dry degeneration, the most common type, shows up with a buildup of debris beneath the retina.
- Wet degeneration is the result of overgrowth of the blood vessels beneath the retina, causing leakage that causes scar tissue.

In either case, vision becomes blurry, especially when viewing objects close at hand, and symptoms often includes the appearance of dark spots in the field of vision. It is a degenerative disease that is avoidable or, at the very least, deter-able.

What Causes Macular Degeneration?

Poor vision does not have to occur with age, as the causes are definable and identifiable. For the most part, vision loss is caused by free radicals combined with poor circulation that damage and break down the eyes. Here are some specific things that can lead to macular degeneration:

- Nutritional deficiency
- Too much ultraviolet light
- Tobacco
- Digestive problems
- Pollution and environmental toxins
- Heavy metal poisoning from food sources
- High blood pressure
- Pharmaceutical drugs

Treatments for Macular Degeneration

First and foremost, increase dietary antioxidants to help strengthen your cells and reduce damage from free radicals, which are created by unhealthy foods and environmental toxins, smoking, drinking, and overeating. Lutein can help reverse the disease. Take 6 mg a day, along with the antioxidant astaxanthin, which can move across the blood-brain barrier to restore cell strength. Chelation therapy has also been shown to help macular degeneration. Also, carotenoid antioxidants are helpful to the eyes and can be found in yellow and orange fruits and vegetables, carrots, blueberries, and lightly cooked eggs. Here are some more treatments:

- Zeaxanthin can be taken in supplement form, or you can get it in corn, romaine lettuce, and tangerines.
- Bilberry improves capillary circulation throughout the eye.
- Take vitamins A, C with bioflavonoids, E, and B2, plus the minerals zinc, selenium, and chromium.
- Use some simple eye exercises, including rolling your eyes, and moving your focus from near to far.
- Drink lots of water.
- Avoid sugars and foods that turn to sugar, such as simple carbohydrates and alcohol.
- Avoid animal products.

Other Considerations

Micro-Current Therapy sends the micro-currents along the meridians to improve circulation in the eyes.

Menopause

Change of Life / Climacteric

See also Hormone Imbalance, Osteoporosis

Menopause is the cessation of menstruation with age (though it can also occur suddenly from a hysterectomy). It occurs when the ovaries stop producing estrogen, causing the reproductive system to gradually shut down. Many women, especially in countries with more natural lifestyles, make it through menopause almost effortlessly, so it is a myth that this time of life must be brutal. In Europe and the United States, however, menopause can be seriously traumatic for women and the men in their lives. There's good reason for this trauma: When a woman hits menopause, her body doesn't slowly reduce the amount of hormones it produces; it alternately stops and restarts producing them. Eventually, the estrogen production level stabilizes itself, but that's after many highs and crashes. Many wonderful natural cures can ease menopause, however.

In addition to irritability and increased osteoporosis risk, menopausal women also experience symptoms such as hot flashes, night sweats, loss of libido, vaginal dryness, weight gain, water retention, depression, palpitations, poor concentration, irritability, the urgent need to urinate, and increased risk of yeast infections, fibrocystic breast disease, breast cancer, and endometrial cancer. A woman can tell menopause is approaching when she has increasingly short, light, and erratic menstrual periods. She may experience sleep disturbances, itching, osteoporosis, muscle pain, atrophy of the breasts, toughening of the skin, and memory loss. It is important for women not to expect this to occur and go into a depression with age, but to take precautions so it does not occur.

The average onset of menopause is around age 50. Some women begin menopause younger if they have suffered from cancer, gone through chemotherapy, or had a hysterectomy. Menopause is considered premature if it occurs before 40. This is rare, occurring in only 1% of women. Autoimmune disorders, thyroid disease, and diabetes mellitus can bring this on.

Treatments for Menopause

When soy meets girl, her life gets better in all ways. Soy is great for the heart and provides nutrients for the building blocks of all hormones. Soy helps with hot flashes and night sweats. Soy is also anticancer, especially estrogen-based cancers such as cancer of the breast, ovarian, and uterine. Soy also helps build strong bones. In general, soy products like tofu and soy protein are better than using soybean oil and soy sauce. As with most foods, the closer it is to its natural state, the better.

Papaya, like soy and soy products such as tempeh, contains phytoestrogens, which are phytochemicals that bind to the body's estrogen receptors, functioning like a surrogate hormone. Some natural medicine practitioners recommend eating papaya once a day.

While eating phytoestrogen-rich foods such as papaya and soy are helpful menopause remedies, estrogen replacement therapy is ineffective because it rests on a theory that most experts now believe is wrong. Physicians used to believe that menopause occurs when a woman's body runs out of estrogen, but this is not the case. As noted, a woman's body continues to make estrogen intermittently, even after menstruation has ceased. Hormone replacement therapy would work if the symptoms of menopause were actually caused by an estrogen deficiency, but they are not. In fact, many women have too much estrogen in relation to their levels of progesterone.

Other Treatments for Menopause

- Supplementing with dehydroepiandrosterone (DHEA), the mother hormone, and pregnenolone, the grandmother hormone, has helped endless women with menopause. Pregnenolone is made from good cholesterol and, in your body, is converted into all your steroid hormones, including DHEA, estrogen, progesterone, and testosterone.
- Many women claim that drinking a glass of cold water at the first hint of a hot flash can keep the flash from hitting full-on.
- For an extra boost to your menopause remedy regimen, try taking black cohosh, alfalfa, sarsaparilla, licorice root, maca root, or blessed thistle. These are all believed to provide some relief from menopause symptoms.
- When it comes to osteoporosis and aches and pains related to menopause, they can be solved with the introduction of bio-available silica. Organic calcium (from silica) builds bones. Inorganic calcium (from cow's milk) leaches the organic calcium from your bones and blood as it links up with the organic calcium in your bones in its futile attempt to be absorbed into your body.
- Vitamin D is key to both the prevention of osteoporosis and the relief of menopausal symptoms. Sunshine is the best source of this nutrient, which is quickly converted into a hormone by the body. One teaspoon of cod liver oil contains 400 IU of vitamin D. The primary avenue for intake of vitamin D is exposure to sunlight.

Other Considerations

A great deal of research recently indicated that soy in any form can be harmful. Much of this is focused on soy's interference with the proper functioning of the thyroid gland, which, in turn, causes hormone imbalances. While scientists continue to deliberate on this subject, validating and invalidating the findings of other scientists, most holistic health practitioners who subscribe to the idea of balance as a foundation of good health believe that soy products are only bad when eaten in excess or when concentrated—such as the case with soybean oil. Bioidentical hormone creams containing natural estrogens, progesterone and testosterone are becoming increasingly popular as safer ways to balance menopausal hormones.

Sexual Hormones

Testosterone keeps men and women younger. When you start to get gray hair, you know your testosterone levels are dropping. If you're a man older than age 35, try 50 mg of DHEA; if you're a woman older than 35, try 25 mg of DHEA. A number of studies link age-related declining DHEA levels to the onset of chronic disorders such as high cholesterol, Type 2 diabetes, obesity, arthritis, heart disease, and autoimmune diseases. Add pregnenolone, pantothenic acid, and vitamin C.

- Many women are estrogen dominant at menopause and the trend of taking more estrogen has luckily stopped. There is already too much estrogens in foods, such as soy, pesticides, and milk. This leads to not only estrogen dominance but also thyroid hormone imbalances.
- Menopausal women should avoid processed foods, which contain artificial hormones, and Xenoestrogens in the pesticides, which are also carcinogenic. Livestock are often injected with estrogen and antibiotics. Men can find themselves becoming feminized, and young girls can begin their menstrual cycles too early because of the hormones in milk and meat.

Menstrual Cramps

Dysmenorrhea

See also Muscle Cramps, PMS

Thirty to fifty percent of women in the United States suffer from menstrual cramps, and at least 10% have such severe menstrual symptoms that they inhibit them from participating in their normal activities. These symptoms include not only abdominal pains, but also backache, nausea, and pain in the inner thighs.

What Causes Menstrual Cramps?

For a long time, experts were unsure. Now, experts know that a decline in progesterone levels causes the endometrium to produce more hormone-like fatty acids called prostaglandins. These prostaglandins then decrease blood circulation to the uterine muscles and blood vessels, so these muscles, in turn, receive less oxygen, leading to a buildup of metabolic waste products such as carbon dioxide and lactic acid. This buildup increases pain and discomfort in the contracting uterine muscles.

However, many women have no cramping at all, due to correct balance of nutrition. Coffee, cola, chocolate, alcohol, diuretics, and a low mineral diet, as well as a lack of exercise all contribute to cramping. People with gluten sensitivity should avoid wheat, oats, spelt, and other foods containing gluten, as it will make cramps worse. Red meats and butter aggravate cramping because of the saturated fat. Many women who have become vegans or vegetarians have found their cramps disappear. Menstrual cramps are often associated with hormonal imbalances, a high fat diet, lack of calcium and magnesium, and stress. The pain is produced by changes in hormone levels that occur during menstruation and cause contractions in the uterus.

IUDs have been associated with cramping, as has a history of sexual abuse.

Treatments for Menstrual Cramps

Some supplements help prevent and relieve cramps naturally.

- Pulsatilla helps prevent and relieve menstrual cramps by correcting the hormone imbalance that causes them. Evening primrose and black currant oils help prevent both premenstrual syndrome (PMS) and menstrual cramps before they start, due to their content of gamma-linolenic acid (GLA), an omega-6 fatty acid. Taking two calcium capsules every four hours may also relieve cramps (a drop in calcium before and during a woman's period can result in irritability and fatigue) as can vitamin B6.
- Magnesium 500 mg taken three times a day is helpful, as is Vitamin E at 400 IU per day.
- Dong Quai is an Asian herb that is considered a tonic for women, curing all sorts of female suffering. It contains vitamins E, A, and B12 and is a powerful anti-spasmodic and anti-clotting agent. It also helps to stimulate the nervous system and regulate blood sugar.
- Black Cohosh herb is great for night sweats.
- Try cotton leaf tea or extract (cleans menstrual blood and encourages menstruation). This has been used as a natural abortive in South America for centuries, so be careful to take this only for menstruation. Peppermint, ginger, and raspberry leaf teas can also help. Many women alternate these with ginger root, passion flower, and chamomile teas.

Other suggestions:

- Drinking water and laxative herbs (see Laxatives) helps move the bowels, as premenstrual constipation is often a major part of the discomfort. See Constipation and Laxatives.
- Many find their cramps stop when they switch from using tampons to using pads.
- Avoid sugar.
- Hydration is important in preventing cramps, so drink plenty of pure water.
- If you have some time to relax, keep a hot water bottle on your lower abdomen and drink a cup of chamomile tea every 15 minutes. This will soothe away pains. A hot bath with Epsom salts may also help.

Mitral Valve Prolapse

Floppy Valve Syndrome / MVP

See also Heart Disease

The mitral valve is a piece of tissue that keeps blood that is leaving the heart from coming back into the heart. It's a one-way valve that keeps blood moving away from the heart. In about 10% of the population (most often occurring in very slender people), the valve becomes deformed and cannot close correctly, causing blood to leak back into the heart. This condition is usually benign, and the heart can generally continue pumping blood normally. However, if extreme, MVP can cause reduced efficiency of the heart, which results in swelling (edema) of the legs, difficulty breathing, heart murmur, fibrillation, and rhythmic abnormalities. It may occasionally become bad enough to require surgery, or lead to congestive heart failure, and even death. Physicians often will tell you there is nothing to be done for MVP, but alternative medicine has found ways to improve the situation.

What Causes MVP?

MVP can be caused by problems with collagen, or connective tissue, or by rheumatic heart disease, which occurs at times because of severe strep throat. The condition is most common in women between the ages of 14 and 30. MVP sometimes appears in several members of the same family, which previously had led to the belief that it is inherited. But many experts now believe that MVP is nutritionally caused. This is good news, as it means that nutritional support can help fix the condition.

Treatments for MVP

If you have been diagnosed with MVP, the first step you need to take is to stay away from caffeine. This popular stimulant can exacerbate arrhythmia in people with MVP.

Once you remove caffeine from your diet, take magnesium and Co-Q10 supplements. Research indicates that anywhere from 62 to 85% of MVP patients suffer from magnesium deficiency, suggesting a link between the disorder and the deficiency. One University of Alabama School of Medicine research study of 92 MVP patients discovered that 62% were deficient in magnesium and that this 62% also experienced tell-tale symptoms of the deficiency: muscle cramps, migraines, and low blood pressure when rising from a sitting or prone position to standing. Similarly, one research study found that 50% to 75% of MVP patients are deficient in Co-Q10. Try adding both magnesium and Co-Q10 to your diet for maximum MVP relief.

Mononucleosis

Glandular Fever / Kissing Disease / Mono / Pfeiffer's Disease

See also Chronic Fatigue Syndrome, Infection (Viral)

Mononucleosis, AKA mono or the kissing disease, has an interesting side note. By the time a person reaches the age of 30, there is a 96% chance that they have had mono in one way or another, whether felt as an overwhelming weakness or a mild malaise. Most people in the latter category don't even realize that they had mono. Typical symptoms include

- Weakness
- Sore throat
- Swollen glands
- Headache
- Fatigue

Early childhood infections often cause no symptoms. People who are symptomatic generally feel ill for about two weeks, though only about four days of rest are required. Adolescence is when most cases appear, and as people usually dating at that age, it has become known as the "kissing disease."

What Causes Mononucleosis?

Mono is caused by the Epstein-Barr virus (EBV) or the cytomegalovirus (CMV). It is most often transmitted from asymptomatic individuals through saliva or blood, by coughing or sneezing, or by sharing glasses, utensils, or needles. It is less contagious than commonly believed.

- Epstein-Barr virus (EBV), which invades the immune system's own B cells, causes 85% of all mono cases.
- The other 15% are caused by cytomegalovirus, which, like EBV, is a herpes virus.

The common school of thought is once you've had mono, you can't get it again. This is not entirely true. Once you catch EBV, you carry it for life in the epithelial lining of your nose and throat, though this doesn't necessarily mean that you are immune from developing mono again. Additionally, since your body releases EBV every so often, there are times when you can infect others with it.

Treatments for Mono

It is important to know that if you have strep throat associated with mono, DO NOT take antibiotics for the strep. It can cause a nasty, red rash over your entire body.

- Mono responds to rest. Get several days of rest.
- Take high doses of vitamin C.
- Take enzymes.
- Get plenty of pure water (Carbon Activated Water is best).
- Try colloidal silver (be sure to use a reputable brand).
- Be sure to get plenty of good nutrition, so your body is well fortified to fight the infection. You can use Spirulina, Chlorella, maca, spinach, kale, and other nutrient-rich foods.

Continued exposure to mono may lead to chronic fatigue syndrome. A simple rule: Know who you are kissing. If someone appears to have a cold or flu, hold off on the smooch until the person is well again. Some viruses are communicable when the person is most sick and other, nastier ones are still communicable post symptoms. Chronic fatigue syndrome is not something to mess with; it makes you feel like the walking wounded. So if you have mono and you get sleepy, do yourself a favor and take a nap. Note that occasionally this virus can cause an enlarged spleen and liver.

Mood Disorders

See also Anxiety, Depression, Energy Enhancement

Mood disorders, an umbrella term used to describe mental/emotional disorders such as clinical depression, bipolar disorder, adjustment disorder, and anxiety/panic disorder, are epidemic in modern society. Mental illness affects approximately 44 million Americans, according to the Substance Abuse and Mental Health Services Administration (SAMHSA), making it one of the most common illnesses affecting public health.

Due to the high incidence of mental illness today, prescriptions for Prozac and other antidepressants have been on the rise for the past decade. Unfortunately, these prescription drugs often have side effects that can actually reduce patients' quality of life. These side effects include nausea, dizziness, anxiety, sexual dysfunction, and uncontrollable facial and body tics. Ironically, antidepressant drugs may even cause a small percentage of patients, mostly children, to become homicidal, suicidal, or both—the same results that antidepressants are supposed to prevent. Fortunately, a number of natural alternatives to prescription antidepressants and sedatives can be helpful.

What Causes Mood Disorders?

It would be difficult to sum up the causes of mood disorders in a simple paragraph. The causes are numerous and varied. However, it is safe to point to two schools of thought on the subject. Western medicine and scientific thought believe that mood disorders are primarily biochemical in origin—that is, that a chemical imbalance is at the heart of the problem. By treating the chemical imbalance, you can cure the problem.

The more holistic and natural-health-oriented practitioners believe, however, that treating the biochemical imbalance is like wearing glasses to improve vision: you never actually cure the cause of the problem, just treat the symptoms by making corrections to the body so the symptoms disappear. They believe that the underlying causes of Mood Disorders are psychological and neuro-emotional—meaning that the emotional wound must be identified and treated. It is difficult to side completely with one school of thought or the other because many patients have had success using both types of treatment.

Treatments for Mood Disorders

A good way to approach mood disorders is to treat both the biochemical and emotional roots of the problem. If you work with a psychotherapist, seek one who will support your natural approach to the biochemical side of the equation. Here are some herbal treatments you can try:

- For mild to moderate depression and anxiety, St. John's wort is by far the most well-known herbal alternative to Prozac and other pharmaceuticals. In two studies, researchers compared the effectiveness of a combination therapy of St. John's wort and the herb valerian against the antidepressant drug amitriptylin. The results were overwhelmingly positive: One study found that valerian and St. John's wort are just as effective as amitriptyline, while the other reported that this combination herbal therapy is actually more effective than the pharmaceutical, with fewer side effects.
- In a French study of 182 people with adjustment disorder (excessive reaction to a stressful situation or event), researchers gave the test subjects a popular French herbal blend of valerian, passionflower, kola nut, black horehound, hawthorn, and guaraná. According to the researchers, the mood disorder patients who took the French product all experienced significant relief from their anxiety symptoms.
- Of course, no mood disorder treatment plan is complete without a balanced diet and exercise. Fill your plate with whole grains, legumes, fruits, and vegetables. Most important, exercise regularly. Exercise naturally boosts the level of endorphins and serotonin (feel-good chemicals) in your brain. Endorphins can give you such a high that they're sometimes called natural heroin. Unlike any drug, prescription or illegal, endorphins are actually good for your body. The best way to raise your endorphin levels naturally is to participate in aerobic exercise. Eating peppers and pure cocoa (not necessarily at the same time) also boosts endorphins.

Mucus

Congestion / Phlegm / Runny Nose

See also Allergies, Colds, Infection (Viral)

Mucus is a reaction of the body to toxins or bacteria either entering or exiting the body. It is designed to trap the toxins in the membranes close to body openings and prevent them from getting farther into the body. In the digestive system, mucus lubricates food passing down the esophagus. In the respiratory system, it prevents foreign matter from entering the body. In the cervix, it prevents infection and moves the spermatozoa. Unfortunately, too much mucus can mean that the body's cleaning mechanisms are not functioning properly or that you are exposed to allergens or bacteria at elevated levels. If mucus continues or is chronic, then treatment is necessary to reduce the slimy secretion and remove the toxins from the mucus membranes.

What Causes Excessive Mucus?

Excessive mucus is generally caused by allergic reactions to food or environmental toxins. If you can identify your environmental allergens (substance to which you have an allergic reaction), get rid of them. Milk is a mucus-forming food even if you don't have an allergy to it, as are bananas, apple juice, and chocolate, so allergies to these substances will easily produce excessive mucus.

- Environmental toxins such as pesticides and hormones may also cause problems for asthmatics and other people who are especially prone to excess mucus formation. To avoid these hidden allergens, use organically grown grains, vegetables, and fruit and organically raised, hormone-free beef and other meats.
- Don't forget about infectious agents such as bacteria, yeast, and parasites. Bacterial infections, in particular, cause the lungs and digestive tract to create excess mucus. Keep yourself healthy and free of germs by washing your hands regularly and avoiding undercooked meat.

Treatments for Mucus

To find the substance causing the excess mucus, try rotating the foods in your diet. Consider everything that goes into your body and on your body as something to which you may be allergic. When you find a substance that appears to be increasing mucus, stop using it. Avoid mold and mildew and fermented foods and beverages, including beer, wine, vinegar, soy sauce, cheese, and pickled foods.

- Taking enzymes on an empty stomach helps digest the mucus.
- Gargle with one teaspoon red sage extract in I cup of water a couple times a day. You can also try hot salt water.
- Chickweed helps remove mucus.
- Many people have had success curing chronic mucus by using colonic cleanse treatments.
- Take Chinese or Ayurvedic herbal combinations. These cultures have looked deeply into the causes and prevention of mucus in the body.
- For mucus caused by viruses or bacteria, use the anti-bacterials St. John's wort, olive leaf extract, and liquid Echinacea. Apply these in liquid form to the back of your throat.

Other Considerations

In Indian Ayurvedic medicine, people identified as having Kapha constitutions are more susceptible to mucus conditions when they get chilled, such as during seasonal changes. These people should take herbs that warm the body, such as cayenne, cinnamon, and tumeric.

Muscle Aches & Cramps

See also Menstrual Cramps

When you experience a muscle cramp, you know it. It can be a painful sensation, especially in the feet or legs. If you are an athlete or work out often, then you dramatically increase your chances of getting them. But a few simple precautions will eradicate cramps.

What Causes Muscle Cramps?

Muscle cramps often are caused by dehydration and/or muscle fatigue, as well as nutritional deficiency. Even a slight calcium deficiency can cause painful muscle cramps, especially nighttime leg cramps. Potassium and magnesium are also required in the body. Here are some other common causes:

- Exposure to cold
- Overexertion of the muscle
- Inadequate oxygenation of muscles or inadequate stretching after exercise
- Dehydration
- Low body sodium
- Mineral deficiencies
- Poor conditioning

Treatments for Muscle Cramps

The first thing to do when you have a muscle cramp is to slowly stretch the muscle while doing some deep breathing to restore oxygen to the blood. Yoga stretches are excellent for this. Apply heat to the muscle, as heat improves superficial blood circulation and makes muscles more flexible. You can massage the essential oils of lavender and chamomile into the cramped muscle (combine these with almond oil if desired), as both are anti-spasmodic. To avoid cramping in the future, try these preventative treatments:

- Take calcium, magnesium, potassium, and vitamin D.
- Drink plenty of water.
- Stretch before and after workouts or strenuous activity.
- Drink plenty of green tea.
- Take magnesium citrate (with food) and a generous dose of skullcap herb to end muscle cramps fast.

Nail Fungus

Nail fungus is easy to get and difficult to get rid of. Some people live with permanent black spots on their toenails because they don't know how, or haven't been successful, at killing the fungus that grows there. Fungus thrives in damp, dark environments, so it's no surprise that our feet are prime real estate for fungi to settle in and raise their families. Closed-toe shoes and damp, sweaty socks only make matters worse.

But we can combat the fungus that lives and grows under our toenails—and evict it forever.

What Causes Nail Fungus?

Fungus is just about everywhere—or at least the potential for it is. Most often, conditions allow fungus to grow and spread. Sometimes, however, fungus such as Trichophyton (the fungus that causes athletes foot) infects the nails (especially toenails), making them brittle and discolored. Tight or poorly ventilated shoes can be a breeding ground for fungus, as are moist or wet socks.

Nail fungi can be difficult to cure fully, so prevention is preferable to treatment.

Treatments for Nail Fungus

If you do get a nail fungus, you can treat it in many ways. Before listing your choices, however, let's cover a few important procedures you should do no matter which treatment you choose.

- Fungus thrives in moist environments, so it is extremely important always to wear clean, dry socks and to keep your feet clean and dry. Add drying agents to your shoes before putting them on in the morning.
- Avoid wearing tight shoes. Instead choose open or at least well-ventilated shoes.
- If you do develop a nail fungus, file or sand the infected nail down—both at the end and top of the nail.
- Rub antifungal oils or other substances on and under your nail every day until the dark part of the nail is gone. Treatments include pure pine oil, oregano oil, or tea tree oil. You can also get positive results from vinegar.

Oral Ulcers

Canker Sore / Aphthous Stomatitis / Aphthous Ulcer

See also Cold Sore

A mouth ulcer is a very painful open sore inside the mouth, caused by a break in the mucus membrane. Don't panic—these sores are not herpes.

They start with tingling and burning, then form a red bump, which opens up into an ulcer, also called a canker sore. The ulcer is light colored with a red border. They sometimes have a white circle around it. The ulcer may cause painful swelling below the jaw.

Small oral ulcers heal on their own in a couple weeks. Even a group of very small ulcers will generally heal before a month is up, with no scars or other negative effects. Larger or more painful ulcers, however, usually take more than a month to heal and you may end up with scar. Natural treatments to reduce the swelling and inflammation are a good idea for these ulcers.

What Causes Oral Ulcers?

Oral ulcers are usually an overreaction by the body's own immune system, which can be caused by food allergies, stress, and exhaustion. You can also get them from injuries such as biting the lip or getting hit on the lip, wearing braces, and passionate kisses. Here are some other causes:

- Hormonal imbalances including menstrual cycles and imbalances caused by coffee, prescription drugs, and stress
- Deficiencies in B vitamins, particularly B2, and in iron
- Candida infection
- Gluten, which is found in wheat, oats, spelt, rye, or barley and can result in chronic mouth ulcers. Many products, even natural ones, include added gluten, so read the ingredients. Even beer is often made from wheat, and of course, most bread products include gluten.
- Vitamin C products, especially ascorbic acid or citric acid
- Chemotherapy
- Illness can bring on the canker sores. If they occur often and you have avoided the known causes, your immune system is not functioning correctly.

Treatments for Oral Ulcers

- Use a highly concentrated solution of sea salt in water as hot as you can stand to hold in your mouth. Keep swishing the solution around in your mouth and on the affected area until the water cools. The salt will sting, but it will clean the bacteria out and help your tissues contract and clot, then grow back together more efficiently. Remember, your body is nearly 1% salt (sodium chloride). This salt mouthwash first expands the tissue at the wound site, then shrinks it naturally.
- Herbalists also recommend aloe vera gel and deglycyrrhizinated licorice (DGL) chewable tablets for oral ulcers. Aloe vera gel soothes and heals the mouth's delicate mucous membranes. Clinical

research suggests that chewable DGL tablets are extremely effective oral ulcer cures. According to one study, chewing on DGL tablets completely healed oral ulcers in 15 out of 20 patients. Best of all, the healing was done within only three days.

Other Considerations

Try Vitamin E oil on the scarred areas to make them disappear.

Osteoporosis

See also Adrenal Imbalance, Hormone Imbalance, Menopause, Thyroid Imbalance

With Osteoporosis, a person's bones become less dense and more fragile. Women who have gone through menopause have osteoporosis most often because hormone changes make it harder for the body to absorb calcium. People with osteoporosis are unusually vulnerable to breaking bones. As people age, they also tend to lose muscle mass around the skeletal structure, which adds to the problem.

What Causes Osteoporosis?

Generally, hormone imbalance is the cause of this disease. Severe hormone imbalance can be caused by medical treatments and surgeries, thyroid and adrenal imbalances, and diabetes. Excessive dairy consumption may contribute to osteoporosis, as well as consuming sodas that contain phosphoric acid.

Treatments for Osteoporosis

Calcium and magnesium go hand in hand for good bone health and osteoporosis prevention. Your bones, cartilage, ligaments, and even muscles need calcium to stay healthy. Your body can't properly assimilate calcium into the bones without magnesium, however, because magnesium prevents calcium from building up in the joints and soft tissue, freeing it up to go into the bones where it belongs.

In order to reduce your body's excretion of calcium and magnesium, you should also take boron supplements. Due to boron's effect on the body's incorporation of these two essential minerals, experts in Germany discovered that boron supplements actually decrease bone loss.

Since dehydroepiandrosterone (DHEA) is a precursor to both estrogen and testosterone, taking 25 mg of DHEA with pregnenolone can help balance the hormones, which, in turn, help your bones absorb calcium. Cow's milk does not build bones. In fact, milk causes gall and kidney stones when it mixes with cholesterol, and leaches organic calcium from your bones.

- Some cases of osteoporosis are actually skeletal fluorosis (fluoride poisoning). If you drink well water, be careful because the development of skeletal fluorosis is associated with consumption of well water containing fluoride concentrations in excess of four parts per million (ppm). Fluoride is a dangerous chemical product and prevalent in some teas, chewing tobacco, snuff, and tap water. It is in some wines, Teflon-coated pots and pans, certain pediatric supplements, pesticides, toothpastes, mouthwashes, and topical dental gels. Even some sparkling mineral waters have unsafe levels of fluoride.
- Keep natural. Think twice before letting your doctor talk you into a hysterectomy, which is usually not truly a required operation; the resulting hormonal changes can lead to osteoporosis. Similarly, don't let your doctor talk you into taking certain drugs that often cause osteoporosis. And don't be fooled into taking synthetic estrogen. See Hormone Imbalance for more details.
- No osteoporosis prevention and treatment plan is complete without exercise. Strength training is essential for strong, healthy bones, since pulling the muscles directly against the bones with gravity working against them drives calcium back into the bones, which helps them retain their calcium.
- Omega-3, such as fish oils, and omega-6 help maintain calcium. Essential fatty acids (EFAs) such as evening primrose oil and borage are also important because of their ability to balance and maintain bone calcium stores.
- Avoid foods that cause your body to become acidic, which pulls the minerals from the bones. Stay away from alcohol, commercially processed foods, particularly soft drinks, caffeine, pasteurized milk and dairy products, fried foods, sugar, and protein. Instead, eat plenty of raw, organic leafy green vegetables, beans, nuts, seeds, and wild fish with the

best oils—these include cod, mackerel, halibut, tuna, and salmon.

- Drink plenty of pure water.
- Take these herbs in capsules or in teas: horsetail, nettle, sage, alfalfa, black cohosh, chastetree, sarsaparilla, wild yam, and dandelion root. If you make tea of roots or barks, like dandelion and wild yam, boil them for 20 minutes. Otherwise, let the teas come to a boil and turn them off.
- Women may apply a natural progesterone cream, which causes none of the harmful side effects of synthetic hormones, reverses bone loss, and helps PMS and menopause symptoms. Pre-menopausal women should use it two weeks a month, and menopausal women should use it three weeks a month.

Poison Oak/Ivy

If you hike or go camping, there's a good chance you've run into the infamous sting of poison oak or ivy. Kids and pets have a natural ability to run through patches of the stuff and bring it back into the house, where it can make contact with the rest of the family. The best thing you can do is educate yourself and your children on how to recognize the plants and avoid them. Pets are a different story.

Poison oak/ivy rash is not life or health threatening, but it very irritating. It should be treated and the rashes dressed and cleaned, or it might get out of hand and cause serious irritation to all areas of your body.

What Causes Poison Oak/Ivy Rash?

You can blame your poison ivy or poison oak rash on the oils in the plants. Like vegetable oil, they're fixed oils, meaning that they don't easily wash off or evaporate. For this reason, if a person or pet is exposed to either plant, you must first thoroughly wash the person's skin or the pet's fur. Then wash the person's clothes as soon as possible, in case they were exposed to the oil as well.

Treatments for Poison Oak/Ivy

Once you get the rash, there is not much you can do to stop poison ivy/oak. You can, however, keep it from getting out of control and encourage the rash to dry up and leave quickly. Here are the main things you should do:

1. Stop the spread of the rash by washing the site and taking Rhus tox orally as indicated, and put full-strength Clorox bleach on the site of the rash. It will sting just a little, but the stinging will dissipate in a minute. Once the Clorox has dried, apply fels naphtha soap with water and let dry. This will stop the spread of the poison oak and dry the oil from spreading under the skin. Be careful, however, as many have allergic reactions to Clorox, causing dizziness and disorientation. You can also try white flower oil, the Chinese remedy made of specific essential oils, to help stop the rash.
2. After you wash the skin or fur, apply any of a number of natural balms to relieve the itching and other symptoms. Lavender oil, for example, both dries the blisters and acts as an anti-inflammatory. For a soothing paste, mix witch hazel with bicarbonate of soda (baking soda) until the mixture is the consistency of cold cream. Apply the paste to the irritated area of skin. Like the lavender oil, this mixture will dry out the blisters and soothe the inflamed skin. For liquid relief, steep 2 tablespoons of dried chamomile in 2 cups of boiled water for 10 minutes. After it cools, dip a washcloth in the tea and rub it on the rash.
3. Fight the antibodies: Combine vitamin C powder and water and put on the rash, as well as take C orally. Also, consume antioxidants from purple berries, lysine, and kelp with iodine.

Other Considerations

A plant called Jewel Weed, which often grows close to poison oak, is useful for treating poison oak, poison ivy and stinging nettles. Just squeeze the juice from the leaves onto the affected area each day until it goes away. The leaves should be as fresh as possible, as the oils in the plant that help treat poison oak/ivy dissipate quickly.

You can build immunity to poison oak and ivy by taking Rhus tox (toxicodendron) 30x potency, three pellets under your tongue three times daily for seven days at the beginning of the year, before the plants come out. This is a homeopathic medicine, so be sure to read the bottle for directions on taking the remedy. Don't touch the delicate medicine with your fingers. Simply pour the pellets into the lid of the bottle, toss the pellets under your tongue, and let them dissolve. Don't take food or put anything else in your mouth 20 minutes before or after taking the remedy. Don't breathe into the bottle. Don't use any camphor-like materials, perfume, or peppermint; these may make the homeopathic medicine ineffective.

> **"Even if you've been fishing for three hours and haven't gotten anything except poison ivy and sunburn, you're still better off than the worm."**
> Unknown

Premenstrual Syndrome

PMS / Periodic Mood Swings / Premenstrual Tension (PMT)

See also Cramps, Hormone Imbalance, Menstrual Cramps

Today, PMS still is often misunderstood and mistreated. Unfortunately, conventional medicine tends to emphasize treatment of PMS symptoms rather than the hormonal imbalance that is the true underlying cause.

PMS is not a disease but a syndrome; that is, it is a pattern of symptoms that may or may not have a logical connection. Symptoms vary from woman to woman, with the most common being cramping, bloating, breast tenderness, leg aches or backaches, nausea and various indigestion problems, diarrhea, headache, pimples and skin rashes, dizziness, fatigue, irritability, weepiness, and increased fastidiousness. It is therefore not surprising that conventional medicine has not found a cure for this syndrome.

PMS is common, occurring in 75% of women of reproductive age. For two to ten days before the onset of menstruation, millions (if not billions) of women are affected by a wide range of physical discomforts and mood disorders, including bloating, depression, insomnia, severe pain, uncontrollable rage, crying jags, and, in the most severe cases, suicidal depression.

Treatments for PMS

Start with foods. Strawberries, watermelon, artichokes, asparagus, parsley, horsetail herb (or organic silica), and watercress are all great natural diuretics, and should be added to the diet during PMS. Other beneficial foods include raw sunflower seeds, dates, figs, peaches, bananas, potatoes, and tomatoes. Avoid sugar and refined carbohydrates and watch your sodium intake (use natural sea salt).

Diet plays a role in PMS, and avoiding the following foods can help to lessen the severity of the discomfort for most women: salt and licorice (licorice stimulates the production of aldosterone, which causes further retention of sodium and water). Likewise, avoid cold and icy drinks/foods. Here are some additional treatments:

- Herbal treatments may work by stimulating the pituitary gland or by affecting dopamine or opioid receptors. There are several herbs that can help alleviate the symptoms of PMS. Dong Quai works for many women by eliminating water retention, and chasteberry and the Chinese herb xiao yao san are great for relief of abdominal cramping. Black cohosh herb is great for counteracting night sweats. You can also take 500 mg of evening primrose oil for an overall tonic and St. John's wort for calming the nerves.
- Maca root is reported to help with PMS and has been used for centuries by women in the Andes region.
- Supplements of vitamin B6 and calcium carbonate have been shown to alleviate some symptoms, and exercise will help reduce depression and anxiety symptoms. Balance B6 with B2 and niacin.
- Stay away from caffeine, which destroys B vitamins, potassium, and zinc while irritating the alimentary canal and increasing the desire for sugar, which further exacerbates PMS.
- Don't drink alcohol, as it depletes magnesium and damages the liver, and like coffee, leads to an acid condition.
- If you eat spinach, beet greens, chocolate, or rhubarb, then take a mineral supplement with calcium at night. These foods contain oxalic acid, which makes minerals non-assimilable and destroys calcium.
- Vitamin D: Take 1,000 IUs. Or, even better, get out in the sunshine.

- Take 250 mg of magnesium with 500 mg calcium: The reason you take more magnesium in this case is that magnesium levels drop before your period.

Prostate Health

Prostate Cancer / Prostate Infection / Prostatitis

See also Anti-inflammatories, Colon & Intestinal Health, Sexual Dysfunction

The size of a mere walnut, the prostate gland is small but critically important to men's health. It produces semen, the fluid that carries sperm from the testicles, and it regulates the flow of urine from the urinary tract, or urethra. It also comes into contact with the rectal cavity and the bladder.

According to Dr. Earl Mindell, almost every man experiences prostate trouble at least once in his life. In fact, a studies show that 1 out of 6 males will develop prostate cancer. That will result in almost 170,000 prostate removals and nearly 31,000 deaths from prostate cancer.

Fortunately, you can, for the most part, prevent prostate disorders if you start a program of good nutrition early. Prostate disorders range from prostate infection to enlargement to prostate cancer. Principal symptoms of prostate disorder include:

- Difficulty urinating
- Dribbling and urgency to urinate
- Increased nighttime urination
- Dramatic reduction of ejaculate
- Weak ejaculation
- Lack of sexual desire
- Difficulty achieving full erection
- Terminal blood in urine

What Causes Prostate Disorders?

The most benign prostate disorder is infection. The prostate can become infected by viruses and bacteria from the rectal cavity (constipation and poor colon health may be a factor), or the urethra (sexually transmitted). Infection could result in painful urination or difficulty urinating (swelling of the prostate). This can be treated with a prostate cleanse and anti-inflammatory herbs and supplements.

It's important to note that oral sex exposes the prostate to more bacteria than vaginal or even anal sex. Also, environmental toxins have been observed in patients with prostate cancer.

The most common prostate disorder is prostate enlargement, known as prostatitis. When the prostate swells, it blocks the flow of urine, making it difficult or even impossible to urinate. This normally is treated with antibiotics or surgery, but natural cures include the use of anti-inflammatories, prostate massage, and dietary changes.

Finally, there is prostate cancer, the most severe of the prostate conditions. Incidence of prostate cancer in America is on a sharp rise. Experts are still unsure as to the exact cause of prostate cancer, but suspect that genetics, nutrition, hormones, and environmental toxins all play a role. Studies suggest that diets high in saturated fat and sodium nitrate increase risk for prostate cancer, as does a sedentary lifestyle. No wonder prostate cancer is so common in the United States!

Treatments for Prostate Health

The best treatments for prostate health are preventative ones. Concerning the prostate, it's much better to eliminate the risk of disease than to treat it after the fact. Here are some key points:

- Eliminate saturated fats and excess sugars and starches from your diet. Reduce the amount of meats and processed foods you eat—especially partially hydrogenated oils. Increase your consumption of fruits and vegetables (lightly cooked or even raw).
- Drink green tea at least once a day. Better yet, trade coffee for green tea.
- Take dietary supplements: Vitamins B, C, and E and omega fatty acids.
- Exercise frequently and engage in sexual activity (including masturbation) regularly.
- Get plenty of movement. A sedentary lifestyle is the enemy of the prostate.
- If your diet has been poor for a long time, consider a colon cleansing as described under Colon & Intestinal Health.
- Combinations of phyto (plant-based) estrogens are useful in treating prostate disorders.

- If you suffer from prostate infection or enlargement, then in addition to the practices listed here, take saw palmetto along with anti-inflammatory and circulation-stimulating herbs and supplements (lemongrass, cumin, tumeric, mistletoe extract, sage, pygeum, pumpkin seed extract, sterolins, and zinc).

Other Considerations

Excess alcohol and caffeine play havoc on the prostate, as do coagulated dairy products (hard cheeses, for example). Excess meat consumption is also a prostate irritation, as meat generally is not completely eliminated and remains in the bowels, infecting the prostate. For this reason, it's a good idea to include plenty of dietary fiber from raw fruits and vegetables, salads, and nuts. Soy products are also helpful.

Avoid excess alcohol and cigarette smoke, including secondhand smoke. Avoid excess caffeine and stress, as they promote hormone imbalances that can affect the prostate.

Receding Gums

Receding gums are generally associated with aging, and dentists assert that a certain amount of receding is expected with age. But you can slow down the process and keep your gums healthy for longer. Receding gums can be painful. They can expose dental nerves, making you sensitive to hot and cold foods, brushing, and even using a toothpick. Touching the exposed nerve can be like receiving an electric shock.

Causes of Receding Gums

Gums require calcium, vitamins, and amino acids to remain healthy and vital. Actually, it's not the gums themselves that require the calcium, but the bone into which your teeth and gums are set. This bone will lose its strength and even recede if exposed to regular bacteria and food particles around the gum line. When the bone recedes, the gums worsen and eventually recede as well.

In addition, a diet of soft foods and/or lack of brushing or flossing can cause the gums to atrophy and make them recede over time. Excessive or violent brushing can also be a cause, as can any prolonged irritation to the gums, including tobacco use (from smoking or especially chewing) or grinding of the teeth. Certain drugs are also known to deteriorate the bone and gums in your mouth over time. These drugs also tend to cause dryness of the mouth

But the single worst thing for your teeth, gums, and bones is drinking sodas. Cola and most other sodas contain phosphoric acid—the same acid used in tile and bathroom cleansers and by dentists to etch away tooth enamel prior to placing fillings. They literally eat away at your enamel and bone.

Treatments

The treatment for receding gums focuses primarily on increasing calcium in your diet, but you can also try some lifestyle and supplement therapies. Here is a quick hit on the essentials:

- Floss regularly.
- Increase calcium in your diet and with natural herbs and supplements, including horsetail herb.
- Increase omega fatty acids and vitamin C in your diet.
- Avoid sodas, or at least brush your teeth after drinking them.
- Rinse your mouth regularly with salt water or hydrogen peroxide.

Restless Leg Syndrome

Electric Leg Syndrome / RLS

People who suffer from restless leg syndrome (RLS) often don't know they have a specific condition, what is causing it, or that many others suffer from it as well. But RLS is quite common and more information is coming to light about it every year. Now, just the phrase "restless leg syndrome" often causes a cry of recognition from sufferers when they hear it for the first time. If you suffer from RLS, you know these symptoms:

- Uncontrollable energy in the legs, especially when lying down
- Difficulty sleeping because of the electric energy in the legs
- Involuntary jerking or movements of the legs during sleep or when falling to sleep
- Inability to calm the legs or "turn off" the energy

- Feeling of pins and needles, pulling, or tingling in the legs

RLS may also affect the arms, although this is usually less intense than RLS in the legs.

What Causes RLS?

The exact cause of RLS is unknown, but many experts believe it may be related to an iron deficiency. Some research suggests that a buildup of lactic acid may also contribute to the symptoms. There may also be an emotional component.

Treatments for RLS

Don't waste your time and pollute your body with remedies that merely tranquilize you to help you get to sleep. These do not cure the cause of RLS, but merely treat symptoms. Instead, try one or more of these treatments and reduce your dependency on sleep aids:

- Take iron supplements and eat foods high in iron and trace minerals, including blackstrap molasses, Spirulina, bee pollen, spinach, thyme, curry, cinnamon, and rosemary. Try folic acid supplements if iron does not work.
- Take magnesium supplements. Research suggests that RLS may be caused by a magnesium deficiency.
- Walk or jog slowly in the late afternoon.
- Do long, stretching exercises or yoga postures before going to bed. If you wake up with RLS symptoms, repeat these stretching exercises until you are ready to sleep again.
- Deeply massage your legs before bed, or try using a vibrating massager.
- Drink at least 10 eight-ounce glasses of water every day.
- Take herbs to relax the nervous system: valerian root, St. Johns wort, skullcap, hops. You can also try bee pollen, ginseng, cayenne, and spearmint.
- Take Cordyceps mushroom extract to reduce lactic acid in the muscles.
- Refer to the Stress section for information on stress reduction.

Sexual Dysfunction

Frigidity / Lack of Orgasm / Premature Ejaculation

See also Erectile Dysfunction

Are you perfectly happy and satisfied between the sheets? Is your partner? Sexual dysfunction is more common than most people like to admit. For men, it involves a number of issues, including, erectile dysfunction (covered in its own section), premature ejaculation, frigidity, obsession, compulsion, and sex addiction.

For women, sexual dysfunction includes such conditions as frigidity, vaginal dryness, inability to reach orgasm, nymphomania, and different forms of enabling their sexual partners.

Causes of Sexual Dysfunction

Sexual dysfunction can be divided into two groups: dysfunction caused by physical or biochemical problems and dysfunction caused by mental, emotional, or psychological problems. Just a few causes include:

- A diet heavy in saturated fats, sugars, and food additives
- Fear of sex and related issues
- Self-esteem issues / lack of sexual confidence and control
- Past sexual abuse or related trauma
- Lack of sexual education
- Anger from puberty issues or past sexual experiences
- Chronic depression

In general, when diagnosing a sexual dysfunction, it's useful to keep an open mind and take a holistic attitude, with the expectation that more than one of these issues will be the cause.

Treatments

Since the most serious kinds of sexual dysfunctions are psychologically based, it's important to seek healing for your mental and emotional wounds. Psychotherapy, energy work, and countless forms of alternative therapies can be used to help.

Tantra is an ancient practice of becoming present for your sexuality and using it to further your health and life force. Tantric exercises and philosophies can break through all sorts of sexual dysfunction.

See Immune System Health for good dietary advice that will help with sexual dysfunction on a physical and biochemical level and the entry for Erectile Dysfunction offers many suggestions for improved performance.

Snoring

Apnea

See also Insomnia / Sleep Disorders

About 40 million Americans snore, causing untold damage to relationships and plenty of lost sleep. When you snore, the fleshy areas of the throat, such as the uvula, vibrate. This vibration causes the buzzing, gargling, rattling, and wheezing sounds known as snoring. Snoring is twice as common in men as in women, but women and children also snore. The figures for men are surprisingly high: 20% of men aged 30 to 35 snore, with that number jumping to more than 60% by age 60.

The most significant drawback to snoring is not the bothersome sound it makes but the fact that oxygen flow to the lungs is being restricted, which can lead to manifold challenges.

What Causes Snoring?

Any number of factors, ranging from mild conditions to life-threatening diseases, can cause snoring. On the less serious side, many factors may lead to the annoying sounds of snoring:

- Simple nasal or sinus congestion
- Swollen tonsils or adenoids
- Nasal polyps
- Loose dentures
- Eating heavy meals late in the evening
- Alcohol, especially if you drink within a few hours of bedtime
- Antidepressants, anti-seizure drugs, antihistamines, and muscle relaxant drugs may cause snoring because they cause the throat muscles to relax, thus reducing the width of airways.

- Age is associated with a high incidence of snoring because aging causes the throat's skin and muscles to become flabby, which partially obstructs airflow.
- Obesity

Some causes of snoring are more serious, such as obesity and heart disease. Sleep apnea reeks havoc with sleeping and can lead to strokes. High blood pressure also causes snoring, and should never be left untreated.

Treatments for Snoring

If snoring is a minor inconvenience, these tips might help cure the problem:

- Sleep on your side instead of your back. Attach a small pocket to the back of your nightshirt and place a golf ball or large marble in the pocket. You will not sleep on your back.
- Blow your nose to clear out congestion before you go to sleep.
- You can try breathing oils, such as peppermint, spearmint, pine, and eucalyptus.
- Develop a consistent sleeping pattern.
- Avoid drinking alcohol close to bedtime.
- Keep your room dust free, and don't let pets sleep with you. You may want to take homeopathic remedies to counter mold, dust, and dander.
- Nasal strips hold the nose open, allowing you to breathe easier through the nose.
- Avoid eating mucus-producing foods like wheat and dairy, and any foods you are allergic to. See Mucus for information on herbs and extracts that may help reduce it.
- Use a humidifier in your bedroom if air is too dry. Or you can use an atomizer if your room is small enough. Add some marjoram oil drops to the water.
- Avoid late meals and overeating. Losing weight also helps.

"Laugh and the world laughs with you, snore and you sleep alone."
Anthony Burgess, author, A Clockwork Orange

Sore Throat

See also Colds, Cough, Infection (Bacterial), Infection (Viral)

Sore throats often mark the onset of colds and flu, so it's important to eradicate them as soon as they appear. Left untreated, even for a just few hours, they can grow out of control and affect, even threaten, the tonsils. In many cases, they may develop into more serious throat conditions and coughs. Scratching or itching sensations in the back of the throat are generally signs of bacteria or viruses. Eating sugar and processed foods can feed them.

Thankfully, there are many natural solutions for eliminating a sore or itchy throat.

What Causes a Sore Throat?

A sore throat is a common first symptom of both colds and the flu. A number of germs, such as streptococcus, and several viruses cause sore throats. Sometimes, however, bacteria and viruses aren't to blame. Basically, anything that inflames and dries out your throat's mucous membranes can cause a sore throat. This means that living in an arid climate, smoking, exposure to secondhand smoke, vomiting, acid reflux, screaming, and allergies can all give you a sore throat.

Sore Throat Remedies

Over-the-counter remedies for sore throat usually just cover up the symptoms of itching and irritation. Many natural remedies, however, can actually eliminate the sore throat. What's important is that you do something right away before it develops into a more serious condition or illness.

- Hit the throat itself with antibacterial and antiviral herbs or tinctures. Some good choices are St. John's wort, liquid Echinacea with goldenseal, and propolis tincture. Use an eyedropper or spray to apply these to your throat.
- Gargle with warm salt water or hydrogen peroxide (diluted in half with water).
- Increase vitamin C supplements, including mega-dosing with 2 to 3 grams per day or more.
- If your sore throat is not caused by virus or infection, you can sooth it with honey and anti-inflammatory herbs.

Sprains & Strains

See also Inflammation

Most active children and adults have experienced a strain or a sprain at least once in their lives. Many people don't know the difference between the two injuries, however, since they share many of the same symptoms: pain, swelling, and bruising. Here are the exact definitions: A sprain is when a ligament, the tissue that connects bones together at joints, becomes stretched or torn; a strain is when either a muscle or a tendon that attach a muscle to the bone becomes twisted or pulled.

Treatments

Here are the steps you should take if you experience a sprain or strain:

1. As soon as you experience the sharp pain of a strain or a sprain, rest the affected limb. If the injury involves your leg, try not to put any weight on it. Next, apply an ice pack to the affected joint or muscle and elevate the limb. The ice pack will numb the pain and reduce swelling.
2. Keep the limb chilled and elevated for about 20 minutes, then compress and immobilize the muscle or joint, using an elastic bandage. Be careful not to wrap the bandage so tightly that you cut off blood supply. You may even lay steamed comfrey leaves on the joint or muscle, and then wrap it up in the bandage. Or you can boil comfrey root for 30 minutes to an hour, cool the tea, and then soak the bandage in the water before wrapping. Comfrey has natural anti-inflammatory properties, so it reduces pain and swelling and helps accelerate healing.
3. As your sprain or strain heals, sitting in warm baths with Epsom salts or massaging the affected area may make you feel better. To support and accelerate your body's natural healing process, add extra amounts of vitamin C, bromelain, and omega-3 fatty acids to your nutritional supplement regimen. Additionally, according to herbalists, drinking comfrey root and spring horsetail tea helps your body heal faster.
4. Use the Homeopathic Traumeel topically to alleviate pain.

Other Considerations

See the Inflammation entry for a list of herbs and extracts that help reduce swelling and inflammation.

Stress

See also Adrenal Imbalance, Hormone Imbalance, Sleep Disorders

Many experts believe that unhealthy stress is the number one cause of disease and poor health. Scientists agree that stress causes actual brain chemistry cal changes, and these changes can influence your health. Stress is or may be a contributing factor in everything from backaches and insomnia to cancer, heart disease, and chronic fatigue syndrome. Heart disease is the number one killer of American women. High blood pressure, heart attacks, heart palpitations, and stroke are often stress-related cardiovascular conditions.

Often, people feel the effects of stress as fatigue, various aches and pains, and headaches, or as emotional disorders such as anxiety, depression, and sleep disturbances. Stress affects others by causing gastrointestinal disorders such as ulcers, lower abdominal cramps, colitis, and irritable bowel syndrome. Frequently, people under the effects of stress will have more colds and infections due to lowered immune system responses. Stress can also cause skin conditions such as itchy skin and rashes.

Why Are We So Stressed Out?

Physical stress may be the result of too much to do, not enough sleep, a poor diet, or effects of an illness. Stress can also be mental: when you worry about money, a loved one's illness, or retirement; or experience an emotionally devastating event, such as the death of a spouse or being fired from work can add an enormous amount of stress to your life.

However, much of our stress comes from less dramatic, everyday responsibilities. Obligations and pressures, both physical and mental, are not always obvious to us. In response to these daily strains, your body automatically increases blood pressure, heart rate, respiration, metabolism, and blood flow to your muscles. This response is intended to help your body react quickly and effectively to a high-pressure situation.

This is why exercise is so vital. In nature, we are designed to be far more active than we are in modern life. The fight-or-flight response is meant to result in a physical activity, such as fighting or fleeing. When you are constantly reacting to stressful situations without making adjustments to counter the physical effects, you will feel stress—which can threaten your health and well-being. Stress significantly ages us, not only cosmetically, but throughout the body.

Stress and Hormones

Stress releases adrenaline into the bloodstream, which converts to cortisol. When there is an overabundance of cortisol in the bloodstream over long periods, it can lead to problems with thinking, raised blood pressure, weight gain in the belly, lowered immune response, muscle mass loss and connective tissue weakening, growth hormone level imbalances, blood sugar imbalances, and hypothyroidism. High cortisol from stress strongly affects memory, and even leaves the blood brain barrier open, allowing toxins to penetrate where they would not go otherwise. A life of stress leaves people more vulnerable to Alzheimer's and other diseases.

High cortisol can be reduced through sunshine, regular rest, exercise, and fun. If cortisol levels become too low, however, stress continues and adrenal depletion ensues. This leads to exhaustion, and is implicated in Chronic Fatigue syndrome and fibromyalgia.

The adrenals also produce too little DHEA when they are busy with cortisol, which can be rebalanced through joy and laughter. You be can be tested for your DHEA levels to see if you need supplementation for either low or high levels of cortisol phases, but careful supervision by a health care practitioner is suggested to make sure DHEA is being used to create the proper hormones in your body. Do NOT use DHEA if you suspect prostate cancer.

Treatments for Reducing Stress

Here are a few suggestions for stress management to help maintain a healthy lifestyle:

- First and foremost, stop thriving on stress. If your lifestyle choices cause too much stress, ask yourself what you gain by continuing to make these choices (or by not changing). Perhaps a larger fear or avoidance pattern is behind the stress.
- Remove caffeine from your diet—completely! Stress is severely worsened by stimulants like coffee, and sugar, even though you may be tempted to use them because your weakened adrenals may need extra stimulation if you are pushing yourself to keep going.

Don't, as that only perpetuates the cycle and you will feel even worse later.

- Noise increases stress response, so find time in a quiet place. Better yet, create a quiet space and use it regularly for introspection, meditation, and relaxation.
- Supplement with DHEA and vitamin B-complex.

Make sure you're eating highly nutritious food if you have a high-stress lifestyle. You can help balance your system by adding super food nutrition from dark green, leafy vegetables, bee pollen, olive leaf extract, pine bark extract, and other nutrient-rich foods and botanicals.

Other Considerations

When you feel stress start to build, take a deep breath! Flood your body with life-giving oxygen and feel the difference immediately. There's a reason Grandma always said take a deep breathe and settle down—because it works! One of the body's responses to stress is to shorten the breath, which will deprive the body of oxygen. Again, in nature we would typically respond to stress in ways that would have us fighting, fleeing, or both. Physical activity (think exercise) following a stressful or threatening encounter will have us breathing deeply and more efficiently using the adrenaline and other hormones and chemicals released by our body. In modern life, we often deal with stress while we are sitting down. We continue the shallow breathing and often keep it all inside. A recipe for disaster!

- Jin Shin Do is a method of working with acupressure points to help release core stresses and help you cope with every-day stressors.
- A good massage will alleviate much stress and muscle tension.
- For many, aromatic baths can do wonders. Fill a hot bath and add Epsom salts and 20 drops of lavender, chamomile, lilac, or neroli essential oils. Breathe deeply while you soak. The aromatic healing properties will melt away your stress.

Stroke

See Cardiovascular Health, Heart Disease

When a person has a stroke, the brain's function is reduced because of injured brain cells. A stroke usually begins when a blood clot or clot of bacteria forms and moves to the brain and blocks the blood flow to areas of the brain. A blood clot also may begin in the brain itself, in a plaque-clogged artery, or the brain may hemorrhage due to age, high blood pressure, or substance abuse.

The first symptoms of a stroke may be a severe headache, perhaps tingling, numbness, or difficulty moving the hands, reflex dysfunction, change in speaking voice, uncoordinated eyes, problems in walking and standing, visual changes, cognitive malfunction and memory loss, and difficulty in movement that affects one side of the body.

Causes of Strokes

Aging, diabetes, tobacco smoke, high levels of the wrong type of cholesterol compared to the good kind, high blood pressure, stress, and being a type A personality all can make one vulnerable to strokes.

Preventative Treatments for Strokes

Studies show that omega-3 fatty acid supplements help prevent stroke in not one, but two ways. The age-related decline of omega-3 fatty acids in the brain leads to increased stroke risk, as well as increased risk for dementia. By supplementing the omega-3 fatty acids you're losing due to age, you reduce your chance of suffering a potentially debilitating stroke. Furthermore, omega-3 fatty acids reduce the likelihood of platelet aggregation in blood vessels, thereby lessening your risk for both stroke and heart attack. Eating fatty fish such as salmon, which is a primary source of omega-3, can cut the chances of strokes in half.

- Bring down high blood pressure with stress management, caffeine reduction, fewer sugars and starches, a weight loss program (if overweight) and less salt in your diet. At the same time, increase your potassium intake and use blood-pressure-stabilizing foods like pure cocoa, garlic, and onion. Garlic in raw trom or extract helps prevent strokes because it is an anticoagulant, and it lowers the bad cholesterol levels as well as lowering blood pressure and improving circulation. Ginger does these things as well, and can be eaten in foods or used in teas—just boil for 20 minutes. You can also use extract form.

- Avoid cigarette smoke, drugs and alcohol, other than a little red wine.
- Carnosine is a great stroke preventative.
- Ginkgo biloba aids overall brain circulation. Interestingly, Ginkgo is a prescription herb in Ireland. Be aware that it is a blood thinner, so take that into consideration if you are taking blood-thinning medications after a stroke.
- Hawthorn berries help the heart as well as the arteries.
- The bioflavonoid quercetin has been shown to reduce stroke risk by cleaning the blood vessels in the brain. Red wine contains quercetin. If you don't drink, use the red wine extract, grape seed extract, or green tea extract.
- Tumeric is excellent for blood pressure and circulation. You may already enjoy this spice in curry, so if you enjoy the flavor, eat plenty of curry (just be sparing with the rice if you have blood sugar issues).

Treatments After a Stroke

Prevention is the best policy when it comes to stroke. If you have a stroke, however, seek medical help immediately, and ask the physician to administer Coumadin (warfarin sodium) within the first few hours of having the stroke. Hyperbaric oxygen delivered immediately after a transient ischemic attack (TIA; temporary interference with the brains blood supply, with no lasting damage) may prevent more serious strokes later. Be aware that TIAs are often warnings that a larger, more damaging stroke may be on its way.

Research shows that, along with Coumadin, giving recent stroke victims acetyl-L-carnitine (ALC) helps normalize brain energy metabolites, a factor that can make a large difference in how well the patient recovers from the stroke. In fact, stroke victims who were administered ALC shortly after the stroke experience better memory, task completion, and cognitive thought than those who did not receive ALC. Chelation therapy is also been found to be helpful.

Here are some more treatments:

- Bromelain breaks up blood clots.
- DMAE improves brain function. The amino acid L-carnitine improves life after strokes.

Sunburn

See also Burns

In the past 30 years, the development of the ozone hole in the Earth's atmosphere has allowed more of the harmful ultraviolet (UV) rays of the sun to reach the Earth—and our skin. Without the full ozone protection, we are more prone to sunburn.

If you are vacationing or live in a sunny climate, be sure to take precautions when going out into the sun. Even dark-skinned people can get skin cancer and other problems because of excessive exposure to the sun's UV rays (or the UV light from artificial sources, such as tanning lamps or industrial lamps).

Sunburn usually goes away in a week or two; even if you've got a bad sunburn, the main discomfort will probably subside after two days. When the skin begins to heal, however, it will be very itchy. Symptoms and damage to the skin can be minimized by using the remedies suggested here. Note that repeated sunburn and excessive exposure to UV light can lead to skin cancer.

Treatments

If you do get a sunburn, here are the basic steps to follow for healing and protecting your skin, and reducing pain:

1. Spray carbon activated water (CAW) generously and frequently on your skin; it will soothe the heat immediately. If you don't have CAW water, try apple cider vinegar.
2. When the pain subsides, smear on aloe vera gel or papaya pulp, followed by a vitamin E cream.
3. While you have the sunburn, drink at least eight 8-ounce glasses of pure water each day to replenish the fluid that the swelling and/or blisters from the burn takes away from the rest of your body.

Other Considerations

Add some calendula or lavender oil to your aloe vera gel or papaya pulp before putting it onto your burn. Before you go into the sun, take extra vitamin C (1 gram added to your normal dose) to helps your protect skin from the sun, while still allowing the rays to get in and produce vitamin D.

Do not soak in water for long periods, as this can dehydrate your skin. To hydrate your skin, put raw plantain or potato pulp onto your skin. This also feels great while helping your skin.

Thyroid Imbalance

Goiter / Hyperthyroidism / Hypothyroidism / Iodine Deficiency

See also Adrenal Imbalance, Chronic Fatigue, Energy Enhancement, Hormone Imbalance

The thyroid is associated with many different diseases, but they all fall into two basic categories: underactive thyroid (too little hormone production) and overactive thyroid (too much hormone production). Underactive thyroid, or hypothyroidism, is by far the more common of the two. In fact, hypothyroidism is fast becoming an epidemic in the United States, affecting well over 50% of the population to some degree. Telltale symptoms include chronic tiredness, low energy, lack of ambition, and being overweight. Further symptoms include decreased sex drive, obesity, cold hands and feet, low body temperature in general, a weak immune system, constipation and slow digestion, allergies, hair loss, and a higher incidence of colds and flu. An underactive thyroid can also raise cholesterol and increase risk of heart problems.

When the thyroid is overactive, secreting too much T3 and T4 hormone, the condition is known as hyperthyroidism. An overactive thyroid is the more serious of the two problems. When this happens, the person's metabolism is raised and energy increases. However, this energy is usually "speedy" and nervous energy. People with this condition may also have sleep disorders, weakness in the muscles, sensitivity to heat, and weight loss. If left untreated, the person may develop goiters, which are enlarged thyroid glands protruding from the base of the neck. Other symptoms may include excessive sweating, increased appetite, weight loss, shaky hands, heart palpitation, nausea, and protruding eyes.

What Causes Thyroid Problems?

The thyroid requires iodine for production of its important hormones T3 and T4. But too much or too little iodine can tip the thyroid into overactivity or underactivity, depending upon other factors. A mild iodine deficiency may produce an underactive thyroid. But too much iodine can also cause mild protrusions in the glands (mild goiter activity), usually associated with overactive thyroid. It's a delicate balance.

Recent studies have also shown that foods known as gointrogens actually block the iodine we get from salt and other foods, making our iodine supplements ineffective. Two of these iodine-blocking foods are peanuts (especially peanut butter) and soybeans (especially soybean oil). Foods in the cabbage family are also gointrogens, but it's unlikely likely that you will eat enough of these to make much of a difference. Here's more information about the causes of thyroid imbalances:

- Selenium deficiency may also play a part in thyroid problems, as selenium is necessary for proper conversion of the T3 and T4 hormones produced by the thyroid.
- The thyroid works closely with both the pituitary and adrenal glands, so deficiencies or imbalances in either of those areas can also affect the thyroid. That means that adrenal depletion caused by too much caffeine can cause thyroid problems as well as adrenal problems.
- Recent evidence suggests that the thyroid is negatively affected by fluoride from toothpaste and water treatment.

Treatments for Thyroid Imbalance

There is no single effective treatment for thyroid imbalance. The best treatment is one that is carefully administered and observed for each person. You must find your own best balance of nutrients, particularly iodine and selenium, for proper thyroid balance. Also, stimulating or inhibiting the thyroid's productivity may actually cover up an underlying problem—treating the symptoms, but not curing the cause. Here are some important keys:

- Remove caffeine, high fructose corn syrup, and artificial substances that may be affecting your thyroid, adrenal, and even estrogen levels.
- Dramatically reduce your intake of peanut butter, soybean oils, and unsaturated vegetable oils in general. Don't replace these with loads of saturated fats. Instead, replace them with coconut oil or refrigerated flaxseed oil.
- Experiment with natural thyroid treatments until you find the proper balance of iodine, selenium, and estrogen for your body. Key foods include kelp and walnuts for organic iodine and garlic, brewer's yeast, and wheat germ for selenium.

- Refer to the section on Adrenal Imbalance to incorporate applicable information into your diagnosis. Your thyroid imbalance may be stemming from an adrenal imbalance.
- Other helpful supplements: Vitamins A, D, E, B2, B3, as well as rosemary leaf extract.
- Maca root from South America can help balance the thyroid.

Other Considerations

The essential oil myrtle, from an African plant, is said to have regulating effects on thyroid hormones. Also, motherwort, valerian root, and ashwagandha are helpful for hyperthyroidism, as they help to counter the energy problems resulting from thyroid and adrenal imbalances.

Be sure to take selenium supplements with iodine to assist in the overall process of T3 and T4 metabolism. Remember, if you use thyroid and/or adrenal supplements in an attempt to balance your thyroid, you should start with low doses and keep a close watch on your symptoms. They thyroid is a sensitive gland and it's easy to go too far with these supplements.

Ulcers (Stomach)

See also Dehydration, Digestion,

Ulcers are painful but common lesions in the stomach or duodenum lining, leading to dull stomachaches, bloating, nausea, and sometimes weakness and severe pain with vomiting, occasionally with blood. Call your doctor if symptoms are severe or if there is blood, as your stomach may be perforated.

Causes of Ulcers

Ninety percent of all ulcers are caused by Helicobacter pylori bacteria, but a little-known cause of stomach ulcers is eating too much sodium (salt). If you consume too much sodium on a regular basis, stomach ulcers, bloating, kidney damage, and a large number of other ailments can develop. If you eat a lot of canned soups and vegetables or eat potato chips, French fries, and other salty foods on a regular basis, look for these early signs of excessive sodium intake:

- Feeling thirsty all the time

- Dark urine and complexion
- Clenching your teeth
- Bloodshot eyes

Here are some other potential causes of ulcers:

- Zinc deficiency
- Too much secretion of hydrochloric acid can eat away the stomach lining, as can excess use of aspirin or ibuprofen.
- Smoking cigarettes weakens the stomach lining as well.
- Until recently, ulcers were thought to be caused simply by stress. Though that opens one up to illness, stress is no longer considered a primary cause. Doctors are still uncertain, however, why some people exposed to the H. pylori bacteria end up with ulcers and some don't.
- Ulcers may be a symptom of dehydration.

Treatments for Ulcers

Whatever you do, get tested first to see what's ailing your stomach. If it is the H. pylori bacteria, it's possible many other conditions may clear up, too, when this bacterium is destroyed. Also:

- Be sure to take a good multivitamin every day and increase your zinc intake when you have an illness or injury. Zinc accelerates healing. Licorice is often helpful in ulcer healing.
- Primal Defense, a probiotic formula, is very useful if your ulcers aren't bleeding.
- The herb slippery elm helps with ulcers, digestion, and Crohn's disease.
- Aloe vera juice (from the filets; don't use whole-leaf aloe because of toxins found in the aloe rind) will cut the burning away and help heal the delicate stomach lining.
- If you want to use herbs, start with garlic, especially freshly crushed clove, in every meal. Drink unsweetened cranberry juice and green tea (without sugar) five times a day. Cranberry juice has been shown to prevent H. pylori from sticking to the stomach wall and the tannins in green tea are active against the bacteria. Then comes the one-two punch: Take both goldenseal and rhubarb root three times daily. Make sure to take these herbs separately, not

together. This herbal therapy takes four to six weeks to work. These herbs can be used long after the infection is gone if you like the effect.

- Honorable mention herbs to add generously to your diet are: cinnamon, thyme, and turmeric. The essential oils of lemon verbena and lemongrass are also effective and make pleasant teas that you can drink regularly. Remember, get checked for H. pylori, the bacteria most commonly associated with benign and malignant ulcers.
- Chamomile tea is actually prescribed by doctors in Mexico for ulcers.

Other Considerations

If you have an ulcer, do not chew gum. Chewing gum activates the digestive juices, which are loaded with acid. Acid secreted into the stomach without any food will only exacerbate the ulcers. Not all gum is bad, however. Guar gum, which is available as a capsule or a powder, can actually help treat ulcers.

Urinary Infections

Bladder Infection

See also Candida, Infection (Bacterial), Prostate Health

About six million Americans are treated for urinary tract infections (UTIs) each year. Women are more likely to develop UTIs than men because there is less urethral distance for infectious organisms to travel from the outside of the body.

The first symptoms are lower back pain, the need to urinate frequently and urgently, while producing only a small amount of urine, and a bit of pain upon urinating. You might have some pain along the urethra. If treatment is begun at this stage, it can cured almost immediately. If you ignore it, you may develop fever, nausea, cloudy or bloody urine, and fatigue.

Other types of urinary infections may include straining to urinate and urinating while sleeping—both caused primarily from prostate problems. Dysuria, or painful urination, is among the most common types of bladder or urinary infections and is caused by bacteria.

Causes of Urinary Infections

Women: Approximately 85% of cases are caused by the bacteria E. coli , since it can easily be moved from the colon to the urinary opening, by wiping from back to front, for example. Sometimes, however, vaginal yeast infections move into the urinary tract by way of vaginal secretions. Also bladder muscle injuries from age or childbirth can cause urinary problems.

Men: Most urinary problems in men are caused by prostate disorders, specifically enlarged prostate. Actual infection can occur in men from sexual contact with infected partners—transferring the bacteria to the new host.

Treatments for Urinary Infections

The most important thing you can do to avoid urinary infections is to be careful during sex. Be sure that you engage in clean and protected activity. To cure infection once it has taken hold, drink unsweetened cranberry juice and green tea, while adding garlic extract and oregano extract supplements to your daily regimen. Also, get at least 2 grams a day of vitamin C while experiencing an infection.

To Prevent Urinary Infections:

- The best way to prevent UTIs is to drink at least six to eight glasses of fluid each day. This steady supply of fluids washes bacteria and other organisms away before they have a chance to stick to the walls of your urinary tract and begin multiplying. Keep in mind that bacteria multiply every 20 minutes.
- On this note, drinking enough fluids won't prevent UTIs if you're not expelling the liquid on a regular basis. Urinate regularly rather than holding it in, and be sure to urinate after sex.
- Be careful when having sex that neither partner touches the anal area and then touches the urinary region, as that is a common way of transferring the offending bacteria. Cleaning afterwards is helpful.
- Eat blueberries on a regular basis.
- Avoid caffeine.

To Cure Urinary Infections:

- For bladder and kidney infections, dilute unsweetened cranberry juice with purified water and drink away. To improve the taste, you can add stevia.

Drink at least 64 ounces per day. Don't use sugar to sweeten it!

- An old English remedy is to chew watermelon seeds during the cranberry juice cleanse. This also strengthens the kidneys. In Traditional Chinese Medicine, the kidney meridian correlates to maintaining youth and a strong immune system.
- Add Liver Tea (see Hepatitis) to the regimen to clean out any stones that may be forming. Simple urinary tract infections can be solved with Alka Seltzer. Just dissolve two tablets in a glass of water and drink it at the onset of symptoms. We've seen dozens of nonspecific urethritis cases cured in a matter of days this way, without the compounding problems of antibiotics.
- Take Vitamin C throughout the day in doses of 2 to 3 grams.
- Uva Ursi and buchu, pipsissewa, dandelion, nettle, horsetail and corn silk are good to take in capsule or tea form. These are also helpful any time you need a diuretic.
- Coriander, Echinacea, goldenrod, and juniper berries may also help sooth the urinary tract and eradicate the bacteria.

Varicose Veins

See also Liver & Gallbladder Health

Varicose veins are much more common in women, leading some experts to believe that the disorder may be related to hormones. The culprit may also be wearing high heel shoes, which cause the blood to pool in the calves. Men aren't immune to varicose veins, however. They're much more noticeable on women, since women tend to shave their legs, yet varicose veins can cause painful throbbing and cramps in both genders.

Causes

Besides the possibilities mentioned above, varicose veins are thought to be caused by standing, sitting, or lying down for long periods of time—in other words, lack of movement. Sitting or lying down for long periods of time causes the blood to pool toward the feet. Ultimately, as a result of this pooling, the heavy, swollen veins protrude, forming varicose veins. There may also be some connection with the health of your blood vessels and arteries and capillaries.

Treatments for Varicose Veins

Preventing Varicose Veins:

Here are a few ways to help prevent varicose veins:

- Though varicose veins are a common hallmark of aging, crossing the 50-year-old threshold doesn't mean you have to develop them. Keep your blood flowing and your cardiovascular system as a whole healthy by staying active.
- Along with staying active, maintaining an ideal body weight is essential to varicose vein prevention. Don't put extra physical stress on the veins in your legs and feet by weighing them down.
- Take enzymes, including bromelain.
- If your liver is congested, your whole circulatory system suffers. Maintain good liver health by not drinking too much alcohol and by ingesting foods and herbs that sustain the liver. These include red grapes, blueberries, cherries, beets, artichokes, dandelion, and milk thistle. Also, eat red grapes, cherries, and blackberries.
- Keep your circulation flowing by eating hot, spicy foods, particularly hot pepper, onions, and garlic. Also Una de Gato (Cat's Claw) is good for circulation.
- Massaging the legs is helpful if you don't already have varicose veins in the area of the massage.

Curing Varicose Veins:

- Varicose veins are much more difficult to treat than prevent, but if you do develop varicose veins, all is not lost. The bioflavonoid rutin strengthens capillaries, and there is some evidence that it can help reduce the severity of varicose veins.
- Horse chestnut herb is useful for varicose vein therapy.
- Take Vitamin C with bioflavonoids.

Waistline

Bloating

See also Digestion, Laxatives, Weight (Over)

Not all problem areas for fat are the same. Where you have fat is just as important as how much you have. Experts agree that it's much healthier to be shaped like a pear, with fat accumulating around the hips and thighs, than to be shaped like an apple, with fat accumulating around the waistline. Research shows that people who store body fat around their waists have an increased risk for heart disease, high cholesterol, stroke, back problems including herniated discs, Type 2 diabetes, and even cancer.

This is bad news for men, who are more likely to store fat around their waists than women. When women do accumulate excess abdominal fat, however, they become high-risk for these diseases much sooner than do men. In other words, even if a woman has just a little excess fat around her waistline, she jumps into the high-risk category for these chronic diseases.

Causes of the Expanding Waistline

You may think you are fatter than you are if you have Candida, as it causes bloating, particularly in the face and abdomen. If you notice a white coating on your tongue, expanded pores, swelling around the eyes, and crave sweets and feel confused and spacey, treat yourself for Candida (see Candida), using herbs and intestinal flora, and avoid carbohydrates and fermented foods.

If your abdomen is too large, you may easily have too much waste solidified in your colon, which can be removed through colon cleanses and colonics. A rounded and bloated abdomen can also be caused by parasites, which most people have, even in developed countries. Some signs are dark circles under the eyes, itchy rectum, worsening of symptoms at full moon, and pale lips.

Kidney weakness, which is associated in Traditional Chinese Medicine with fear and also with sexual depletion, can cause edema (puffing of the cells due to excess moisture), particularly in the ankles, around the eyes, under the chin, and throughout the abdomen. Also, fat will accumulate in the abdomen to protect the kidneys. Adrenal deficiency also adds to the size of the waistline because of cortisol production, first too high, then too low once the reserves are used up.

Hypothyroidism also can lead to difficulty with weight, and cause a rounded abdomen.

Treatments for an Expanding Waistline

Here are the keys to curing a puffy midsection:

- Avoid fatty foods, dairy products, processed foods, alcohol, and sodas. Also avoid sweets; risen and fermented foods such as alcohol, cheese, bread and pizza, vinegar; and avoid mushrooms.
- Reduce consumption of meats and sugars.
- Eat more nutrient-dense foods, such as Spirulina, Chlorella, bee pollen, Spanish gooseberry, and dandelion.
- Stay active. Sweat at least three times per week.
- Consider a parasite cleanse or general cleansing program or product.

Other Considerations

Aside from crunches and other forms of core strength-building exercises, conjugated linoleic acid (CLA), a fatty acid from animal sources, has been almost miraculous for some people, especially men, at removing the roll around the abdomen that accumulate as soon as a person becomes more sedentary. Drink plenty of pure water to transport the broken-down smooth fat out of your system.

Eat raw pumpkin seeds and take Una de Gato (Cat's Claw) herb, black walnut hulls in capsule or extract form, and raw garlic for cleansing. Keep your body alkaline, and keep your intestines scrubbed with fiber. For more cleansing herbal treatments, see Constipation.

Sprinkle dulse and seaweed (especially fucus kelp) over your food for extra iodine to help your thyroid and metabolism. You may want to take the amino acid L-tyrosine to raise the thyroid function as well. Also, chickweed helps the body get rid of fat, and spicy foods can keep the metabolism up.

Taoist and Tantric practices promote orgasms without ejaculation as a way to maintain kidney meridian strength.

Warts

See also Human Papiloma Virus

Warts are contagious skin tumors, bumps, or growths that are most commonly found on hands and feet. They typically disappear after a few months, but can last a lifetime, and can also recur. Certain types of warts, depending on location and cause, can be contagious from body region to body region, but are not transferable between species (so don't worry about touching a frog).

Warts can occur singly or in clusters. Their appearance and size varies tremendously depending on where they erupt on the body and the degree of irritation or trauma they receive through daily wear of the skin and clothes. Warts often disappear on their own, without any treatment, within several months. However, in some individuals, they may continue for years or reoccur on the same or different parts of the body.

Of the many types of warts, the most common wart is the Verrucae vulgaris. It presents as a well-defined, rough-surfaced, round or irregular growth that is light gray, brown, grayish-black, or yellow. It is usually firm to the touch, and most commonly appears on the knees, elbows, fingers, face, and scalp.

Periungual warts occur around the nail beds. Plantar warts occur on the sole of the foot, are very common, and often appear flattened due to the pressure of walking on them. When several plantar warts are close together, they appear as plaque-like and are called mosaic warts. Pedunculated warts are stalk-like and are common with age. They most commonly occur around the neck, chest, face, scalp, and armpits. Genital warts appear on or around the genitalia and are highly contagious. For more information about genital warts, see Human Papilloma Virus (HPV).

Natural healing of warts may require one to two months of care, with the wart disappearing suddenly in one to three days.

Causes of Warts

- Warts can be caused by any of 35 viruses. The viruses usually take hold because of poor diet and nutrition.
- Poor hygiene is sometimes implicated in having warts, and the viruses are somewhat contagious.

- You can test for the microscopic warts by putting vinegar over an area and watching for white spots. This is useful for spotting tiny genital warts, which can actually exist anywhere in the pelvic region.
- Many health care practitioners believe that warts can be caused by stress.
- Warts also become more common with the diminished immune function that corresponds to aging.
- Warts and moles also are thought to be the effect of potassium deficiency. Melons are the foods highest in potassium.

Treatments for Warts

- Useful homeopathic remedies for warts include: Thuja, Causticum, Calcium carbonate, Ruta Graveolens, and Graphites.
- A topical application to the wart of the milky latex from a dandelion stem each morning and night can be helpful.
- Lemon essential oil applied topically can speed healing, as can grapefruit seed extract applied directly on the wart. Drinking water with a few drops of these extract helps kill the virus from inside. Have a chaser ready—they taste awful!
- Thuja oil is also effective for dealing with warts.
- Another topical recipe for treatment is a solution of garlic oil, vitamin E, castor oil, and zinc oxide cream.
- Try applying these oils or solutions to a piece of cotton covering the wart.
- Apple cider vinegar is recommended both topically and internally, but if you are guarding against Candida infection, be aware that vinegar is fermented and could exacerbate Candida.

Other Considerations

Dietary changes also can help resolve warts. An organic, whole-foods diet, emphasizing foods high in vitamin A (such as dark green and yellow vegetables, cold-water fish, and eggs) and sulfur (such as onions, garlic, Brussels sprouts, cabbage, and broccoli) can be helpful. Avoid all refined and processed foods, sugar, unhealthy fats, excess animal proteins, and milk and dairy products.

Recommended nutrients include vitamin A, beta-carotene, vitamin B complex, vitamin C, vitamin E, zinc, garlic capsules, and L-cysteine. All foods that boost the immune system will help fight off warts because warts are caused by viruses. Try nutrient-dense foods like maca, Spirulina, Chlorella, and green leafy vegetables.

Weight (Over)

Obesity / Overweight

See Thyroid Imbalance, Waistline

Being overweight is the single biggest health risk in the United States. Fifteen percent of American kids are obese, or more than 35 pounds overweight. Thirty-seven percent of all Americans are obese. Eight percent of Americans are morbidly obese, or more than 100 pounds overweight. Being overweight makes people susceptible to illness and debilitating diseases such as diabetes, heart attack, and stroke. Obesity also is associated with a higher risk of prostate, breast, and colorectal cancers. Being overweight costs us all money with the doubling in health costs and higher incidence of diseases that could easily be avoided.

Being overweight is an insidious cycle. For those who do not feel secure, it can eat away at their self-esteem. If your mood depends on your weight, you can become depressed and eat even more. Reacting with depression to being overweight can lead to taking dangerous antidepressants, creating a loss in libido, which can create further problems with the psychological underpinnings in relationships. It's best to first look at any emotional causes for overeating to address the core issues.

Being overweight is relatively easy to overcome if there is no underlying health condition causing the problem. Of course, hypothyroidism, genetics, and being born with a lower amount of brown fat can make weight loss more of a challenge. Obese people often have abnormal metabolism, and can't eat what others eat and stay slim. It has been found that overweight people often don't eat more than thin people. But a few simple changes in food choices and eating right for your blood type (see appendix), then slowly adding exercise, can help most people without a serious health disorder overcome their weight problem.

Causes

Americans on average eat more than 125 pounds of refined sugar per person per year. (Note that overloading on simple carbohydrates such as sugars also leaves you more susceptible to viruses, bacteria, molds, and fungi, allowing them to grow more prolifically in your body.) These make you crave more carbs to feed them.

Any excess food, whether it's protein, carbohydrates, or fat, will be stored as fat when not burned. Overeating, even if it's healthy food, can cause weight problems. One common reason for being overweight is not eating the appropriate portions of foods to fuel your body correctly.

Finally, a slow metabolism can be caused by thyroid dysfunction, which is usually caused by dietary problems.

> **"I don't exercise. If God wanted me to bend over, he'd have put diamonds on the floor."**
> Joan Rivers

Treatments for Obesity and Excess Weight

Diet is the king and exercise is the queen, and without both you can't feel like royalty. Start with mild exercise like walking. If you start too fast and too hard, you may get discouraged. Getting your weight to the level it belongs is a life-changing experience, so do it gradually and make it last for the rest of your life. Building muscle burns stored, smooth fat six times faster than fat that just has been ingested. Here are more keys:

- Take a nutrient-dense super-food supplement every day before meals. Some good ingredients for high-nutrient supplements include: Maca, Spirulina, Chlorella, spinach powder, kelp, and bee pollen.
- Get plenty of omega-3 fatty acids from fish oils or flaxseed oil.
- Drink lots of pure water and avoid fruit juices that contain corn syrup.
- Add olive leaf extract, pine bark extract, and dandelion extract to your supplements for better nutrition and immune system health.
- Exercise regularly, focusing on aerobic movements that make you to sweat.

> **"The second day of a diet is always easier than the first. By the second day you're off it."**
> Jackie Gleason

The Ultimate Secret of Natural Weight Loss

The first and last secret of natural weight loss can be wrapped up in a single word: nutrition. That's right, nutrition is the ultimate cure and the ultimate secret to weight management. A lack of proper nutrition can cause everything from low energy and a weak immune system to virtually every disease known to man! Nutrition provides the foundation for every living cell, every organ, and every metabolic chemical in your body. Nutrition provides strength, energy, and vitality while empowering you to fight disease and illness. Most important, it's the reason we eat in the first place. The lack of proper nutrition is the bottom line reason why we gain weight.

Hunger is more than just a craving to consume food. Hunger is really your body communicating its desire and basic need for vital nutrition! Taste buds are actually nutrient receptors designed to tell you what foods are nutritious and good for you. We are constantly fooling these receptors with sugar, salt, chemical food additives, and artificial flavorings that make nutrient-depleted foods taste good and appear healthy and nutritious. Your body doesn't want to be FOOLED. Your body wants FUEL. When you eat and fill up on nutritionally deficient food, of course you feel full. But there's a huge difference between being full and being satisfied. When you eat natural, nutrient-dense foods, you satisfy your body's need for fuel.

Every day we consume processed garbage food that lacks the vital nutrition our body is screaming for—and what happens? We feel full temporarily, but we have not satisfied our body's fundamental need for nutrition. As our body struggles to digest what we've eaten, it doesn't find this vital nutrition because IT'S NOT THERE! So we are fundamentally still hungry—hungry for more nutrition. Our bodies tell us we need more nutrients and send the appropriate signals to get more nutrition. We feel hungry again and WE EAT AGAIN!

At the core of every weight loss program should be a diet of super nutrition. With proper food nutrients and an element of control over toxic foods, you can eat small portions and never feel hungry. And if you add plenty of water and exercise, you'll feel energy like you haven't felt since childhood. If you consume nutrient-dense, health-forming foods, you won't be suppressing your appetite, you'll be satisfying it.

Wounds

See also Bee Stings & Insect Bites, Burns

We all want open-skin wounds to heal as quickly as possible, and keeping healthy overall, getting plenty rest and nutritious foods, avoiding chemicals both internally and externally, and keeping the wound clean and covered will help enhance the wound-healing process.

Each wound goes through a natural healing stage, and no matter how well you treat it, you can expect some tingling, itching, and puffiness in the Inflammation process, blood clotting; and fibrin cross linking, and new collagen and capillary production that produces scarring, and then remodeling, which smoothes the scar into the surrounding skin—all part of the normal healing process.

If you feel heat at the wound site or see that redness is spreading around the wound, it is likely that infection is setting in. It is important to start taking natural antibiotics such as goldenseal internally immediately upon receiving a wound and applying it topically to avoid this.

Treatments

There are many internal and external alternatives to help wounds heal quickly. Of course, when you get a cut, first clean the wound with water (research indicates that hydrogen peroxide actually damages tissue, so many health centers advocate using only water to clear debris from cuts).

- Plantain is excellent for dressing wounds, as are the pulps from papaya and aloe vera. It's a good idea to keep aloe vera plants in the home, as it particularly helps sunburn and other minor burns and cuts. Aloe bought from stores does not always perform in tests as does fresh aloe vera. The luscious papaya is a lovely way to treat bee stings and bug bites, as the papain enzymes disintegrate the skin eating poisons. You may also be tempted to eat some of it in the meantime. Papaya is also good for burns, as it moisturizes the skin and prevents scarring.
- For external aid, apply a topical povidone-iodine cream. It accelerates the healing process and has

antibacterial, antiviral, and antifungal effects to help ward off infection.

- Additionally, goldenseal has been used as a healing aid for centuries. To make your own therapeutic paste, mix goldenseal powder with a small amount of water. Then put the paste right on the wound and cover it with an adhesive bandage.
- You can facilitate wound healing internally by adding vitamin E, zinc, and beta-carotene to your nutritional regimen. Adding vitamin E oil topically to the wound can help prevent scarring.
- Vitamin C and zinc picolinate are a wonderful one-two punch for healing.
- Placing turmeric powder directly on bleeding cuts causes the blood to clot almost immediately.
- Grape-seed extract helps wounds heal more quickly and cleanly. It regenerates blood vessels and clears the bacteria from the area.
- Raw honey may be the handiest thing around to put on wounds—it is both antibacterial and antiseptic, and has chemical properties that help the skin heal more quickly.

Other Considerations

Avoid all sugars, as these allow bacteria such as staph to proliferate. Sugar reduces the immune system response immediately, and provides an acid condition that nourishes bacteria. Smoking cigarettes slows your immune system, and thus wound healing. Also, putting urine directly on wounds may save your life if it is all that is available. Urine is antiseptic and pure, and contains antibodies to fight infectious agents.

Wounds don't heal as quickly with the condition of hypothyroidism, so taking supplements to raise your metabolism may be indicated if your wounds do not heal in a typical timeframe. Diabetics must pay particular attention to wounds in the legs and feet; people with diabetes often have peripheral nerve damage and not realize they have wounds on their feet and legs until they are badly infected. In addition, these wounds are slow to heal, and can lead to gangrene if they are not treated aggressively.

About the Authors

Reno R. Rollé

Mr. Rollé currently holds the position of CEO for Studio Store Direct, Inc., a direct response entertainment marketing company that has developed a patent-pending process for empowering DVDs and new media video with direct response television/infomercial methodology. More information is available at www.studiostoredirect.com.

Rollé previously held the position of CEO for Shop America USA, a leading infomercial marketing firm based in Bradford, England, and operating in the United States. During this time, Mr. Rollé co-created the historical bestseller *Natural Cures 'They' Don't Want You To Know About*. This experience inspired Rollé to go a step farther and create a complete and comprehensive volume of natural health. The result is *The Ultimate Guide to Natural Health*. The book you have in your hands is an abridged "Quick Reference" version of that complete volume.

Prior to his experience at Shop America, Mr. Rollé was a founding principle of the National Lampoon Acquisition Group, LLC, and in 2002 he founded the Home Entertainment division to produce and distribute National Lampoon branded DVDs.

Rollé was Chairman and CEO of Synergy Worldwide, Inc., an award winning product engineering, design, and marketing company. Mr. Rollé also co-founded HSN Direct, a joint venture with Home Shopping Network, Inc., where he helped develop and launch several major consumer successes, including the Ab Isolator and EZ Crunch exercise products.

Mr. Rollé has been a proponent of natural health and nature-based, organic trends for many years. He currently lives in Southern California with his wife Lynn and two teenaged children, Reno II and Ryann.

James W. Forsythe, M.D., H.M.D.

James W. Forsythe, M.D., H.M.D., received his B.A. degree in biochemistry and physiology from University of California, Berkeley, in 1960, and his M.D. from University of California, San Francisco, in 1964. In 1965, Dr. Forsythe spent two years in residency in Pathology at Tripler Army Hospital in Honolulu, Hawaii. He completed his residency in medicine at Childrenâ€™s Hospital San Francisco, California, in 1971. In 1971, he received a two-year Fellowship in Oncology-Hematology at the Cancer Research Institute, University of California and San Francisco General Hospital and is board certified in Internal Medicine, Medical Oncology, Utilization Review and Quality Assurance. He is board eligible in Clinical Pathology and Medical Gerontology.

Dr. Forsythe spent 26 years in the U.S. Amy Medical Corps and is a retired Full Colonel. He is the former state surgeon of the Nevada Army National Guard and started the cancer centers at three hospitals in Northern Nevada.

Since 1986, Dr. Forsythe has been interested in integrating conventional and alternative medicine. Dr. Forsythe currently maintains both a homeopathic practice (Century Wellness Clinic) and a conventional medical clinic (Cancer Screening and Treatment Center) located in Reno, Nevada. He has also been the Associate Professor of Medicine at the University of Nevada, Reno Medical School and has done original, chemical outcome-based studies on many natural substances.

Dr. Forsythe has been married for 29 years to his wife Earlene, an advanced nurse practitioner and business manager of their clinics. They have raised five children.

. . . for the evolving human spirit.

THE
ULTIMATE
GUIDE TO
NATURAL
HEALTH
BY RENO R. ROLLE
&
DR. JAMES WILLIAM FORSYTHE M.D., H.M.D.

Everyone Needs Boku Super Cleanse

...to receive the full benefits of Boku Super Food!

A clean colon and regular bowel movements are the foundation to better health. Years of eating nutrient-depleted, processed food takes its toll on our colon, the body's main detoxification route. The combination of plaque and toxic build up can impede the absorption of vital nutrients, which the body so desperately needs!

Here's what you can do...

Boku Super Cleanse Steps 1 and 2

Boku Super Cleanse Steps 1 and 2 are effective, gentle and non-habit-forming formulas that work to nourish and cleanse the colon and all body cells. You only have to commit a long weekend (or 3 days) **and** you can take these formulas while living your normal life. No special diet is required (although the better you choose to eat during the cleanse, the better your results will be).

BOKU CLEANSE STEP 1 in capsule formula is created to gently yet powerfully move the bowels, relieve constipation, help with digestion and the elimination of gas. These capsules can be used on their own, or in conjunction with Boku Cleanse Step 2.

BOKU CLEANSE STEP 2 is an intestinal drawing formula in powder form created to draw in and hold onto a huge array of toxins that collect in the colon. It also helps heal the intestines as it moves through.

Ingredients in Boku Cleanse Step 1:

- Rhubarb root – Organic
- Peppermint Leaf – Organic
- Fennel Seed – Organic
- Nopal Cactus – Wildcrafted
- Thyme Leaf – Organic
- Oregano Leaf – Organic
- Whole Leaf Aloe Ferox (cape aloe) – Organic
- Enzymes (amylase, lipase, protease, cellulase)

Ingredients in Boku Cleanse Step 2:

- Slippery Elm Bark – Organic
- Nopal Cactus – Organic
- Marshmallow Root
- Fenugreek Seed
- Activated Charcoal
- Organic Flax Seed Meal
- Organic Whole Stevia Leaf
- Organic Kelp
- Wildcrafted Carob
- Natural Zeolite Clay
- Volcanic Bentonite Clay

Call: 800-215-9887 to order Boku Super Cleanse or order online at www.bokusuperfood.com

TM
Bōku